D1548279

THE SHAPING OF AMERICAN ETHNOGRAPHY

Critical Studies in the History of Anthropology

Volume 2

Series Editors: Regna Darnell and Stephen O. Murray

The Shaping of American Ethnography

The Wilkes Exploring Expedition, 1838–1842

Barry Alan Joyce

University of Nebraska Press   Lincoln and London

Library of Congress Cataloging-in-Publication Data
Joyce, Barry Alan.
The shaping of American ethnography: the Wilkes
Exploring Expedition, 1838–1842 /
Barry Alan Joyce.
p. cm—(Critical studies in the history of anthropology series)
Includes bibliographical references and index.
ISBN 0-8032-2591-1 (cl.: alk. paper)
1. United States Exploring Expedition (1838–1842)
2. Ethnology—United States—History—19th century.
3. Ethnology—Oceania. 4. Indians of South America.
5. Indians of North America—Northwest Coast of North
America. 6. Racism—History—19th
century. I. Title. II. Series.
GN663 .J69 2001   305.8'09'034—dc21   00-059963

Reproductions of figures 1, 6–10, 12–17, 19, and 23–27 are courtesy of the Navy Art Collection, Naval Historical Center, Washington DC. Reproduction of figure 2 is courtesy of the University of Nebraska–Lincoln Libraries Archives and Special
Collections. Reproductions of figures 3, 4, 11, and 18–22 are
courtesy of the Yale Collection of Western Americana, Beinecke
Rare Book and Manuscript Library.

CONTENTS

Illustrations

Figures

Maps

Regna Darnell and Stephen O. Murray

We are proud to introduce the second volume in the Critical Studies in the History of Anthropology series. *The Shaping of American Ethnography: The Wilkes Exploring Expedition, 1838–1842*, by Barry Alan Joyce, responds directly to a need, widely perceived among anthropologists, historians, and Native American scholars alike, for historicist perspectives exploring the continuing relevance of past events and ideas to contemporary anthropological theory and praxis. Disciplinary history has too long restricted itself to names, dates, and places in the past without the interpretive context of either their own times or ours. Contemporary critical perspectives, in contrast, use the older kind of history as primary data for alternative and often contested interpretations of a past in which contemporary practitioners have considerable stake.

Joyce's book innovatively combines insights into the history of anthropology, American history, and Indian history. Very few anthropologists are well informed about the expansionist period of mid-nineteenth-century American social and political history. The Wilkes Expedition of 1838–1842 was perhaps the single most important exploring expedition in expanding American cultural horizons to include Polynesians and South Americans among the "inferior races" already known to Americans of the Jacksonian era—African American slaves and Native American "barbarians." As new peoples were encountered, they were assimilated into existing classifications alongside "wild" Indians and "naturally docile" Africans in a racial hierarchy topped by white Anglo-Saxon Protestant Americans. The Protestant utopian vision of "God's chosen people" in the "new Zion" of the United States dovetailed with the ostensibly scientific notions of "race" and the aptness, indeed the virtual predestination, of American dominion over the continent and even beyond.

This sense of the mission of the young American republic to rule the continent and guide the world would come to be called "manifest destiny."

Its mandates were justified by the purported objectivity of its commitment to science and by the obvious diversities of culture and custom discovered by American explorers. The United States government itself sponsored the expedition led by Lieutenant Charles Wilkes, hoping to prepare the way for imperial expansion and presumably benign leadership of other, less fortunate peoples from barbarism to the enlightenment of Christian-American civilization. Cultures that could not meet the new standards of republican civilization faced assimilation or extinction.

The story is a dramatic one, with individualized characters whose actions and interactions changed the way America viewed itself. Charles Pickering, the bookish zoologist, contrasts with the more flamboyant cowboy entrepreneur Titian Ramsay Peale. Pickering's influential uncle John Pickering insisted on the appointment of recent Yale graduate Horatio Hale as philologist, arguing that specialized skill was necessary for collecting more than superficial vocabularies. Wilkes himself attained the leadership commission because more seasoned officers were discouraged by delays of the grandiose plans for the expedition. His autocratic manner and scientific ambition produced more than one near mutiny and a complex trial involving charges and countercharges. By the time the expedition returned, however, its initial unpopularity had been reversed, to the extent that political appointees tampered with the crates of artifacts shipped home in advance of the expedition itself. Much of the story can be told in the words of the actors because each member of the expedition was required to keep a journal.

The new American science was understood to be both useful and accessible to the observational skills of any committed would-be scientist. And the American public was eager to read eyewitness accounts of such scientific studies of newly encountered cultures around the world. American scientists had conferred with the expedition personnel before their departure, providing scientific instruments, books, and questionnaires for collection of everything from natural history specimens to human skulls to linguistic texts. The American Philosophical Society and Academy of Natural Sciences of Philadelphia were particularly active in the preparations and later interpretations.

The Wilkes Expedition documents shed little direct light on "the native point of view." Far from espousing a contemporary cultural relativism, Wilkes himself was bloodthirsty in seeking retribution for the death of his nephew. Nonetheless, the results of the expedition's four-year search for new data and collections fed into ongoing debates in an American anthropology that was moving headlong toward more systematic observations and eventually professional training for cross-cultural observers. Particularly influential were Wilkes's five-volume official record of the expedition, Pickering's *Races of Man*, and Hale's linguistic collections.

Pickering's standoff with Samuel George Morton, founder of what was called in the mid–nineteenth century the American school of anthropology, engages debates over scientific racialism that continue today between cultural and biological explanations of human diversity. In Pickering's time the clash was between the basic unity of the human species, or monogenism, and a separate creation or development of incommensurable racial "natures," or polygenism. Pickering boldly challenged the Americanist status quo in refusing to categorize the American Indians as systematically inferior to white Americans. Joyce's narrative tacks adroitly between Native American and African American exemplars of racialist positions (the "dissimilar bookends" to compartmentalize all indigenous cultures encountered), demonstrating how "race" was defined by preexisting stereotypes about savage customs and character types more than by skin color or physical features.

Joyce's carefully researched, insightful, and absorbingly written critical history reveals the details and context of a formative moment in American self-consciousness. Observation of inferior others who needed to be ruled and guided by civilized white people is the historical basis from which anthropology emerged, not only in the United States during the nineteenth century but also in the colonial and neocolonial anthropologies of the twentieth century and beyond.

Acknowledgments

I have received assistance and encouragement from many individuals during the course of this endeavor. I am particularly indebted to Sharon Salinger and Clifford Trafzer at the University of California, Riverside, for their interest, advice, and faith shown in my work. Both were inspirational islands of encouragement during my graduate years; both have continued to offer support, friendship, and collegiality in the ensuing years. Scott Martin, Richard Lowy, Sally Ness, Rebecca Kugel, Marta Savigliano, Edward Beasley, Bud McKanna, Arthur Schatz, and Thomas Cox helped me to articulate and develop my ideas. Michael Moon kept me safely on the road and out of the poorhouse. My mother, father, and Rachel fed and sustained me in many ways. As always, I am grateful to my friend and mentor James Nauman. His editing is invaluable; his energy in the pursuit of knowledge contagious.

Those who contributed to the publication of this book at the University of Nebraska Press have graciously put up with my naiveté and my mistakes while infusing me with the confidence I needed in my own work. I hope that the final result justifies the encouraging and valuable comments and critiques I have received from UNP editors, referees, and the copyeditor.

I visited many repositories during the seven years I have devoted to this book. The American Philosophical Society (APS) and the Academy of Natural Sciences of Philadelphia stand out for the enthusiasm of their staff. Marty Levitt and Roy Goodman at the APS were especially encouraging at the early stages of the project. My research at these institutions was made possible by a Mellon Fellowship from the American Philosophical Society, as well as two fellowships from the University of California, Riverside, to conduct research in Philadelphia and Washington DC. I also had the privilege of being granted a fellowship from the Beinecke Rare Book and Manuscript Library, as well as a minigrant from California State University, San Bernardino, to conduct research in the later stages of the project. This assistance was particularly valuable in locating the illustrations included in this book.

Curators George Miles at the Beinecke and Gale Munro at the Navy Art Collection (Naval Historical Center) provided copies of this artwork. My thanks to them and to those who also assisted me during my visits.

Finally, Angela and Joe Joyce gave me their love, faith, and approval. They sacrificed some of their needs so that their dad could achieve his goal.

"The just shall live by faith."

My faith has been justified.

THE SHAPING OF AMERICAN ETHNOGRAPHY

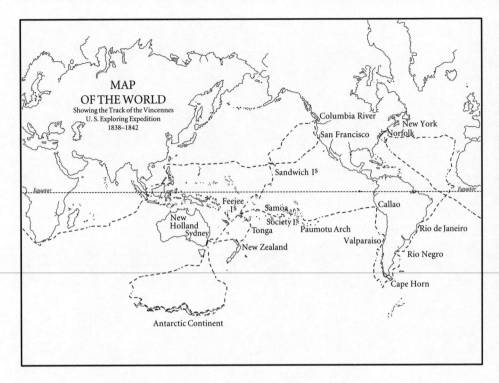

MAP
OF THE WORLD
Showing the Track of the Vincennes
U. S. Exploring Expedition
1838–1842

Equator

Columbia River
San Francisco
New York
Norfolk
Sandwich I^s
Feejee I^s
Samoa
Callao
New Holland
Sydney
Society I^s
Tonga
Paumotu Arch
New Zealand
Valparaiso
Rio de Janeiro
Rio Negro
Cape Horn
Antarctic Continent

Equator

The route of the Wilkes Exploring Expedition: Track of the USS *Vincennes*

INTRODUCTION

The Shaping of American Ethnography focuses on the construction of American ethnological and anthropological tenets during a period when the United States government was actively sponsoring naval scientific expeditions to various parts of the globe. I have analyzed journals, published narratives, correspondence, and scientific data pertaining to the ethnological observations of those who served on the most extensive and far-reaching American scientific endeavor of the nineteenth century—the United States Exploring Expedition to the Pacific under the command of Charles Wilkes.

In August of 1838 the United States Exploring Expedition set sail from Norfolk Navy Yard, the squadron consisting of the flagship *Vincennes* and five other vessels. The voyage encompassed such a wide range of objectives that it required over seven hundred men, officers, and technicians plus seven scientists on board to fulfill them. Over the course of four years, the expedition made stops on the east and west coasts of South America, visited Australia and New Zealand by way of the Paumotu group, Samoa, and Tahiti, headed farther south and discovered the Antarctic land mass, then returned to the South Seas to chart and explore the Fiji Islands, Tonga, and many other island groups. From the Fijis the voyage proceeded to the Sandwich (Hawaiian) Islands and from there to the northwest coast of America. The expedition returned to the United States in June of 1842 after a journey of nearly four years.

By reconstructing the narrative of this voyage, I am particularly interested in the process by which Americans on this expedition filtered their observations of the world's indigenous people through the lens of their peculiar constructions of "savagery" as shaped by the American experience. I have not attempted to judge the veracity of their efforts or whether their scientific method of compartmentalizing and classifying humans is a valid one. In fact, many of the challenges they faced in making sense of their experiences continue to confound ethnological observers today. The debate over the past two decades swirling around anthropological theory and methods serves to emphasize this fact.[1]

Remarks and discussions at a 1994 meeting of the American Anthropological Association also brought home the point that scholars continue to struggle with many of the same issues, influences, and attitudes that the Wilkes Expedition faced. Presenters at the various sessions pondered such questions as just who was setting the criteria and agenda for discussing cultures—scholars or fallout from the "culture wars" of the 1990s? During the conference Clifford Geertz noted the tendency of experts to dismiss and trivialize the work of their predecessors once a new general model has been accepted. He found the subtitle of his session, "Beyond the Imperialisms and Parochialisms of the Past," to be "peremptory, over-excited and self-congratulatory. Our predecessors," Geertz concluded, "were not as blind as we sometimes portray them."[2]

I believe that nineteenth-century explorers shared the attributes that characterize the discipline of anthropology in any age—a reliance on synthetic systems constructed with a self-assurance that masks the fact that its foundations and conclusions are period- and culture-dependent. In essence, politics, social mores, religious beliefs, funding, research agendas, and even the intrusion and interaction of the researcher into and with the society being studied all tug at the best intentions of the researcher-observer. Whether the intent is to correlate, differentiate, or "thickly describe," we often ignore the fact that the observers themselves may be the constant in the equation that most influences what they see.[3] Why should the experiences of the Wilkes Expedition in the nineteenth century have been any different in this respect?

That said, by examining the exploratory encounters of the Wilkes Expedition, I hope to shed light upon the process by which American observers in the nineteenth century—including scientists—ordered *their* world through their perceptions of what *others* are like. It will be shown in this study that, similar to today's fieldwork, a curious dialectic also developed between the constructed image of the "American savage" and the explorer's observations of the native people encountered during the voyage.

In the course of my study of this important expedition, I have found that native people around the world were identified, compared to, and subsequently classified according to American perceptions of Indians as "wild" and black slaves as "docile." In essence, American explorers used the constructed images of these two groups as dissimilar bookends for the compartmentalization of all indigenous cultures they encountered. These images provided a "working definition," prescribed the boundaries, and theoretically allowed for gradations of barbarity and possibility for improvement within these limits. The resulting observations, expressed privately in their journals and publicly through scientific reports, popular narratives, and ethnological exhibitions, in turn produced images of world cultures with which all Americans could readily identify and comprehend, while at the same time remaining true to the broader schools of anthropology emerging in the nineteenth century. A rather startling discovery was that while nearly all of the people the expedition encountered were considered "of color," the importance of the hue of the skin as a classificatory tool was in fact subordinated to the *image* of the prototypical "savage" that had evolved out of the American experience.

The prevailing use of savagery as an anthropological category stemmed from the work of eighteenth-century scientists such as Blumenbach and Linnaeus. According to their system of racial classification, humankind could be grouped into four or five divisions based on skin color and "features." Not surprisingly, these categories usually paralleled European concepts of "stages" or "states" of societies around the world. Societies were separated into five categories—enlightened, civilized, half-civilized, barbarous, and savage.⁴ These became the commonly accepted criteria in Europe for evaluating societies, cultures, and nations by the nineteenth century.

These theories were adopted and quickly put into practice in the United States. They found their way into American publications by the first decades of the nineteenth century. For example, American students in the early republic were taught from geography texts that were organized around the "five races of mankind" and the "five stages of civilization." These images were used as part of an emerging pedagogical method of teaching geography—that of comparison and classification. By using this method of instruction, an instructor could teach the vast subject of world geography in a rational, organized fashion, enabling students to make connections and relate to the material. While this method indeed seemed to make much more pedagogical sense than rote memorization of geographical facts, the actual result was that the rest of the world became a foil for creating images of American nationalism, uniqueness, and superiority in all categories—one professed goal of public education in America. Americans, it seemed, had their own way of looking at things.

This book is divided into three unequal parts. Chapter 1 covers the conception of and preparation for the Exploring Expedition. In order to put the importance of the voyage in its proper historical and scientific framework,

4

Asiatic. Malay. European. African. American.

A. They are five : the European or Caucasian, Asiatic or Mongolian, American, Malay, and African or Negro.

299. How may they be classed in regard to their colour ?

A. Into the White, Yellow, Red, Brown, and Black races.

300. What nations does the European or White race include ?

A. The nations of Europe, Western Asia, the North of Africa, with all the white inhabitants of America and other regions.

301. What nations does the Asiatic or Yellow race include ?

A. All the nations of Eastern Asia, (except the Malays of Malacca.)

302. What other nations belong to this race ?

A. The Finns and Laplanders of Europe, and the Esquimaux of America.

303. What constitutes the Copper-coloured or Red race ?

A. The Indians of America.

304. What nations does the Malay or Brown race include ?

A. The people of Malacca and Malaysia, with those of Polynesia and New Zealand.

305. What part of the earth does the African or Black race inhabit ?

A. All Western, Central, and Southern Africa, with a considerable part of Madagascar and Australasia.

306. A large number of this race are found in both North and South America, where they are chiefly in a state of slavery.

307. The European or Caucasian is the most noble of the five races of men. It excels all others in learning and the arts, and includes the most powerful nations of ancient and modern times. The most valuable institutions of society, and the most important and useful inventions, have originated with the people of this race.

Which is the most noble of the five races of men ?
In what does it excel all others ?
What does it include ?
What has originated with the people of this race ?
To which of the races of men do the greater part of the people of the United States belong ?
To which race do you belong ?
F

"Races of Men." Source: Samuel Augustus Mitchell, *A System of Modern Geography*, 4th rev. ed. (Philadelphia: Cowperthwait & Co., 1853). Note questions and answers in number 307. This is one example of the pedagogical "system" of comparison and classification prevalent in academic texts. Mitchell's 1853 edition included illustrations and information culled from the Wilkes Expedition.

this chapter analyzes the interest shown by prominent anthropologists and ethnologists such as such as Samuel George Morton and members of the American Philosophical Society in the ethnological aspects of the proposed expedition. This chapter also introduces Charles Pickering and Horatio Hale, the two scientists who were assigned to report on the ethnologic and philologic contributions of the expedition.

The bulk of this work—chapters 2 through 5—covers the actual voyage itself. This chronological narrative includes the events, observations, and evolution of ideas pertaining to ethnology, and relations with the various people and cultures encountered. The final chapter analyzes the immediate reaction, impact, and interpretation of the ethnological data generated by the expedition upon its return to the United States in June 1842, particularly in relation to the broader "schools" of anthropology in the nineteenth century on both sides of the Atlantic. Finally, I contrast Horatio Hale's and Charles Pickering's work and its reception and impact in nineteenth-century circles. Most importantly, I analyze why the former was lauded while the latter's work was rejected by his peers.

In the process of researching, writing, and discussing this book, I have found that most anthropologists and historians of anthropology tend to regard the development of the discipline in the nineteenth century within a series of dramatic shifts or "leaps"—from philology to Darwinism to "Boasian" anthropology. In doing so, they disregard the period that is the focus of my book. The works of George Stocking, William Stanton, and Reginald Horsman have been overshadowed by those stressing the impact of Darwin, Lewis Henry Morgan, and Franz Boas, the "father" of American anthropology. The earlier "American school" of anthropology in the 1830s and 1840s, if addressed at all, is seen as an aberration in this shift—a scientific "wrong turn." Indeed, anthropologists and historians alike appear to hold their collective noses and step over the quasiscientific excrement of this era onto the cleaner, firmer, and more pleasing footing of Boasian anthropology. Obviously this might be considered a period belonging to the "imperialisms and parochialisms" of past efforts.

For example, in 1997 I participated in an American Philosophical Society conference on "Surveying the Record: North American Scientific Exploration to 1900," where anthropology received prominent attention—except for the American school of the 1830s and 1840s. One such presentation seamlessly moved from the Jeffersonian school of linguist-philologists such as Albert Gallatin and Peter Du Ponceau to John Wesley Powell, L. H. Morgan, and building up to Boas, omitting the American school entirely.

Another stressed philologist Horatio Hale's influence on Boas but ignored the former's work on the Wilkes Expedition.[5] Intrigued, I later went to my university library to conduct an informal survey of college anthropological textbooks in order to ascertain how anthropologists perceived and projected their own history.[6] Nearly all began their discussion of nineteenth-century work with either Darwin, Morgan, Edward Tylor, or Boas—the "classical era," as one author put it. One book jumped from Linnaeus to Tylor in one sentence—a leap of one hundred years! Two books left out the nineteenth century entirely in their background chapter. Not one book mentioned Samuel George Morton, Charles Pickering, or others of the American school. My conclusion was that an "anthropology of anthropology" was needed. Maybe the trace left by these discredited and avoided anthropologists and observers of the 1830s and 1840s should be analyzed in order to better understand Americans, anthropologists, and American anthropologists of that era and our own as well.

I believe that a distinct American school or national ethnology developed in the nineteenth century—one that cannot be compartmentalized into philological or anthropological stages. Rather, it was determined by (1) the interplay and competition with science and religion, (2) the aspirations of an expanding nation, and (3) unique American images of American blacks and Indians (a focus of my work). These images often transcended skin color and were used to measure and compartmentalize the remainder of the "uncivilized" world. Finally, I have found that the views of two nineteenth-century scientists crucial to my study—Horatio Hale and Charles Pickering—continue to be misrepresented by scholars in this field, when they are not ignored entirely, that is. A careful examination of Hale's and Pickering's written output from their experiences on the expedition, their interaction with their peers, and subsequent scientific work shows that labels such as "relativist," "polygenicist," or "racist" are of little value when measuring their work and contributions. The ideas of Hale and Pickering, taken together, represent a microcosm of the scientific and sociological debates of that era in America. Before I proceed, it is essential to describe the historical context of these debates within American society, as well as to prepare the backdrop for the United States Exploring Expedition itself.

While often swayed and inspired by the siren song of Anglo-Saxon romanticism wafting across the Atlantic, America's sense of immediacy regarding the frontier and its relationship to the past, present, and future of the emerging nation caused American naturalists to develop perspectives on natural history and ethnology divergent from those of their European counterparts. The intimate contact with Native Americans and blacks was producing a parallel perspective emanating from the West and South. Southern plantation owners chafed at the audacity of outsiders who criticized their "peculiar institution" devoid of any firsthand knowledge of the workings of the southern system. At the same time, American settlers on the vanguard of the western frontier—the contested turf running north to south along the eastern drainage of the Mississippi River that was the scene of bloody conflict between Indians and settlers—were sending a starkly pragmatic message eastward to the "seats of American civilization" in Philadelphia and Boston. The message was this: The Indians—considered treacherous, indolent, savage, and incapable of assimilation—simply had to go, either through emigration or extermination.[7]

Following the War of 1812, a new image of American nationalism that ran counter to the goals of many early nationalists emerged from the bitter confrontations with the British and the Indians. This vision, epitomized by that "backwoods commoner," Indian fighter, and hero of the Battle of New Orleans Andrew Jackson, rejected European civilization as antiquated and decadent and embraced the west as pure, unadulterated, and wholly American. The proponents of the new nationalism narrowed their eyes to allow only the barest generalities to filter through—expanses of land they considered theirs to possess and subdue by virtue of some natural, manifest birthright, land temporarily inhabited by a doomed human adversary. The Native American civilizations that were so greatly admired by some, and romanticized by most, were no longer considered part of America's heritage but its antithesis. Thus began the Jacksonian era.[8]

The story of the Jacksonian period in America is the story of a nation entering pubescence: growth pangs and mood swings abounded, together with brash assertions of adulthood when in the company of more mature nation-states—exemplified by the Monroe Doctrine, the boom-and-bust economic convulsions, and the plethora of religious revivals and cults springing forth from this period. The fount of strength from which such assertiveness flowed emanated from two sources: one was the nation's immense wealth of natural resources, land, and labor; the other a sublime confidence in the superior institutions engendered by the Declaration of Independence and the Constitution. Behind the democratic bravado of the Jacksonian period, however, a swell of conflict and tension began to percolate within American society that muddied the waters of the supposedly pristine republic with rivulets of doubt and insecurity.[9] A fluctuating social and economic system sent many to seek spiritual relief in the Second

Great Awakening, while many others rejected traditional religion and a materialistic society to follow Joseph Smith, William Miller, Mother Ann Lee, Robert Owen, or a multitude of other millennial and utopian pied pipers. After an uneasy truce of some two centuries, religion and science again began to lock horns. At issue was the origin of human life and the antiquity of the earth. The uncovering of disturbing and unmistakable (even to those encumbered by the mental restraints of their day) archeological and fossilized evidence pointed to an antiquity far in excess of Archbishop Ussher's calculations.[10] To make matters worse, that great contradiction of American liberty, the chattel system of the South, was being challenged vicariously in the free states by abolitionists such as William Lloyd Garrison and violently in the heart of Dixie by Bible-toting slave insurrectionists Denmark Vesey and Nat Turner. Threatened by these events, intellectuals north and south of the Mason-Dixon Line hastened to erect a bastion constructed of an alloy of religion, race, and economics in an attempt to bolster their potentially unstable social system.[11]

At this point it was science and not religion that stepped forward to rescue Americans from the siege of conflict and uncertainty over race that threatened to rend the fabric of American society. American science had, from its inception in the eighteenth century, prided itself in the "promotion of useful knowledge." In the nineteenth century, nothing could have appeared more useful to scientists than to determine the origin of mankind. While this quest was common on both sides of the Atlantic, there was in America a sense of immediacy brought on by the close interaction of the "black, white, and red races," a veritable laboratory of humanity from which to construct a racial model demanded by American society. There was, in fact, a long tradition of racialism in America dating back to early English colonialism. As Edmund Morgan so eloquently argues in *American Slavery, American Freedom*, the use of race to construct an American social system can be traced back to the turbulent era of Bacon's Rebellion in the 1670s.[12] What nineteenth-century science contributed to this model was the supposed objective and empirical proof of white racial superiority. It is no coincidence that the Jacksonian era witnessed the rise of the American school of anthropology, led by Philadelphia physician and naturalist Samuel George Morton.[13] In 1839 Morton published *Crania Americana*, in which the inherent capabilities of a race of people was scientifically determined by skull size and capacity. In its most extreme form, such work rent asunder the biblical and Enlightenment notion of the unity of mankind in favor of the theory of polygenesis, or multiple creations—even separate species—of humans.

A seemingly more moderate and generally accepted variation of scientific racialism adapted the naturalist's penchant for classification by imposing value and gradation upon the categorized races. There was unity, perhaps, but within a fixed and immutable hierarchy. Responding to the urgent social, economic, and political need for denying certain groups the privileges of the Constitution and the rights of a republican government, scientists contributed the building blocks for the construction of an American racial worldview.[14] They sought out and found the physical, empirical evidence demanded of it by American society—evidence that, to no one's surprise, placed the Anglo-Saxon as the most intellectually developed, morally aware, and physically beautiful creature of God's creation.

In an important sense, the study of humankind differed from the other sciences of its day. Within a culture that was increasingly receptive to the "objective" pronouncements of the trained scientists, ethnology, in its own way, stood apart as an egalitarian discipline. The savants of the nineteenth century had increasingly distanced themselves from the general population in terms of training, expertise, and specialization in fields such as zoology, geology, and botany.[15] The study and observation of people and culture, however, was still within the domain of the layman (much to the consternation of many scientists). For instance, all officers and scientists of the Wilkes Expedition were required to keep journals of their observations, which were collected by the government at the end of the voyage. In essence, these accounts, nearly all of which focused upon the cultures they encountered, qualified each voyager as an ethnological observer at some point. And certainly, with its component of blacks, Indians, and Mexicans, as well as white immigrants such as Irish and Germans, no other population in the world was better equipped to comment on other cultures as a result of firsthand experience than were Americans as a whole in the nineteenth century. This phenomenon, according to historian William Stanton, "tended to make every citizen, if not an ethnologist, at least a speculator on matters of race."[16]

This "multicultural" background set American explorers of this era apart from British and French observer-explorers during the same period. With the notable exception of philologist Horatio Hale, it is highly unlikely that the images and attitudes concerning American Indians and blacks carried across the Pacific by officers and scientists of the expedition were based on significant direct contact with either racial group back in the United States. The vast majority of these men were born and raised either in New England or along the eastern seaboard—areas largely depopulated of Native

Americans through war, disease, and relocation. No doubt some of the men had had limited contact with slaves working in the major southern seaport cities; virtually none would have visited southern plantations from whence popular images of Jim Crow and other minstrel imagery had supposedly been derived. Therefore, their images of Indians and black slaves would have been based not on personal observation but much more likely on the images engendered by popular literature, public performance, the above-mentioned geography texts and, for a few, scientific literature.[17] It was an image that I believe was in many ways uniquely American.

By the time of the United States Exploring Expedition, America, a nation bereft of kings, queens, and princes boastful of the absence of a rigid European class system, had instead created a unique democracy that not only justified the removal and extermination of Native Americans and the bondage of African Americans but also held promise for application beyond the boundaries of the Union as well. By applying American images of savagery to world cultures, American scientists and explorers helped construct the foundation for an American racial *weltanschauung* that contributed to the implementation of manifest destiny in this period and laid the ideological foundations for future American imperialism. The richly illustrated reports and published narratives, together with the popular museum exhibits subsequently generated by the United States Exploring Expedition upon its return, served as ethnological primers on the world's indigenous cultures and can be seen as precursors of later popular scientific publications such as *National Geographic*. Written and read in the context of a society already primed by generations of contact with blacks and Indians, these eyewitness accounts enabled readers later in the nineteenth century to further define themselves as members of an Anglo-Saxon, and superior, race in comparison to the indigenous people depicted in the narratives.

Until you have a skull, until you can look into one of those big orbits or hold a cranium in the cup of your hand, some people are not really satisfied that you have a new species.—Donald C. Johanson, president of the Institute of Human Origins, 31 March 1994

Americans by the nineteenth century were already old salts on the high seas. Boston merchants had been reaping huge profits from the China trade since the late eighteenth century. These latter-day Marco Polos wrapped their ships around Cape Horn and up the coast of America to the Pacific Northwest to purchase furs from the Indians, which were then exchanged in Canton and other Chinese ports for the silk, spices, and tea so much in demand back home. New Bedford, Nantucket, and Newport served as home ports for whaling, one of adolescent America's most profitable industries.

Just as surely as the landlocked explorers and fur traders of America's western interior, the captain and crews of these cruisers of commerce depended to a large extent upon the goodwill of those people upon whose land and waters they were encroaching. Fleeing from the hearth of white civilization for months or even years at a time, a whaler's only refuge was often an island port where supplies, rum, and sex spiced the monotony of the voyage. Many a South Sea islander filled out the crews of vessels depleted by death and desertion, no doubt driven by the same mixture of wanderlust and curiosity as their white shipmates. A few made it back to America. The equivalent of Melville's Queequeg was not an uncommon sight in the streets of Nantucket in the early nineteenth century.[1]

While sailors and sea captains were somewhat familiar with the Pacific islanders, Americans at home were, as a rule, ignorant of the languages and cultures of this vast region outside of the well-trod (by the British and French) areas of Tahiti and the Sandwich Islands. A whaler's spicy tale or a missionary appeal occasionally made its way into print; none of these remotely approached Captain Cook's narratives of his voyages through the islands in the previous century. *Omoo, Typee,* and *Moby-Dick* were still decades away.

Within the United States government in the 1820s there was a growing movement in favor of exploration on the high seas. Among the most staunch advocates of such oceanic endeavors was John Quincy Adams. This New Englander, an unflagging expansionist and nationalist throughout his multifaceted career as diplomat, congressman, secretary of state, and president, had long admired the expeditions of Cook, La Pérouse, and the Russian Bellingshausen. He was eager to see America take its place in the race for discovery and national glory over the seas.[2] Money was certainly available for an expedition of such scope; the coffers of the Bank of the United States were bulging from land sales, tariff duties, low government overhead, and a tiny military establishment. America was in the midst of the market revolution; technology was being dramatically welded to trade and commerce to produce cotton textiles and sundry manufactured goods. Nationalism and pride in the uniquely American lifestyle, a viewpoint incubated during the wars against England, had blossomed with a desire to further define themselves in relation to a perceived decadent Europe and the "savage" western frontier.[3]

It was this quest for the consummation of American destiny, economic opportunity, and a dash of "fallacious folly" from 1828 onward that nurtured and eventually clinched final appropriation for a national expedition in 1836. As for folly, there was just enough to pique the adventurous, too.

John Cleves Symmes was one of those eccentric backwoods philosophers whom America was spawning in abundance in the 1820s, not only in "burnt-over" upstate New York but in the newly settled West as well. Symmes, from Ohio, concocted a recipe of homespun history, rudimentary scientific observation (Where *do* martins migrate to when they head north?), native folklore, and his own ample imagination, declaring in 1818 "that the earth is hollow and habitable within; containing a number of solid concentric spheres, one within the other, and it is open at the poles twelve or sixteen degrees."[4] By traveling north through and beyond the halo of polar ice, Symmes was convinced that explorers would eventually find the entrance to a warm, inhabited inner earth. Perhaps those inhabiting this inner paradise would turn out to be Israel's ten lost tribes, a noble tribe of Indians, or perhaps another, new race of men.[5] Symmes spent the ensuing years lecturing and touring American towns and cities in hopes of winning over the general public and scientific community for a voyage to the poles.

Both the stately Adams and the dreamy Symmes were aided in their endeavors by a midwestern journalist named Jeremiah N. Reynolds. A landlocked publicist-enthusiast with, as Daniel Henderson has put it, "a gift for winning the respect of truly learned men," Reynolds became an early and valuable convert to Symmes's theories.[6] Largely through his efforts, a voyage to discover Symmes's hole nearly won congressional funding; failing that, it received official State Department encouragement as a private voyage of discovery.[7] Quickly outstripping the more introspective and unpretentious Symmes in his ardor for a national expedition, Reynolds eventually jettisoned the "holes in the poles" theory in the late 1820s for more tangible arguments in favor of a national exploring expedition. Whalers and sealers, naturalists, and nationalists such as Adams all lined up in support of Reynolds, flooding Congress with memorials on his behalf. A star-crossed three-year private cruise (Reynolds was "chief scientist") in 1829–31 failed to dampen his enthusiasm or quell his proselytizing for a larger, federal undertaking.[8]

In a speech before the House of Representatives in 1836, Reynolds capped the lobbying efforts of a number of interested groups, detailing in a lengthy compendium the benefits of undertaking a national expedition on the high seas. Reflecting the growing interest of the American scientific community in such an undertaking, Reynolds urged America "*as a nation* to add to the accumulated stock of knowledge," to "collect, preserve, and arrange every thing valuable in the whole range of natural history," and to "study man . . . in order to trace his origin."[9] From this developed the plans for the voyage that eventually set sail in 1838—the United States Exploring Expedition under Lieutenant Charles Wilkes.

On 14 May 1836 Congress took the first official step, authorizing the president to "send out a surveying and exploring expedition to the Pacific ocean and South seas, and for that purpose to employ a sloop of war, and to purchase or provide such other smaller vessels as may be necessary and proper to render the said expedition efficient and useful."[10]

Soon after, the Navy Department appointed Captain Thomas ap Catesby Jones to the command of the expedition. In addition, young Lieutenant Charles Wilkes was sent to Europe to purchase scientific instruments needed for surveying, exploring, and conducting experiments.

The purposes of the proposed voyage encompassed such a range of endeavors that a bevy of officers, technicians, and scientists was required on board to fulfill them. Ostensibly, the major task of the voyage was to promote the whaling industry by traversing and charting the areas where

American whalers roamed. In time, however, the objectives multiplied. The expedition was to round Cape Horn and, by way of Tahiti and Australia, head for the Antarctic in search of the landmass that supposedly lay hidden beneath the ice. Following a stay in New Zealand, it was next to continue to the South Seas to chart and explore islands such as the Fijis. From the Fiji group, the voyage was to continue to the Sandwich (Hawaiian) Islands and from there to the northwest coast of America for more charting and exploring.

The expedition was also to serve a military purpose. A new threat to American trade in the Pacific had appeared with the presence of a French fleet in the South Seas. The British, of course, had long been there. In 1836 Captain Jones, in a letter to Secretary of the Navy Mahlon Dickerson, foresaw the necessity of establishing American colonies in the region to counteract English expansion.[11] In addition, growing United States interest in the northwest coast of America increasingly ran counter to those of the Hudson's Bay Company operating under the protection of British warships. But it was not these perceived threats that prompted the expedition to include armed vessels such as *Vincennes*, a 780-ton sloop of war, and *Porpoise*, a 230-ton brig. The Navy Department, despite Jones's recommendations, insisted that the expedition was "entirely divested of all military character" and posed no threat to European interests.[12] The military firepower carried on the expedition was instead meant to send a message to the native inhabitants of the South Pacific, to make "impressions on the natives as to our *military power* and *national strength*."[13] Responding to petitions from American commercial interests in the Pacific, the navy intended "to hold intercourse with the native islanders and endeavor to put a stop to their savage habits and barbarous treatment of shipwrecked mariners, and to rescue such as are believed to be now in captivity among them," affording "protection to persons and security against loss of property from causes complained of by the various memorialists from Massachusetts, Rhode Island, Connecticut," employing military might "for the imposing effect such a ship would have on the minds of the natives."[14]

Then there was the enticement of California—a plum seemingly ripe for picking from the weak grasp of the new and debt-ridden government of Mexico. Charles Wilkes, the eventual commander of the expedition, later admitted that "the chief object of his visit to California was to obtain and report accurate information in regard to the bay of San Francisco to the government at Washington, with a view of future acquisition."[15]

Announcement of the voyage set off a wave of excitement within the

American scientific community, which was called on to recommend peers suitable for such work as well as to offer suggestions and proposals for fields of study. Many of the cream of America's young scientific talent, among them geologist James Dwight Dana, botanist Asa Gray, and zoologist-naturalist Charles Pickering, eagerly signed on to serve the expedition. In the course of the proposed expedition it would be their responsibility to collect specimens of flora and fauna as well as to observe objectively the habits of native peoples that were encountered. In October of 1836 the American Philosophical Society responded with a list and description of the major areas of scientific study that its members felt should be addressed during the expedition; these included astronomy and physics, geology, botany, zoology, medicine, philology, and ethnography. Peter Du Ponceau authored the section on philology, or "the Comparative Science of languages."[16] According to Du Ponceau, further study of "the variety of languages which exist on the surface of the Earth" would allow science "to trace as far as possible, the history of Mankind." He also added that such work "tends also to facilitate Commercial intercourse." He saw American philologists as being at the forefront of their field by virtue of their proximity to Native American cultures. It was these scientists who had brought to light "the forms and character of our Indian languages." He further asserted that the time was ripe for an American expedition. Philology had only recently been rescued from the dabblings of missionaries and travelers. A trained philologist, in contrast to a lay observer, would not be a mere compiler of random words but would systematically range from group to group taking care to utilize the same words in each collected vocabulary. Grammar, sentence structure, and the conjugation of verbs should also be noted as time allowed. Du Ponceau particularly recommended the use of the Lord's Prayer as a collecting tool (apparently oblivious to its cultural implications), "not because it is the best in a Grammatical point of view, but because it is that which Philologists have chosen from time immemorial, and therefore, is the best to serve as an object of comparison."[17] He reiterated that Americans had undertaken similar work before, referring to an attempt by Albert Gallatin and John Quincy Adams to collect and publish a "National Work . . . of all the languages spoken by the Indians in the United States."[18]

Interestingly, Du Ponceau considered ethnography as a separate science from philology, consisting of

the knowledge of the habits, manners, and customs of the different Nations of the Earth. Their manner of making War and Peace, their food, their dress, their festivals, their marriages and funerals, the education of their children, the rank by which their Women hold in Society, the division of labour among them, their mode of living, by hunting, fishing or agriculture, their traditions, their laws, their industry, their exercises, all these and other analogous subjects offer a vast field of information which it is important to collect as much in detail as possible.[19]

In light of their experiences with Indians in America, the gentlemen of the American Philosophical Society considered Americans providentially positioned to accomplish great things on the upcoming expedition through comparative philology. Such a study might also answer lingering questions concerning Indians and even blacks. At the same time that the society was briefing the government, Raynell Coates wrote to Dickerson that the ethnographical and philological data from the upcoming expedition may "shed a very desirable light on the question of the origin of the American Indians." He also held out the hope that "a careful examination" of the "diversified localities" of the Pacific Islands may uncover "points of analogy . . . to the negro race."[20]

For some, the importance of identifying and classifying both the American Indian and the South Sea islander took on an even more urgent tone. Many Americans in the 1830s, from the most erudite scholar to the backwoods circuit rider, felt acutely the pulsating crescendo of the millennial timepiece, tracked through biblical scripture and confirmed by the plethora of latter-day prophets arising from the ashes of the "burnt-over" district of New York to the camp-town revivals of the frontier. Truly America was fulfilling God's word as set forth in Joel 2:28: the sons and daughters of the nation prophesying, the old dreaming dreams, and her young seeing visions. Many would have testified to the beliefs and concerns that Sherlock Gregory expressed in his letter to the Navy Department concerning the exploring expedition: "From numerous of the prophecies of the scriptures I have been led to believe (and there is not wanting many imminent and learned men that believe the same) that there is to be without doubt a literal restoration of the descendants of the Hebrews to the land of their fathers, or to Palestine. This of course embraces the House of Judah . . . and the House of Israel, the Ten Lost Tribes."[21] Fearing that those nations impeding the restoration would be punished as were the ancient Egyptians, it was imperative for Christians to locate the present whereabouts of the lost tribes. Gregory felt not only that "the Aborigines of America are of those tribes" but that "very numerous islands in the Pacific Oc. are inhabited by the same."[22] Citing Jeremiah 31:10 as his source,[23] and working under the assumption (not uncommon) of their Indian-Jewish ancestry, Gregory compiled a lengthy list of physical and cultural comparisons to be made in order to determine the connections between the Hebrew sojourners and the islanders, touching upon rituals (circumcision, "firstfruits" ceremonies), "mournful" appearance ("it has repeatedly been observed that the American Indians strongly resemble the acknowledged Jews. Is anything of the kind been viewed with regard to the islanders of your acquaintance?"), residence ("The American Aboriginese generally reside in tabernacles or wigwams"), and language.[24] From letters such as these it is apparent that much was expected from the Exploring Expedition in the way of ethnology, even to the point of transporting America full sail into the prophesied chiliastic millennium.

By the summer of 1837 most of the appointed scientists had gathered in Philadelphia in order to collect books, materials, and hardware for the impending voyage, making frequent use of the libraries and facilities of the Academy of Natural Sciences and the American Philosophical Society.[25] It was during this time that they met with one of the most respected men of American science, Dr. Samuel George Morton, who took a "lively interest" in the upcoming expedition.[26]

Morton was a professor of anatomy at the University of Pennsylvania who was at that time immersed in a work that was to set the tone and direction away from philology and toward the emerging American school of anthropology.[27] Throughout the first decades of the nineteenth century, European anatomists had been hard at work in search of some quantifiable, physical characteristic with which to compare, classify, and rank the various types of humanity as they had done to the rest of the natural world. Such pursuits reflected a move away from Enlightenment notions of the essential similarity of humanity toward a compilation of essential differences. Pieter Camper, Lambert Adolphe Quételet, and Anders Retzius, among others, applied their calipers and yardsticks over the width and breadth of the human body, calculating and comparing bodily angles, ratios, and proportions.[28] Invariably their inquiries became focused above the shoulders. Scientists made comparisons of facial angle, location and size of protuberances, and cranial size and configuration among specimens from among Johann Friedrich Blumenbach's five races.[29] In a slightly different but not unrelated thrust, the Viennese physicians Franz Gall (1758–1828) and Johann Spurzheim (1776–1832) sought to map the contours of the skull so as to determine the over- or underdevelopment of the various compartments of the brain.[30] These first phrenologists concluded that, concerning the brain, "size, *other conditions being equal*, is a measure of power in the manifestations; that is to say, that

XVIII.

TABLE OF THE MEASUREMENTS OF THE NATIVES OF THE SEVERAL GROUPS OF POLYNESIA.

NATIVE OF	Height.	Facial Angle.	Front Line.	Upper Line.	Lower Line.	Length of Arm.	Length of Collar Bone.	Number of Teeth.	Length of Hand.	Length of Foot.	Circumference of Head.	Number of beats of Pulse in a minute.	REMARKS.
Terra del Fuego . . .	5 ft. 4 in.	64°	3 in.	in.	in.	29 in.	8 in.	32	in.	10½ in.	25 in.	66	About 22 years of age. Pecherai tribe.
Raraka	5 8	72	4¼	6	6¼	34½	6	32	7	10	22	61	Chief.
Tahiti	5 11	70	4	7	7½	30	5	30	8	11½	23	71	Chief.
Navigator's (Eastern) .	5 10	75	3¼	8	7	36	6	31	7	10½	24	65	Native.
Navigator's (Western) .	6 10	70	4½	7	6½	36	7	32	8	11	27	72	Chief.
New Holland	5 2	62	*1½	4¼	6½	30	4½	31†	6	12	20	66	
New Zealand	6 3	75	5	7	6½	36½	7½	32	8	10½	24	67	Pomare (chief).
New Hebrides . . .	5 1	64	3½	6	6½	30½	5	28	7½	10	11	68	About 13 years of age. Natives.
Tongataboo	6 4	70	3¾	7	7¼	36	7	32	4	11	24	66	Native.
Feejee	5 2	63	4	5	5½	32	3½	30	8	10¾	21	67	Native (Kai-si).
Feejee	5 11	67	6	7	8	34	5½	32	7½	11½	22	65	Vendovi (chief).
Rotuma	5 7	77	3½	7	7	35	4	32	8	10	24	74	Native.
Marquesas	5 6½	70	4⅝	6¼	6	28½	5½	32	7½	10¼	22½	66	Native.
Sandwich Islands . .	5 6	72	4	6½	6¾	35	6¾	29‡	7¾	12	22	66	Native.
Nisqually	5 9	61	4	5	5½	*18¼	4¼	30	7	10½	22	70	Native.
Californian Indian . .	5 4	70	4	6	5¾	*19½	4	32	7	10¾	19	77	Native of Sacramento Valley.
Luzon	4 7	64	*2½	4	4¾	27	4	30	6	9	12¾	70	Between 14 and 15 years of age. Native.
Malay	5 6	78	4¾	7	7½	27	4	32	7	11½	22	72	A native of Sooloo.

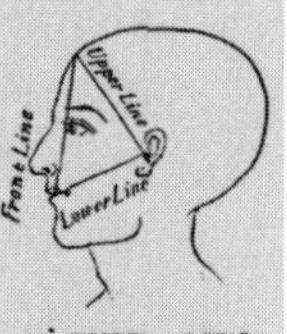

MEASUREMENT OF HEAD.

* The numbers in the table with this sign affixed are believed to be erroneous, but I preferred giving them as they were, to making any change. The table is from a copy the original record having been lost.

† One knocked out on his attaining manhood, as customary in New Holland.

‡ *Three knocked out on the death of Liho-liho*

"Table of the Measurements of the Natives of the Several Groups of Polynesia." While skulls from the various regions of the world were acquired during the expedition, little mention was made of the scientists and officers taking body measurements of native people. Obviously they did, as evidenced by this table, which is included in the appendix of the *Narrative of the United States Exploring Expedition* (vol. 5). Such statistics were valued by anthropologists such as Samuel George Morton. Source: *Narrative*, 5:539.

if age, health, exercise, and temperament be *equal* in two individuals, but if in one of them the mental organs be *small*, and in the other, *large*, the latter will manifest the mind most powerfully."[31]

Morton, as well, was fascinated with the possibilities for objective measurement and classification of humanity presented by the cranium, a part of the anatomy seemingly impervious to climatic variation and other environmental factors that might cause change to external features, such as with skin color darkened by the sun. In the early 1830s he set out to test the viability of this method by methodically collecting human skulls from the four corners of the earth in order to compare the cranial capacity of whites with that of other races. His method was to plug up the cranial orifices, then fill each skull to capacity with white pepper seed (later, lead shot) in order to determine its total volume, assuming a direct correlation of cranial volume with brain size and intelligence.

To be sure, Morton had no desire to conduct his own fieldwork, nor did he seemingly need to. An immensely popular and respected educator, physician, and scientist, Morton had only to sound the call to naturalists, explorers, friends, and colleagues in order to acquire skulls by the score from around the world. Then, surrounded by this macabre collection at home in Philadelphia, the doctor could impassively and calmly measure, sort, pour his pepper seed, calculate the results, and objectively organize mankind into a fixed hierarchy.

The work of gathering cranial specimens, however, did not always proceed so systematically. His associates in the field, however enthusiastic, encountered numerous problems collecting their grisly specimens. In 1833 Dr. William Ruschenberger, Morton's colleague at the Academy of Natural Sciences, reported from Callao that "The difficulty of obtaining skulls is much greater than you would suppose, from the prejudice existing with sailors and even officers against anything of the kind being brought on board ship. . . . The skulls I now send [from Arica] were dug up with my own hands, and I forward them in all their envelopes—They cost me a deal of labor, having dug up eight or ten graves to find them."[32] Despite these obstacles, Ruschenberger continued to collect skulls for his colleague, reporting from Batavia three years later that he was shipping "a Malay, an Amboince [Indonesian] and a Chinese, all in fine order."[33]

As much as Morton prized these additions to his collection, he was even more interested in obtaining crania of American Indians. His *Crania Americana*, published in 1839, heralded the rise of the new American school of anthropology, reflecting a scientific fixation upon American Indian origins as well as a response to the prevailing American racial environment. His hopes were twofold: to establish the uniformity of Indians as a separate race that had originated in America and to objectively quantify their inferiority compared to Caucasians. As to his beliefs concerning the future of the American Indian, Morton left no doubt when lecturing to his students at the University of Pennsylvania: "We found them a wild and erasable [*sic*— a Freudian slip après la lettre?] people—passionate, crafty and vindictive. We found among them a disinclination to the arts of civilized life, and to education and its requisite restraints." The American Indian, according to Morton's research, was the very epitome of savagery. "In fine, we observed that the unsophisticated Indian embodies in his character all the elements of the savage condition which only come into contact with civilization to be reduced yet lower in the scale of humanity; for it is justly observed that the Indian readily adopts the vices of the white-man, without imbibing his virtues."[34]

It was Morton's aim to objectify these beliefs. His correspondent-contributors in America, however, found that collecting skulls in the field could be anything but an objective exercise. Zina Pitcher reported from the Mississippi River at Fort Gibson that he was invariably at the mercy of the guide or interpreter when attempting to gather information on the identity of each unearthed skull.[35] Collectors could easily be deceived. From the banks of the Ohio River—an early archeological gold mine of mammoth bones and Indian mounds—local resident William Wood complained about the entrepreneurial spirit of the local residents: "There is a negro burying ground in the neighborhood which the inhabitants call *old indian*; but the interments have certainly been of a comparatively recent date. Were a stranger not careful in his examination, he would be deceived, as the neighboring people think everything in this vicinity of the *mamoth* kind, either in *time* or *size*, besides, they expect *pay for* pointing out *the best places*."[36] Others frankly admitted confusion over identifying the nationality of skulls that they sent to Morton; many specimens were acquired secondhand by those in the field from less than trustworthy sources.[37] Nor did everyone agree with the viability of Morton's hypothesis and method of generically grouping Indian skulls. While eager to add to Morton's collection, William Bird Powell was skeptical of its worth. He argued that "concerning the pure nationality of such specimens as you have . . . you must be aware that every Indian head does not any more represent his tribe than does that of every French or German head." Nevertheless, he conceded that "each tribe has a well marked national form of head, and between the several tribes there is frequently an immense difference of cranial configuration; and to obtain this *form* for *you* in every instance should be a prime object."[38]

Noted ornithologist John Townsend was one of Morton's most valuable and enthusiastic collectors, supplying the doctor with many Indian crania from the Pacific Northwest of America. Morton, writing to Townsend in 1836, was particularly adamant about acquiring several of the notorious "flathead" skulls. "With respect to *skulls*, you know how much I desire them for my projected work. You must not fail to bring me some Flatheads—no matter about expense—I will gladly repay it all and more. Any aboriginal skull from that remote region will be highly prized by me, or the skull of *any* animal whatsoever."[39]

Townsend proved equal to the task, forwarding to Morton Clickatat skulls with their "characteristic flat occiput," along with "some quadrupeds and birds." His accompanying letter illuminates his zeal for such work but also reveals that the natives took a dim view of American scientific methods.

It is rather a perilous business to procure indians sculls in this country—
The natives are so jealous of you that they watch you very closely while
you are wandering near their mausoleums and instant and sanguinary
vengeance would fall upon the luckless . . . who should presume to interfere with the sacred relics—I have succeeded in hooking one however. . . .
[I]n the course of winter I shall get more—there is an epidemic raging
among them which carries them off so fast that the cemeteries will soon
lack watchers—I don't rejoice in the prospect of the death of the poor
creatures, certainly, but then you know it will be very convenient for my
purposes.[40]

Duly impressed with Townsend's ardor, Morton attempted to secure for the
ornithologist a position on the upcoming Exploring Expedition.[41]

Though unsuccessful in this endeavor, the doctor still had many friends
slated to sail on the voyage who could keep him apprised of its progress.
Some, like conchologist Joseph Couthouy, had previously contributed crania
to Morton's collection.[42] Others such as James Dwight Dana corresponded
with the doctor. Certainly the best known to Morton was his colleague at the
Academy of Natural Sciences, Charles Pickering, whose early appointment
to the expedition must have lent an ample measure of luster and credibility
to the scientific nature of the voyage. Described by Asa Gray as "retiring and
reticent," with a penchant for scrupulous accuracy, this physician-naturalist
was renowned by his peers for his "encyclopedic and minute" grasp of
science, "looked up to as an oracle, and consulted as a dictionary by his co-
workers."[43] Of slight build and extremely nearsighted, Pickering nonetheless
had exhibited from boyhood a thirst for knowledge through exploration.
Born in 1805 in the wilds of northwestern Pennsylvania, he was raised by his
widowed mother and grandfather on a farm in Massachusetts, where as a boy
he would often lead botanical excursions into the White Mountains to study
and collect not only plants but insects, birds, and various quadrupeds.[44]
At age eighteen he entered Harvard College but soon turned his attention
toward medicine, earning an M.D. degree from Harvard Medical School in
1826. Early the next year the young doctor moved to Philadelphia, ostensibly
to practice medicine but more likely to avail himself of the facilities available
there for the study of natural history, his real passion. In October 1827 he
presented his first paper to the American Philosophical Society, "On the
Geographical Distribution of Plants," which was later published in their
Transactions. Even at this relatively young age, Pickering possessed a broad
vision of the interplay of man and nature. His study of the history of human
impact on the dispersion of plants throughout the world predated those

of twentieth-century ethnobotanists. Although he was elected to both the American Philosophical Society and the Academy of Natural Sciences in 1828, he felt more at home mingling with fellow naturalists within the library of the academy, located one mile west of the Philosophical Hall. It was while serving as curator of the academy in 1836 and 1837 that Pickering became involved in the planning for the upcoming Exploring Expedition. Even before being chosen for the expedition, he served on a three-man committee along with Samuel George Morton, who was then president of the academy, to formulate recommendations similar to those tendered by the American Philosophical Society for the prosecution of the scientific aspects of the voyage.[45]

Thirty-one when appointed to the expedition as zoologist, respected for his modest, even-tempered demeanor as well as for his vast breadth of knowledge—the "highest authority in the science of natural history, generally, to be found in the United States"[46]—Pickering was not without his detractors. A small but influential group of gentlemen scientists at the American Philosophical Society championed their own candidate for the position of zoologist—the sharpshooting artist, taxidermist, and family museumkeeper—Titian Ramsay Peale. According to society president Robert Patterson, Peale was everything that the bookish doctor was not. He warned that, compared to Peale, Pickering was "entirely inefficient in the procuring of the specimens—the observations of their habits in their native habitat—making drawings of them from the life, and preserving the skins etc., Dr. Pickering is no hunter,—is exceedingly near-sighted—cannot draw,—and knows nothing of taxidermy. It is only in the *book-knowledge* of natural history, that his superiority is supposed to be."[47]

Such was the influence of the American Philosophical Society that Peale, toting his arsenal of six double-barrel fowling pieces, rifles, one ton of assorted shot, and five hundred pounds of powder, was eventually included in the expedition as a generally unwanted companion zoologist to Pickering.[48] Indeed, this appointment may have influenced Pickering's decision to focus—at least as much as his nature would allow—upon anthropology during the voyage.

The assembled scientists considered the start of the voyage to be imminent; in fact they were only at the midpoint of a two-year period of setbacks and delays for the expedition. These problems emanated from political rivalries between the Democratic and Whig parties, competition among scientists for positions on the cruise, and chronic government inefficiency. Eventually Commander Jones ran out of patience and resigned his command in mid-1837. The navy subsequently discovered that, as a result of the ongoing difficulties and delays, few others were interested in command of an expedition that likely would never set sail. As something of a last resort, the command was offered to Lieutenant Wilkes, who accepted in March 1838.[49]

Wilkes, nearing forty at the time of his appointment, was the son of a wealthy New York City businessman. He had entered the navy in 1818 as a midshipman, spending his early years in the service aboard a variety of cruises to Europe and South America. Promoted to lieutenant in 1826, he began to study in earnest the various aspects of naval science, which included hydrography, geodesy, and astronomy. He received excellent instruction from Ferdinand Hassler, the first superintendent of the United States Coast Survey, and noted scientist and mathematician Nathaniel Bowditch. Few if any naval personnel could match Wilkes's grasp of naval science or his application of state-of-the-art surveying techniques in 1838.

The placing of a mere lieutenant in charge of an expedition that promised to endow its leader with some lasting renown was certainly controversial. The fact that this lieutenant happened to be Charles Wilkes added to the consternation within naval circles. The young officer's talents in hydrography and surveying were well known and respected. However, these abilities were offset by his reputation as the "stormy petrel" of the navy; as David Jaffe has put it, Wilkes was "known in scientific and naval circles as inordinately ambitious, arrogant, and defiant of authority" and a martinet who dwelled upon petty perceived slights.[50] As a result of Wilkes's appointment, many officers and scientists previously assigned to the voyage, including Asa Gray, submitted their resignations. Undaunted, Wilkes took stock of his position and quickly proceeded to reorganize and streamline the expedition.

In spite of the complex nature of this mission, Wilkes determined to rid the roster of scientific "bulk" by removing some of the civilian scholars. In turn, he assigned all scientific departments that in any way pertained to the naval profession—hydrography, geography, astronomy, territorial magnetism, meteorology, and physics—to a rising core of young naval officers trained in such duties. It was also his opinion that carrying a philologist on the cruise was unnecessary, as his officers could just as easily collect basic vocabularies and jot down unusual customs and practices of the natives they encountered.[51] His intention to drop the appointed philologist— twenty-one-year-old Harvard graduate Horatio Hale—elicited considerable protest within the scientific community, however. John Pickering, the highly respected former president of the Academy of Natural Science in Philadelphia (and uncle of Charles Pickering), appealed Wilkes's decision to the

Charles Wilkes. Engraving from a painting by T. Sully.
Source: *Narrative*, vol. 1, frontispiece.

secretary of the navy, explaining that "a knowledge of the languages of different tribes and nations is now an object of the *highest interest* among the learned of Europe, and of course will contribute essentially to the *eclat* of the Expedition as well as to the promotion of Science—and that this knowledge, to be good for any thing, must be *exact*, just as much as should be the case in astronomy, hydrography or other branches."[52] As to the argument that anyone could collect this sort of data, Pickering bluntly rejected it. Such efforts would amount to "meager vocabularies (such as we find in old voyages and sailor's narratives collected by persons wholly ignorant of the questions which are the subjects of discussion among the learned)." Finally, he warned that neglecting this science would "most certainly expose us to ridicule throughout Europe."[53] For most Americans, whether or not they had an interest in science, it was imperative that the United States must not come up second best in any endeavor.

Pickering's assertions reflect the rejection of the "grand Baconian principle" of induction through mere mass accumulation of data, so common to naturalists in the eighteenth century, in favor of bringing into the field "questions" that would in turn give the data its relevance and meaning: questions such as the "history of our race" and "the origin and relationship of nations" that weighed on the minds of scientists and theologians alike.[54] Not surprisingly, these were the same questions being asked by comparative anatomists such as Samuel George Morton. Eventually Wilkes was overruled by Secretary of War Joel Poinsett and the philologist was retained.

It is interesting that few quibbled with the appointment of Horatio Hale to this position, despite his youth and lack of familiarity with the reigning heads of American science. Hale had already established a reputation as an Indian linguist and ethnologist when, while only seventeen, he had gleaned an Algonquin vocabulary from his sojourns among Indian villages on the edge of the forest. Professor Josiah Gibbs of Yale had highly recommended the New Hampshire native and Harvard undergraduate for the expedition even before he had graduated in 1837 and defended his protégé when Hale was in danger of being dropped. Besides Hale's great intellectual capacity, Gibbs was impressed with "the urbanity of his manners, his devotion to his department, his cool and investigating mind," and—an essential trait for any nineteenth-century scientist—"his indifference as to the amount of his compensation."[55] Like Charles Pickering, Hale's father had died while Horatio was a child. He was raised by his mother, the noted editor and author Sarah Josepha Hale, who had hoped that Horatio would become a lawyer. Instead, Hale, like Pickering, was inexorably drawn to the forests, streams, and mountains of rural New England, often canoeing with neighboring Indians into the wilderness of Maine, upper New York, and Canada.[56] These early experiences proved to be a defining influence upon his professional methods of philological investigation.

Hale, for his part, desperately wanted to be included on the expedition.

Eager to make his mark among his peers, he viewed the expedition to the South Seas as "the opportunity of accomplishing what has been for many years an object of desire with me—viz.—the completion of the only department of philology (or rather ethnography) in which there is an entire deficiency."[57] Here was the opportunity to provide for science the missing link in the study of man and his origins and migrations, to carry civilization across the threshold of understanding by providing tangible answers to "questions" through scientific inquiry.

Finally, in August 1838 the United States Exploring Expedition set sail from Norfolk Navy Yard, the squadron consisting of the flagship *Vincennes* and five other vessels—*Relief, Porpoise, Peacock, Flying Fish*, and *Sea Gull*. Their goals were grandiose indeed, unabashedly echoing a theme that had served as the anthem of western exploration from Columbus to Cook: to thrust out across the ocean, carrying "the moral influence of our country to every quarter of the globe where our flag has waved," "pushing her discoveries furthest by opening the paths by which the benefits of knowledge and the blessings of Christianity and civilization may be extended throughout the Isles of the Sea. Besides reaping the rich harvest of present and contigent [*sic*] commercial advantage, we will acquire the proud distinction of Benefactors of the Human Race."[58]

As recommended by the American Philosophical Society, all officers and scientists were required to keep daily journals. Wilkes warned the more recalcitrant scribes that he expected "full and complete memoranda of all observations" and "not a mere copy of the log-board." They were to make particular note of "the habits, manners, customs, etc., of the natives, and the positions, descriptions, and character of such places as we may visit."[59]

Special arrangements were made to prepare for the anticipated encounters with the various natives along the voyage. Along with the usual assortment of beads, tobacco, and fish hooks, the ship's holds contained more "exotic" items such as accordions, jew's harps, carpet slippers, and vermilion. Sundry examples of a burgeoning American manufacturing community—cotton cloth, iron hoop, knives, and muskets—were also brought along to entice the natives into the market economy. Lists had been compiled in advance setting fixed rates on the items to be exchanged: for instance, it was expected that in the Fiji Islands, two pigs could be obtained for one American axe; a bushel of yams for a handful of blue beads, and so on.[60]

Finally, the Navy Department felt it necessary to instruct the expedition members in the etiquette and propriety of dealing with "savages and barbarians." They were reminded that the expedition was "not for conquest, but discovery." It was imperative that the first impression should be a positive one, since "much of the character of our future intercourse with the natives of the lands you may visit, will depend on the impressions made on their minds by their first intercourse with your vessels." Because "savage nations" were as yet unacquainted with the sacred American rites of private property, precautions were to be taken to prevent theft. If punishment was in order, "all due moderation and forbearance" were recommended. Anxious to get off on the right foot with the natives and aware of past indiscretions by sailors, the department warned that the rights of these people "must be scrupulously respected and carefully guarded." They were not to "interfere, nor permit any wanton interference with the customs, habits, manners, or prejudices . . . nor take parts in their disputes, except as a mediator." They were also instructed not to "commit any acts of hostility, unless in self-defence, or to protect or secure the property of those under your command, or whom circumstances may have placed within reach of your protection." The crew was advised "to display neither arrogance nor contempt" for those deemed lower on the scale of humanity and were encouraged "to appeal to their good-will rather than their fears, until it shall become apparent that they can only be restrained from violence by fear or force." The expedition was reminded that Americans were to stake no claim to any territory nor erect any colonies in native lands. For Americans, unlike the English and French, the "objects are all peaceful," echoing the commonly held view that a nation born out of colonialism should not inflict the same injustice upon others. American explorers would avoid hostilities merely by striving "to extend the empire of commerce and science."[61]

The government offered what they considered a sagacious summation of the generic characteristics of "savages," drawing from their constructed images of American Indians and blacks. First, they were treacherous, this being "one of the invariable characteristics of savages and barbarians." Second, "it is the nature of the savage, long to remember benefits, and never to forget injuries." While the United States Exploring Expedition would further embellish this definition of "savagery" over the next four years, it was never to be abandoned.

The Savages that call this place [Tierra del Fuego] home—better leave them un-honored and unsung. Yet they are no worse than the Fijians and Tahitians, or even than the dusky denizens of fair California.—Hubert Howe Bancroft, *The New Pacific*

The expedition first struck east from Norfolk, crossing the Atlantic on a shakedown cruise to Madeira, then following the curvature of Africa southwestward to the Cape Verde Islands. Following the trade winds, the small fleet cut diagonally across the equator and arrived in Rio de Janeiro during the last week of November.

Standing on the deck of the *Peacock*, Captain's Clerk Frederick Stuart admired the one-thousand-foot mass of perpendicular rock—Sugarloaf—thrusting out of the bay. Stuart then shifted his gaze toward the city and was struck by the remarkable configuration of mountains that formed the backdrop for the bay. A student of phrenology, his eyes beheld on the horizon terrain that bore "a great resemblance . . . to the face of a man while lying down, especially in that part which forms the forehead and nose."[1]

The expedition bided its time in Rio for over six weeks, repairing its vessels and making preparations for the first attempt to enter the icy seas surrounding Antarctica in search of a landmass. Generally, the scientists were disappointed to be marooned in an area that had been relatively well trod upon by earlier scientists of many nations and were anxious to move on to virgin climes. The philologist Hale found the urban environment around Rio devoid of true native inhabitants, and any attempt to foray very far into the interior was stymied by Wilkes. Instead, Hale and others focused their ethnological sights on the transplanted Africans held within the bondage of Brazilian slavery, a system the expedition members found to be quite distinct from their own "peculiar institution." For Americans unacquainted with Africans in their "natural state," such observations and comparisons with "their own negroes" proved enlightening.

The slave trade remained a thriving business in Brazil in the 1830s, despite British efforts to curtail it by patrolling the African and South American coasts. Thousands of slaves were imported annually into Brazil from various locations throughout Africa. Because so many slaves had been only recently wrenched from their villages and relocated in an unknown and hostile environment in America, there had not been sufficient time for acculturation nor significant loss of cultural identity to occur among these people. Unlike slave owners in North America, Brazilians made little headway and indeed expended little effort to strip Africans of their ethnic heritage, allowing those of similar ethnicity or tribal affiliation to associate together and retain their distinct languages and preserve elements of their culture—a phenomenon virtually nonexistent in the United States. Therefore, expedition members were afforded the opportunity to observe for the first time the broad range of physical and cultural characteristics of black Africans. Hale went to work collecting as many of the various vocabularies as time would allow.

Wilkes seemed befuddled by the variation, and after "the most cursory examination" referred to them henceforth as the "different races" of African slaves, remarking that some had "little of the distinctive negro character and others more of it than any human beings we have seen."[2] By the "distinctive negro character," Wilkes meant those traits supposedly inherent and common for blacks back in the United States. Time and again he utilized such comparisons. According to the captain (Wilkes had promoted himself from lieutenant during the first days of the voyage), the Minias and other tribes who had resided to the north of Equatorial Africa, were typified by their intelligent and dignified bearing and countenance, betraying "little of the levity usually ascribed to the negro race."[3] On the other hand, blacks from the southern regions of Africa "have the usual form of the negro, agreeably to our ideas . . . in general, short, badly formed, or clumsy, with narrow foreheads, flat noses."[4] Groups such as the Mudjuna, who had resided hundreds of miles into the central interior, were considered "among the ugliest of the African tribes. . . . [They are] short and ill formed, with the usual negro features in their most exaggerated forms."[5] Wilkes seemed genuinely surprised when confronted with evidence that the "negro stamp" was not impressed upon all Africans. It is not surprising that his assumptions of "usual negro features" harmonized with those of that shuffling caricatured favorite of the stage, Jim Crow, an American phenomenon just then coming into its own throughout the northern states.

Most expedition members considered the Brazilian system of servitude much more severe than their own "peculiar institution." While strolling the streets of Rio, Fred Stuart stepped aside while "half starved and naked" slaves passed by in gangs of eight to ten, "each bearing a burthen of from 2 to 3 hundred lbs. on their heads," singing in their native tongue "perhaps to put them in mind of better days and drowned if possible the thoughts of their present situation, which at best is but miserable."[6] To Yankees weaned upon minstrel shows, Jim Crow, and the "happy slave" of the southern plantations, such sights and sounds were grim indeed. One officer, possibly a southerner but obviously never a witness to a southern slave auction, sat before his journal on Christmas Day, 1838, pondering the contrasts: "Could the abolitionists of the U.S. behold the evils of slavery as it exists here, they might justly preach up their favorite doctrine. Indeed one who has been accustomed to slavery in the U.S. from his childhood might be shocked in walking the streets of Rio, at the abject condition of the slave and the brutal manner in which they labour and are treated. They are also bought and sold like cattle, and perform all the drudgeries of the ox, and at work like him, wear the yoke, not indeed of wood but of iron."[7]

Charles Erskine, a common sailor before the mast, was initiated into the horrors of the African slave trade while on board the *Vincennes*. When two slavers were apprehended by an English man-of-war brig and brought into the bay, the curious Erskine received permission to board one of the tiny vessels. At first he refused to believe that three hundred slaves were confined within the ship's hold, until he saw for himself: "When the hatches were opened, such a cloud of steam and such a horrible smell issued that it staggered everybody on deck. They found only thirty living human beings out of three hundred."[8]

Other aspects of race relations in Rio would have raised the ire of any northern or southern gentleman in the 1830s. According to George Colvocoresses, "their color operates less to their prejudice than with us."[9] Charles Pickering, in his rambles through the long and narrow streets of Rio, acknowledged that while most blacks were harshly confined, conversely the Portuguese gentry held no aversion toward allowing freed black men and women to penetrate Portuguese social circles—a philosophy only the most radical abolitionist would even dare to suggest in the States. Black police officers could be seen arresting white lawbreakers; ordained black Catholic priests gave daily communion to their parishioners. Pickering was also informed that blacks held positions of honor and trust within the government; some were even practicing attorneys. He found that intermarriage—the great phobia of the American plantation South—was not uncommon among the gentry. Black women moved freely "with their Portuguese husbands, in the first circles of society."[10] Wilkes was struck by "the indiscriminate mingling of all classes, in every place, all appearing on terms of the utmost equality . . . black and white, mixing and performing their respective duties, without regard to color or appearance. . . . There are many wealthy free blacks, highly respectable, who amalgamate with the white families, and are apparently received on a footing of perfect equality."[11] The paradox of such a harsh system of slavery coexisting with the "indiscriminate mingling" of black and white in Brazil baffled the American explorers. Their perceptions, however, were most likely colored by a misconception of the realities of the slave system in the United States; the myth of the "happy slave" being expounded on stages across the eastern seaboard was just that—a myth. Slavery in Dixie was harsh as well. Even more telling was the expedition's reaction to miscegenation and other social "mingling." Society in the United States had cordoned off the "savage"—whether they be slaves, free blacks, or American Indians. They had assumed that other "civilized" cultures did likewise. Evidence that challenged those barriers were bound to be viewed anxiously.

On 6 January the ships left Rio and commenced working south. After spending a week in the mouth of the Rio Negro, the ships of the squadron each made their own way against inclement weather and contrary winds to rendezvous at Orange Harbor on the southern cusp of South America before making a dash for the Antarctic in hope of discovering a landmass. The plodding storeship *Relief* had been sent ahead of the squadron and was the first to enter Tierra del Fuego, the frigid, windswept extremity damned by Magellan as a forbidden "land struck with eternal cold."[12] Its inhabitants, the Onas and the Yahgans, were considered so despicable and degraded as to be off the scale of humanity. Charles Darwin, who encountered the Fuegans when the *Beagle* had plied these waters just a few years previous, was so disgusted by their appearance that he seriously questioned whether these people—"short, misshapen, filthy, and certainly cannibals"—were indeed members of the human family.[13]

The *Relief* found the going tough, dense fog shrouding the shoreline as the heavy-laden storeship inched its way through the fitful elements and dangerous seas. In the first light of 22 January, Lieutenant Commander Andrew Long anchored the *Relief* in Good Success Bay, seventy-five miles northeast of Orange Harbor. Soon several Indians could be seen on the beach, apparently beckoning the Americans ashore. These were the Onas, a stout, copper-colored people wearing only short reddish brown robes made of guanaco pelts.[14] Long landed several boats of men to meet them.

The encounter was quite friendly. The officers were greeted warmly by the eldest Indian, assumed by Long to be the "chief" of the gathering of about seventeen natives, many of whom had their faces daubed with red and white paint.[15] Like Darwin, sailors raised on the tales of the "noble savage" of America's woodlands grappled with the new images of Indians who now stood in the flesh before their eyes. Despite their disturbing appearance and the ferocious reputation of these inhabitants, one officer was disarmed by their friendliness and pronounced them "very harmless." He was impressed by their distaste for the whiskey and tobacco that Long had offered them for exchange.[16] The commander was surprised at their calmness, confidence (they were unarmed), and lack of curiosity during the encounter, as "nothing seemed to attract or cause them surprise." The Onas exchanged bows and arrows only for hoop iron and nails, exhibiting considerable "cunning" during the negotiations, according to accounts.[17]

Other officers were not as charitable in their appraisals. Assistant Surgeon Edward Gilchrist dismissed the Onas "as dirty and stupid as they have always been represented."[18] They were deemed inordinately jealous, particularly of their women and children. No doubt this "jealousy," which was described as "their principal characteristic," was an unfortunate byproduct of European contact. According to Wilkes's narrative, "None of their women or children were seen, but they were thought to be not far distant in the wood, as they objected to any of our people going towards it, and showed much alarm when guns were pointed in that direction. They seemed to have a knowledge of firearms, which they called *eu*, or spirit."[19] Whenever the officers ventured in search of the Ona women, they were "immediately intercepted." Still the Ona showed "no marks of hostility" in doing so. Long finally had to order the men neither to approach the interior nor to search for the Ona dwellings.[20]

The *Relief* spent two days among the Onas, then weighed anchor and was reunited with the squadron on 18 February in Orange Harbor after a typically harrowing passage through the straits. The rendezvous was brief, as *Porpoise*, *Peacock*, and the schooners soon began their southward trek into the ice-clogged seas of Antarctica, leaving *Vincennes*, *Relief*, and most of the scientists behind in the windswept yet beautiful environment of Tierra del Fuego with its inhabitants, the Yahgan Indians.

The naturalists were eager to explore the verdant, forest-laden hills enclosing the harbor, a traditional rendezvous and rest stop for circumnavigators and whalers from Magellan to Cook. Such sojourners collected wood from the beech, birch, and willow groves and hunted the abundant fowl and fish among the coves and inlets. Overhead the somber gray Magellan clouds, appearing as "three burnt holes in the sky," cast their leaden shadows upon a frigid and alien land of mock suns, moons, and halos, brightened only by the aurora australis.[21] The environment was seemingly so hostile and foreign to their sensibilities that Passed Midshipman Joseph Perry Sanford pondered how "something having the shape of 'God's noblest work' may be found here" at the extremities of His creation.[22] Yet the Yahgans managed to survive and thrive in their surroundings.

First contact with the Yahgan Indians was made when a narrow birch bark canoe containing, in Wilkes's characteristically generic terminology, "an Indian, *his squaw* [italics mine], and four children" paddled out to the ships, a fire from a pile of sand and embers glowing in the center of the frail craft.[23] The explorers, peering down into the canoe, deemed the Yahgans even more debased and revolting than the Onas to the north. A closer inspection seemed to confirm their opinions. Diminutive—none reaching five feet in height— and extremely filthy by Western standards, their long, lank black hair fell upon shoulders deprived of even the skin of the guanaco for protection from the elements. Except for a slim piece of sealskin, they were "quite as naked and destitute and more so, then [*sic*] the baboon in the forest."[24] Their countenance was dominated by a broad, flat nose and a mouth described as so large that "you could not open them any wider, unless the almighty set their ears back."[25] Barrel-chested and spindly limbed, the Yahgans were judged "an ill-shapen and ugly race," a people "but little above the brute creation, and are the lowest in the scale of humanity."[26] A few of the officers and scientists waxed philosophic when attempting to reconcile what they saw with what they believed. Lieutenant George Emmons concluded that appearances notwithstanding, "they [the Yahgans] form a component part of the living, & it would appear, are necessary to complete the variety."[27] The New Englander James Dana was repulsed by such "an extremely degraded and filthy race of beings . . . probably one of the most debased races on the globe."[28] Obviously, for scientist and sailor alike, their preconceived and idealized notions of human beings in their "state of nature" had taken quite a jolt.

This disillusionment and disgust, however, was tempered with pity. "Poor creatures," Long soliloquized, "You do not seem to be so well provided for as the beast in the forest. . . . God protect you."[29] Dana, as a scientist, could not fathom how or even why they had managed to exist in such an environment; yet, unlike his contemporary Darwin, Dana the Christian saw in the condition of the Yahgans a cause for hope and an opportunity for his comrades. Echoing the age-old call of the missionary, Dana wrote that

"Fuegians and Canoe." Source: *Narrative*, 1:123. From a drawing by Joseph Drayton. "Poor creatures, you do not seem to be so well provided for as the beast in the forest. . . . God protect you." Andrew K. Long, Journal, 31 January 1839.

"it is difficult to imagine how they exist—they call loudly on the Christian world for instruction both as to what concerns their temporal comforts and spiritual interests, for they are not but little above the brutes—But they inhabit one of the most inhospitable climates in the world. . . . No people on the globe stand more in need of the renovating principles of the Bible."[30]

Prior to the expedition's departure from Norfolk in August, the young geologist had undergone an emotional religious conversion, and his perceptions were those of one who had but recently tasted the heady wine of salvation that flowed throughout America during the second Great Awakening. Whatever his professional opinions concerning the Yahgans, as a witnessing Christian he was not willing to deny their humanity. Dana waged a personal duel between the spiritual and temporal that reflected the larger struggle between religion and science in Western society. Dana, for example, was both "somewhat amused, though at the same time shocked" when one of the marines on board *Relief*—an "infidel" by Dana's estimation—remarked to anyone within earshot that surely " 'God never made these people—He would never make such filthy brutes.' "[31] Dana would have none of this. Instead, he considered the Yahgans a tragic and extreme example of just how far humanity had fallen since the Garden of Eden—an ethnological perspective out of the Enlightenment that explained the "degeneration" of cultures by their centuries of sinfulness and rejection of God's grace. The Yahgans provided a counterimage: They represent both God's disappointment with the human race and an example of what "civilized" Americans should not become. Where once there was Paradise, "man, who was made in the image of his maker, has been reduced by sin" to the fate of the Yahgans. Regeneration was possible but only through Christ: Dana's prayer was that "God grant that these wretched beings may soon learn of the ways of salvation."[32] Fewer and fewer scientists after Dana were able to resolve personally these ethnological dilemmas without sacrificing portions of either their spiritual or temporal ideas. As the bonds between religion and science degenerated and dissolved into separate spheres during the nineteenth century, scientists from Samuel Morton to Charles Darwin concocted other formulas that held no such hope for people like the Yahgans.

Meanwhile, curiosity, scientific and otherwise, soon overcame distaste and revulsion. When a few Yahgan men were coaxed aboard ship, quite an interesting banter developed between explorer and native. The women, however, steadfastly remained in their canoes, hunching over and tending the fires while sailors dangled presents over the railing as enticements. Some were impressed by this apparent spark of virtue and "an uncommon share of modesty" among the women.[33] No doubt they would have been even more surprised had one of these naked Yahgan women—as they were wont to do—stood up, only to dive into the frigid kelp beds in search of shellfish.

The natives astonished and amazed the scientists and crew with their uncommon ability to mimic virtually every sound and word they heard, down to the precise inflection, accent, and rhythm. Simultaneously, however, such a talent completely thwarted Hale's attempts to glean even the barest vocabulary from the Yahgans, who mimicked his attempts to have them identify any object "with an extraordinary accuracy."[34] Dana was equally nonplussed: "The only native phrase they spoke was something like *yamoskanak*, and this was always in their mouth. Whatever question was asked them they would repeat it, word for word, enunciating each syllable distinctly and almost as correctly, as if a native of New York—ask them, what do you want?—they say 'what do you want, yamoskanak,' laughing at the same time, apparently as much diverted with us, and our novelties, as we with them."[35]

One can only guess at the natives' refusals to share any of their language with the Americans. Later in the century, an English sheepherder named Lucas Bridges, while living among the Yahgans, compiled a dictionary of thirty-two thousand words. "Yamoskanak," however, represented the lone entry in Hale's Yahgan dictionary.

Meanwhile, the men who ventured on board continued to astound the crew with their feats of mimicry. "Their imitations of sounds," Wilkes wrote, "were truly astonishing." To his amazement, "one of them ascended the octave perfectly, following the sounds of the violin correctly. It was then found he could sound the common chords, and follow through the semitone scale, with scarcely an error."[36]

Wilkes was perplexed by the seeming incongruity of Indians "continually singing . . . very talkative, smiling when spoken to, and often bursting into laughter," and he was annoyed at what he considered their "truly ridiculous" mimicry. He preferred Indians to maintain their "natural serious and sober cast," as in the classic image of the American Indian.[37]

When the rest of the squadron returned from the Antarctic in late February, they received a visit from the Yahgans as well. On board *Peacock*, a fifer serenaded the natives with " 'My Bonny Lad,' 'Sweet Home,' and 'The Girl I Left Behind Me.' They did not understand these songs, but when he struck up 'The Bonny Blue' they were all immediately in motion, keeping in time to the music."[38] Joseph Couthouy presently took a native in his arms and waltzed about the deck, a scene that greatly amused some but angered others of his shipmates.[39]

Such gaiety disintegrated into a more debased humor, however, as sailors commenced to dress up the natives "as soldiers and sailors," then parading their "new recruits" before a mirror to observe their reactions. One such native, rechristened with the moniker "Jim Orange," was kept on board ship for a week, dressed and fed, "washed and combed," until he became "dissatisfied, and was set on shore, and soon appeared naked again" to the disappointment of the crew.[40]

Although such "amusements" were enjoyed by the expedition's crew, they did little to expand their knowledge of Yahgan life. So little information was gained that the scientists were unable even to discover their means of obtaining fire. If the Yahgans purposely intended to draw a veil over their culture, they were certainly successful. Like the Onas, and probably for the same reasons, they seemed particularly anxious to prevent the Americans from locating and entering their huts. Finally, artist-draughtsman Joseph Drayton and purser J. C. Waldron were able to finagle their way to the entrance of a Yahgan dwelling. Despite this intrusion, they were greeted warmly in the Yahgan tradition of locking arms and jumping up and down while face to face for a minute or more to the accompaniment of a native song. Once inside the cramped habitation, facing a semicircle of natives three-deep around a smoldering fire, Drayton, through signs, attempted once again to probe into the culture of his hosts. His queries focused on whether the Yahgans believed in a Supreme Being, a question which reflected well his own culture's concerns and agendas for study. To their surprise, they received a favorable reply from one man, who "clasping his hands as in our mode of prayer . . . said Eloah Eloah," which was taken as sufficient evidence of their belief in God.[41] As a result of this rather dubious revelation, Hale was able to jot down a second entry alongside "Yamoskanak," which of course doubled the size of his sparse Yahgan dictionary.

The Americans as a whole generally felt kindly toward the natives, their pity bolstered with large doses of condescension. To most, the Yahgans were merely "poor, inoffensive creatures," a "timid race," described as "inno-cent . . . beings that did not touch any article that was not given to them."[42] Wilkes was less impressed. He accused the natives of "stealing" a windsail that had been left on shore to dry. To compound this breach of Western taboo, the Yahgans, in Wilkes's eyes, were obviously bad capitalists on account of their having "little or no idea of the true [i.e., Wilkes's] value of articles."[43]

Whatever their feelings were toward the natives of Tierra del Fuego, none but the most positive and hopeful of the expedition—Dana, for example— could bring themselves to imagine the possibility of their becoming "civ-ilized." For some, like Passed Midshipman William Reynolds, romantic notions of the "noble savage" living in an idyllic state of nature were dashed upon the frigid crags of Cape Horn. "If *they* be the children of Nature, I am thankful that I am a member of a more artificial community, & will waive forever the belief, that those barbarous ones who have the fewest wants, lead a more enviable existence, than the great civilized mass, who are always wanting."[44]

Despite their inability to compile a vocabulary or delve into Yahgan ways, the expedition did manage to make some ethnological headway. Fish spears, bows, quivers and arrows, slings for throwing stones, a paddle, guanaco wool, and assorted necklaces were traded for and packed away.[45] Physical measurements were taken of the natives, these tabulations representing the first entries in the expedition's "Table of Comparative Proportions."[46] Finally, in the spirit of Samuel George Morton, the first human remains found on the expedition were exhumed—burnt bones were dug up and removed from a solitary cave near Orange Harbor. The new American science had penetrated "even unto the ends of the earth."

Before the expedition was to strike out onto the South Pacific, two more ports remained on the agenda along the western face of this continent. From late April to early May 1839 Wilkes reassembled the squadron in the Chilean harbor of Valparaíso. Here they were feted by a round of parties and banquets for over a month. Pickering, upon observing the racial makeup of the Chileans, noticed the scarcity of pure Indians—"white blood," he felt, "evidently getting the upper hand."[47] Considering the ignominious and violent legacy of his own native country toward indigenous people, it is not surprising that he found it both "novel and interesting [in Chile] to perceive one physical race thus quietly giving place to another, without outrage or oppression," a perception expressing a certain naïveté about the Spanish conquest.[48]

While the bulk of the expedition thus lingered in Chile, several of the scientists made their way to Callao and Lima in hopes of exploring the Peruvian highlands. They were finding it hard to stifle their impatience at being confined thus far to locations previously well gleaned by earlier scientists, and they longed for something to titillate their scientific palates. Peru held much for those interested in the origins of the races. Its artifacts had already yielded important and controversial data for Samuel George Morton and his ongoing construction of a racial hierarchy. The glories and achievements of the Inca civilization were well known to scientists in the 1830s. Indeed, the apparent contradiction between how such genius could germinate and spawn from the diminutive Incan skulls such as the ones sitting in Morton's "American Golgotha" pointed to an aberration in Morton's findings, a discrepancy that was obvious to contemporaries such as the phrenologist George Combe.[49] Thus the expedition was anxious to add to the existing body of knowledge of Incan physiology by inspecting and gathering more data—in the form of Peruvian skulls—for comparative analysis.

For Charles Pickering, contemporary Peru was nearly as fascinating as its ancient Incan ancestors. Perhaps reflecting upon the tales of Sir Walter Scott and the other romantic paragons of his day, he found that "Ever since I had been in Peru, I had not been able to get it out of my head, that we had somehow gotten back into those old times that Poets and Novelists are so fond of, familiarly called the 'Dark Ages'—the Knife produced at the slightest affront, the mode of travelling, the frequency of highway robbery, a walled city, women covering their faces; the language I heard spoken, so much like the Latin, even the forms of the Roman Catholic Religion, etc."[50] Wealthy and mysterious *señoras y señoritas*—seductive, veiled "black Apparitions" hidden beneath the *Saya y Manto*—hearkened back to the fictional times of Ivanhoe.[51] William Reynolds, no doubt voicing the opinions of many a sailor, found these women "lovely beyond belief."[52] Pickering also painted a vivid depiction of the lower-class woman of Peru—cigar or cigarillo in her mouth, shaded from the intense sun by a broad, round straw hat while sitting astride her donkey, exuding a "striking air of independence."[53] Charles Wilkes, however, construed such apparel as both "awkward and absurd." When he witnessed a performance of the "national dance," the *sambacueca*, the prim commander was struck speechless, later writing that "no words can describe its vulgarity and obscenity."[54]

Both Pickering and occasionally even Wilkes found themselves reflecting favorably upon a culture so at variance with their own, particularly at sunset, when the sounding of the cathedral bell summoned the ancient rite of *Oraciones*. "Every-one within doors quits whatever he may be about, everything in the streets stop and the men uncover; which continues for about a minute, when at the second signal everything goes on as before. I do not know what habit may not do, but if anything would teach men reflection, seems to me it is some such observance as this.—In their zeal for church reform, it may be well for Protestants to inquire, whether they have not left out too much."[55]

During their stay in Peru, Pickering led a group of fellow scientists and officers to the ancient pre-Columbian ruins of Pachacamac, located on the coast twenty miles southeast of Lima, in search of skulls and other artifacts that might shed additional light on the ancient Peruvians. They survived a harrowing landing through a high surf that capsized their whale boat. The walled ruins sat on a hill near the shore. Passing through the gates, Pickering was immediately struck by the "Egyptian like shapes" of the apartments and pilasters. Midway between the great temple and the town, the party halted at what appeared to be the burial grounds and commenced collecting specimens à la Morton from among the rectangular, stone-lined pits.

According to Pickering, the site was in disarray.

> Skulls were laying here and there, and the ground was strewn with fragments of antique cloth and buried in dust, the evidence of various excavations which have been made by visitors. Skulls from this place are known to present a remarkable point of symmetry, probably the result of some mode of carrying the new born babe, or attempt to alter the natural conformation. Others presented the usual character of the Ancient Peruvians, vertical elevation, or the raised occiput:—while others had the forehead and top of the head decidedly depressed.—a selection of eight was made for the Government.[56]

Temple of Pachacamac. Skulls and artifacts were collected by Pickering and others at this anthropological site. Source: *Narrative*, 1:279.

Pickering, however, found the various vegetable substances that had been buried along with the dead of even more consequence than the octet of skulls bagged for the government. For in his grand, Humboldtean perspective of nature, determining the various races of man was only a single step toward answering a question of much greater interest and import: the history of humankind and its interaction with the environment, particularly plants and their comigrations with humans. This had been the topic of his first scholarly paper, delivered before the American Philosophical Society in 1827, and remained his intellectual quest throughout his lifetime, culminating in the publication of his magnum opus, *The Chronological History of Plants: Man's Record of His Own Existence, Illustrated through their Names, Uses, and Companionship*, nearly fifty years later in 1878. So, while the rest of the expedition party rummaged through the Incan graveyard for intact skulls, Pickering declared that "what interested me more particularly were numerous vegetable substances. Here then was evidence of the existence of these vegetables here before the arrival of the Spaniards."[57]

Meanwhile, back in Lima, Titian Ramsay Peale, on the outs with most of the other scientists, whiled away his days in and out of the churches and public buildings of the city. He soon found, however, that he need not leave Peru empty-handed. Visiting the great Cathedral of Lima, Peale ventured below the high altar to the burial vault, which contained the remains of all the prior archbishops of Peru, dating back to the sixteenth century (excepting one, who had had the audacity to support the forces of revolution against the Spanish Crown). There, in the musty chambers of these departed spiritual patriarchs, Peale found that one did not necessarily have to ascend the Andes to collect skulls for the United States government. "In vaults under the great altar all their bodies . . . are interred in the niches of the sidewalls. Many of the coffins are open, exposing the dried up remains, of which the Sextons made no difficulty about disposing for a small compensation—'if I will give you a dollar will you allow me to take that skull?' 'Como no' says the Sexton."[58] Later, when the expedition finally departed Lima for the South Pacific, Peale mused that "two [skulls] at least are now tossing over the waves of the Pacific toward the islands, where probably they will receive the company of some equally honored cannibal, *sic transit gloria mundi.*"[59]

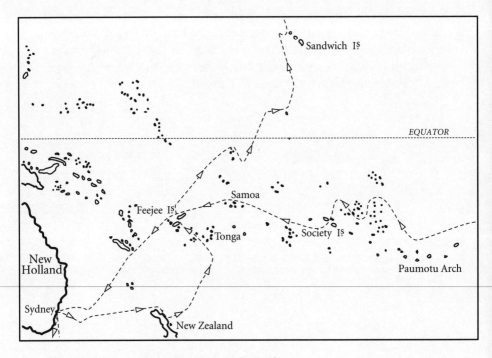

The United States Exploring Expedition in the Pacific

Heaven help the "Isles of the Sea!"—The sympathy which Christendom feels for them has alas! in too many instances proved their bane.—Herman Melville, *Typee*

Leaving Callao in late July, the squadron bore southwest toward the "fairy islands" of the eastern Pacific.[1] The Paumotu group, consisting of the Dangerous, Disappointment, and, nominally, the Society Islands, were for the most part circular coral outcroppings that freckled the eastern Pacific.[2] Only the latter cluster—including the now legendary Tahiti—had been seriously explored and exploited by Europeans by the 1830s. The members of the expedition anxiously anticipated their first taste of coconuts and breadfruit, white sands and ringed lagoons. Most had had their appetites whetted by poring through the popular narratives of Cook and Wallis. Tahiti, of course, was the staple fantasy and geographical locale of many a sailor's yarn, where sailors become gods in a heavy-lidded nirvana of roast pig, poi, and permissive women. Ships' captains kept one eye on the blue waters, nervously navigating through submerged coral castles that could tear open the bowels of a sailing vessel like a jagged knife, and another to detect the outcropping of mutiny and desertions that spread like a disease whenever vessels entered these waters.

Captain Wilkes eagerly anticipated exploring these waters. Hedonism, however, made no headway in motivating this stern officer. Instead, he knew that though these islands had been known to Europeans for a century or more and were well trafficked in parts, little accurate surveying had been accomplished—possibly a result of the tempting distractions that enticed mariners. Wilkes intended to correct this. While the expedition had been at sea for one year, he felt its work was only now entering its most important phase, not only concerning surveying and hydrography but also in matters of natural science. Wilkes reflected philologist Hale's aspirations in declaring that the expedition's sweep across the Pacific "would thus enable us to trace the inhabitants from one end of Polynesia to the other," thereby shedding light upon origins and migrations of the "races."[3]

To ensure that intercourse with the natives would be devoid of "any misdemeanors, and [to] insure a correct deportment in both officers and men," Wilkes issued an abbreviated version of the general order concerning the treatment of the natives of the Pacific Islands, stressing that "neither contempt of nor interference with, their customs, habits, manners, and prejudices, nor annoyance over them" would be condoned, "that no act of hostility will be committed, and that an appeal will be made rather to their goodwill than to their fears." He promised that any violations of this policy "will meet with the most exemplary punishment."[4] Such orders assumed that the expedition would be welcomed or at least tolerated at each locale they visited. Already they had found that it could be annoying and aggravating when natives, such as those in Tierra del Fuego, courteously but pointedly attempted to shield their homes and ways from foreign encroachment. The commander was later to insist that "no opportunity has been omitted to land on the islands and establish a friendly intercourse with the natives."[5] But in fact, when put to the test by recalcitrant islanders of the Paumotu group, it was Wilkes himself who took the lead in disobeying his own directives, his general orders tossed overboard into the sea of good intentions.

On 14 August the first "dull white coral strand" of the Dangerous Islands appeared on the horizon: Clermont Tonnerre, according to the charts (called Reao today).[6] Wilkes promptly launched the survey boats and granted permission for a few of the naturalists to go ashore. Soon, Pickering and others were splashing through the crystal-clear surf, excitedly observing the "brilliant hues of the myriad submarine life of the coral isles."[7] After two hours of collecting in this rich environment, the naturalists swam back to the ships without, however, coming into contact with the inhabitants. The next day would be very different. When Wilkes dispatched three boats toward shore, they were "welcomed" by a large group of men and boys brandishing long javelins, "calling to us and motioning us to be off."[8] Wilkes, who was in one of the boats, sent John Sac ashore to talk to the natives. Sac, a native New Zealander and Maori "chief" who spoke the Tahitian language, only worsened the situation, according to Wilkes. Seemingly as a result of Sac's diplomacy, the natives were now shouting at Wilkes to "go to your own island. This belongs to us, and we do not want anything to do with you."[9] Wilkes blamed the contrariness of the natives not on the threat and danger of foreign encroachment by the expedition, or on previous hostile actions by whites, but on Sac's inherent "savage" character. By doing so, Wilkes

Natives looking out to sea. The inhabitants of the islands in the Paumotu group had good reason not to welcome the arrival of the Wilkes Expedition, based on their prior experiences with whalers and merchants. Watercolor by Alfred Agate.

effectively redirected the responsibility for the unpleasant encounter away from the expedition and those foreigners who had preceded him. In his eyes, civilization is blameless—the fault lies with and within the "savage."[10]

Though considered "generally a well-disposed fellow" who had "imbibed some feelings of discipline," beneath this thin veneer of "civilization" Sac was, in Wilkes's estimation, "truly a savage." He watched from his launch as the Maori became more and more agitated with the obstinate natives. Soon the veneer was shed and the sailor had, in Wilkes's eyes, reverted to the "fierce majestic-looking warrior" of his native New Zealand, confronting the islanders with such a ferocity that "the one appeared as savage as the other."[11] Though Sac later denied inciting the natives, Wilkes was convinced where the blame lay.

An hour passed and still the boats lingered off shore. Wilkes, hoping to divide and conquer, split the three vessels and attempted to land elsewhere on the island. The natives, however, likewise split up and again met the boats as they approached the beach. George Emmons encountered twenty natives making "gestures that were evidently intended to induce us to land—

This scene was repeated numerous times in the Paumotu Islands. Here Agate captures a naturalist—gun and collecting bag in hand—wading ashore. An islander awaits to usher him back into the surf and off the island. Watercolor by Alfred Agate.

and at one time appeared to be going through drill—marching in Indian file."[12] Impatient, Joseph Couthouy and two others leapt from the launch and made for shore, bearing trinkets as their passport. Emerging from the surf, Couthouy was met by a man he assumed to be the "chief" of Clermont Tonnerre. The man motioned to the naturalist not to proceed further. When Couthouy continued to advance toward the native despite this warning, the "chief . . . with a shout and distortion of countenance" lunged at the naturalist with his spear and chased the fleeing Couthouy back into the ocean. Emboldened by their success, the islanders, who up to that point had limited their defense to emphatic words of warning, now began hurling bits of coral at the piqued crews. Wilkes was affronted by the apparent temerity of such a people, and while he insisted that he "felt no disposition to do them harm," he had no idea of letting them see and feel that they had driven us off without landing."[13] And so the captain, frustrated and not a little embarrassed that the expedition's first Pacific encounter was going so poorly, proceeded to disobey his own general order. First, upon his command, several blank cartridges were fired toward shore to frighten the islanders but with no effect. (Wilkes later found out why: European pearl fishermen had used the natives of Clermont Tonnerre for target practice in earlier years, which also helps to explain the expedition's less-than-cordial reception.) Next, he loaded his pistol with mustard-seed shot and fired at the nearest natives but missed. Finally, Wilkes turned to the sharpshooting naturalist Titian Peale and ordered him to draw a bead on the spear-wielding "chief" who had caused Couthouy to turn tail. Peale complied and quickly peppered the legs of his target with painful mustard shot. Seeing their comrade in pain, the islanders finally yielded the beach. It was a small victory for the expedition, however. So much time had been consumed that a subsequent landing proved fruitless in the dusky, waning afternoon, and the crew shortly thereafter returned to their ships. In describing this encounter, Wilkes, though irritated at the failure of the landing, was favorably impressed with the physical features of the islanders of Clermont Tonnerre—at least from the vantage point of his launch. This "fine athletic race," dark skinned, with straight raven-like hair, Wilkes felt, closely resembled "our Indians."[14] It is impossible to ascertain just how much personal contact the men of the expedition had had with "their" Indians in the United States. With few exceptions, it would be safe to assume that these men of the sea had little firsthand knowledge of either the physical features or culture of the American Indian. At best, a few may have, in their youth, gained a regional sampling of the remnants of one or another Atlantic coast tribe. It is obvious, however, that Americans considered themselves expert judges of what comprised an Indian—"our Indians."

At daylight on 18 August the squadron left Clermont Tonnerre for Serle Island (present-day Pukarua), another low coral atoll twenty-six miles to the northwest. Upon arrival, boats were dispatched for the usual surveying and reconnaissance. Lieutenant James Alden, in charge of one of the boats, was soon surrounded by natives friendly in the extreme. These islanders gladly exchanged their valuables—plumes from the frigate bird, tapa, coconuts, and the like—for bits of iron and various trinkets. Though willing and friendly traders, they could not be enticed aboard the survey boats. For that matter, despite assurances by the natives of their good intentions, none of Alden's party would venture ashore. "After leaving as far as the beach they sent all their spears away and made signs for us to come on shore—we should have been very glad to have *rubbed noses* with them but as we had no arms in the boat to cover the landing thought most prudent not to accept their polite invitations."[15] One native made off with Alden's notebook but returned it "upon seeing the anxiety of the owner."[16] Wilkes deplored such "arrant thievery" but was encouraged by the hospitality of the Serle Islanders. Due to some less-than-skillful sailing by the captain, however, by the next morning *Vincennes* found itself to have drifted out of position for further exploration of the island—another opportunity lost for the naturalists.[17]

From the Dangerous Islands the expedition continued northwest toward the Disappointment Islands. Along the way they paused at an uninhabited atoll, possibly to atone for the scientists' lack of collecting time at the preceding stops. Sifting through the species *Scaevola* and wiry *Suriana*, Peale found the birds so tame that he need not resort to his musket to gather them up; he could just shinny up a pandanus tree and take them by hand. Peale no doubt wished that the natives of these parts were so obliging.[18]

On the morning of the 24 August, while still several miles from land, the crew awoke to a song emanating from the water, a tune "though wild, [was] not only musical but something fine and pleasant." Several small sewn canoes stealthily glided toward the squadron, rowed by natives harmonizing "with the utmost accord."[19] "Peculiar" looking, according to Wilkes, with "strong wiry beards and mustaches and a different physiognomy," their "wild" appearance led Pickering at first glance to judge that at last the scientists had "really got among 'savages,' such as are depicted in the imagination of writers."[20] For once, it seemed, reality was coinciding with the literary imagination. Soon they were skirting the ship, singing, laughing, and gesticulating to the crew. Since the natives seemed reluctant to come aboard *Vincennes*, Wilkes directed various articles to be thrown down to the canoes. In response, the islanders broke into song, with an occasional pause to "look up and return the laugh of the crew by a grin, apparently enjoying the sport as much as any of them."[21] This was the expedition's introduction to the natives of Wytoohee (present-day Napuka), the larger of the two Disappointment Islands. The Americans found these people to be shrewd and sharp traders who refused to part with their spears and paddles in trade, instead offering tapa—the coin of the island realm in those parts.[22] Peale attributed such reluctance to the islanders' inherent "thievish" and "dishonest" nature.[23] Stuart, observing how the natives interacted with each other, disagreed. He watched as the canoers "showed the utmost degree of honesty *one with another*, for in 2 or 3 cases articles being thrown to one who might by chance miss it and another get it—it would be immediately passed to the one which it was intended for," a trait, he judged, that was "a credit to all mankind, let alone the savage." Stuart with his cranial fixation was correspondingly impressed with the topography of the Wytoohee skull:

"According to Phrenology, I never saw a more manly looking race . . . having well built, splendid features, apparently possessing all the qualities desirable."[24]

Later that evening, while recounting the day's activities, Peale groped for analogies to describe these islanders, which led him back to his American racial models for a context. "These natives," he wrote, were "of a dark brown color, redder than Negroes, but blacker than N. Amn Indians."[25] Meanwhile, nearby, Pickering was making similar comparisons. "Their complexion was brown, of decidedly a deeper tint than our Indians," a "deeper hue and more European style of feature, than in the aboriginal American." These features he attributed to a probable ancient East Indian or Middle Eastern migration.[26] He felt that the expedition was just now penetrating the far eastern wave of the great Polynesian (or Malay) migration. Like Horatio Hale, Pickering now discounted any western migration of American Indians into the Pacific, the book of Joel and Sherlock Gregory notwithstanding: "There was no longer any ambiguity about the origin of these people. They have nothing to do with any of our Indian tribes, but belong to the genuine Malay Race, a portion of the Hindoo, or in other words the ancient Egyptian, as distinct a variety of the human family as any whatever."[27]

Early the next afternoon three launches skimmed toward Wytoohee in hopes of finding an opening through the verdure and into the lagoon. Pickering, Couthouy, and Reynolds pulled close enough to the shore for Couthouy, gifts in hand, to swim to the beach safely. Although he was greeted quite cordially in the Polynesian fashion—broad smiles and rubbing noses— he was not allowed to advance beyond his tiny foothold in the surf. Another boat, commanded by Wilkes, was more successful. They landed, managed to gain the confidence of the wary but friendly natives, and walked briskly through the pandanus and coconut groves to the small village, where they were received quite warmly. Wilkes saw evidence of previous white contact in the attitudes of the villagers, particularly in that no one seemed alarmed at the sound of gunfire. Also, in what was becoming an annoyingly common circumstance in the travels of the expedition, there were no women to be found in the village. When inquiries were made about the whereabouts of the Wytoohee women, the men "burst out into a knowing laugh," informing Wilkes that "they had penetrated our motive for visiting their island—That as we inhabited an island without any women, we wanted to have some." The commander, in his narrative, assures the reader that "nothing more was said to them on the subject."[28]

The next day found the expedition lying off Wytoohee's sister island

"Native of Wytoohee." Sketch by Alfred Agate. "These natives," wrote Titian Peale, were "of a dark brown color, redder than Negroes, but blacker than N. Amn Indians."

of Otooho, a square-mile lagoonless atoll twelve miles west-northwest of Wytoohee. Frustrated with their lack of opportunities to perform their duties, the naturalists conspired to make a concerted effort to storm the island in order to add to their heretofore rather insignificant collections. The Otoohoans, however, were fully equal to the challenge. When Drayton, Couthouy, the botanist William Breckinridge, and Pickering rowed in through the rising surf, they were greeted by friendly but firm natives, who promptly relaunched their boats with a shove into deeper water. Switching to their alternative plan, Pickering and Breckinridge took to the water and swam to shore. The result was familiar: cordial greetings, rubbing noses, kissing and shaking of hands all around—but still, no one was allowed to plant his feet on dry sand.[29] Whenever one tried to advance and make contact with an islander, the natives jumped but then quickly composed themselves and attempted to placate and soothe the foreigners, "continually pawing and whining over him [one of the naturalists]," according to Wilkes, "making a kind of purring noise, not unlike that by which we propitiate or soothe the feelings or doubtful temper of some beast."[30] Indeed, it must have been quite an awkward experience for these men of science to be the ones under observation, to be handled and feared like an unpredictable animal, just as they had done to all previous native people they had encountered during the voyage. The tables had been turned.

Breckinridge made one last attempt to penetrate the shore. He somehow landed unopposed and made a low dash for the interior in a frantic attempt at collecting some new plant specimens. Much too soon he was detected, creating another frustrating though humorous scene:

> Two stout natives came running up, and made him understand, by very intelligible signs, that he must return to the boat; he pretended not to understand them, and endeavored to proceed, but they went before him, and crossed their clubs, determined that he should go no farther. This caused him to laugh, in which the two natives joined. . . . The rest of the party having gone up to the huts, were at once seized and shoved down towards the boat, and into the surf, where they presented a rather ludicrous appearance, with the danger of drowning on the one side, and the natives on the other. . . . No harm, however, was done them.[31]

Whatever reasons the natives had for thwarting the attempts of the expedition to explore these tiny islands, thus far the Exploring Expedition had been stymied in their scientific pursuits ashore. This failure could have been the result of prior depredations by foreigners, a limited supply of food and water, or perhaps just a strong sense of privacy or provincialism. No one seemed to consider that the islanders might have decried the "arrant thievery" of the collecting naturalists as well. But at least in the case of the natives of Wytoohee and Otooho, the defense was accomplished with a such a noticeable lack of violence, hostility, and ill will that it seemed as if the islanders had determined to carry out Wilkes's general order, even if he had not. One can even (almost) detect a slight smile animating the face of the taciturn Wilkes as he recalled the odd hospitality of these people in his narrative.

Still, not everyone thought the natives so innocent. A few men thought that the kissing and nose rubbing was only a prelude to an invitation to dinner, in which *they* were to be the main course. Sailing Master George Sinclair imagined he detected "something in the expression of one of the old men's countenance that seemed to say 'you would make a good roast and I would like to be at the roasting.'"[32] Pickering himself fanned the flames a bit when he returned to the ship on one occasion with what was assumed to be a large human bone (no other animal larger than a rat inhabited the islands besides the natives).[33]

At any rate, Tahiti was still beckoning, so Wilkes departed from the Disappointment Islands and sailed *Vincennes* southwestward through the western cluster of the Paumotus, island-hopping along the way. Their recent experiences still vivid, the naturalists "had now learned caution" when going ashore. They often stopped to cast anxious glances over their shoulders, expecting the imminent appearance of native escorts to usher them back into the sea.

On 30 August the expedition reached Raraka, an island within the outer fringe of the "watery kingdom" of Tahiti, where they were welcomed by "an emblem of civilization" rising from the coconut trees: the Tahitian flag.[34] Here at last could Wilkes detect "the dawning of Christianity and Civilization" among the islanders.[35] All the masonry of these twin pillars of Western society was in place at Raraka. Native missionaries enforced orderly and proper behavior among the clean-shaven, respectable inhabitants. Habitations were tidy and laid out in queues resembling a military camp. Cocoa palms were planted regimental style in similar rows. Even the pale spotted terns that congregated about the "encampments" seemed to Pickering to be "half-domesticated."[36]

Wilkes became "great friends" with the "old chief of Raraka," a one-handed tattooed veteran of the pearl fisheries. He and his entourage were frequent companions of the commander when Wilkes toured the island. The old fisherman, however, refused an invitation to visit *Vincennes* until assured that no expedition members would be allowed ashore while he inspected the ship. Wilkes presided over the tour of the vessel, a favor designed to suitably impress the natives of the power and superiority of the expedition and the society that it represented. At the end of the tour, a brother of the old man was given a piece of chalk and proceeded to draw "with considerable accuracy" nearly all the islands of the Paumotu group, positioned correctly, each with their native name. Included was an atoll that Wilkes had "discovered" just the day before and named Vincennes Island, and three other islands not found by the expedition until 1840.[37]

The expedition discovered that, unfortunately, another residue of civilization—alcohol—had made equally strong inroads into Rarakan society. The "chief" and his entourage refused to leave the ship until supplied with the new vogue in Rarakan hospitality—whiskey.[38]

At last, on 11 September, Tahiti hove in sight. The picturesque shoreline was capped by verdant summits that pierced the ceiling of heavy, moisture-laden clouds. A true island, it was quite a contrast to the doughnut-shaped atolls of the eastern Paumotus. Before sundown the first Tahitians boarded *Vincennes*, enabling Pickering and the other scientists to take stock of the physical traits of these islanders. Pickering followed the "chiefs" about the deck as they solicited the expedition laundry—a coveted concession in the Tahitian-European market system that effectively reduced all islanders, regardless of class or gender, to washerwomen for the whites. Even the queen was said to gather sailors' dirty laundry for a price. He was surprised at the imposing physical size of these people compared to his own. At last he got the joke of which he had been the butt: a "left-handed compliment" given to him by the women of Raraka, "viz., 'that we were good looking men for women.' "[39] Horatio Hale concurred with the doctor. He considered the Polynesians of these parts to be, "as a race," physically superior to any other, a confession that would have made Samuel George Morton blanch.[40]

Pickering's invariable attempt to compartmentalize the physical features of the Polynesians was floundering. He found their physical variations too great to generalize. Hale, as well, found few "general characteristics" with which to label these people. From these and other observations, Pickering was later to conclude that it must be *civilization* that breeds commonality of features and not vice versa. Such a conclusion was an interesting and novel concept for a member of a natural science community bent upon formulating and fixing a concrete generic image of the "savage," whether they be found in the plains and forests of North America, the jungles of Africa, or the islands of the Pacific. Unable to fit the Polynesians as a single entity within the accepted categories of race and savagery, Pickering instead turned to the tried and true models used by American anthropologists—Indians and blacks—to describe the variations among the islanders. Some, he felt, with their "Orang expressions . . . might have passed in the streets of our cities as containing Negro blood." However, others closely resembled "our Indians," except for the slight curling of the hair. Pickering eventually concluded that he had come upon a distinct "race" that required classification.[41]

There was general agreement that the Tahitians, after fifty-plus years of continuous European contact, had evolved into the most "civilized savages" in the Pacific. The building blocks of civilization—Christianity and commerce—had been fortified by a half-century of missionary work among the Tahitians, sealed by the mortar of the Protestant ethic. By the 1830s, according to Wilkes (or at least his missionary sources), a "naturally indolent" people had been transformed into a clean and industrious population with "sound moral and religious principles."[42] Thievery, for instance—that bane of savagery—had been abolished, though now the Tahitians had become "inveterate beggars."[43] The vehicle for change in Tahiti was the Protestant concept of labor—hard, regular, and above all, regulated—"so powerful an aid in the promotion of civilization."[44] Young and old alike were seemingly obsessed with learning to read and write. Missionary schools had been established all over the islands to encourage and facilitate this desire. What they were exclusively allowed to read was, of course, the Bible, translated into the Tahitian language. The religiosity of these people astounded the expedition. The Sabbath was strictly observed, more so than back in America: "More quiet and Sunday-like . . . than in our cities and towns." It was "truly the Lord's Day" there, Erskine continued, "and the people not only recognize it as such, but keep it sacred. . . . No labor or games of any kind are allowed: no, not even the picking of a coconut, or the paddling of a canoe is permitted on that day."[45] Natives would quietly file into church "neatly and decently clothed, although in very bad taste" but "behaving in a very becoming manner" and giving their full attention to the preacher. Wilkes and his officers attended one such service, conducted in Tahitian. Though admittedly feeling some misgivings about not being able to discern whether the songs and sermon were "the promulgation of divine truth or pagan superstitions," their fears and spirits were soothed by the familiar old melodies of their own wood and brick sanctuaries back home—"Old Hundred" and "St. Martin's."[46]

The Tahitians certainly fared well when compared to the behavior of certain crew members. George Emmons witnessed a performance on tierra firma of an American naval tradition, the intraservice brawl. Drunken sailors and marines grappled before a curious Tahitian crowd. This scene reminded Emmons "to bear witness to the uniform peaceable & good natured conduct of these people whom I have never yet seen engaged in any quarrel whatever." He wondered whether "this be attributed to their life of indolence & the absence of excitable things."[47] Happy, indolent, peaceable, spiritual, impressionable—all were common adjectives used to describe these people.

Even the celebrated moral laxity of the Tahitians was considered by many of the expedition to be largely a thing of the past. Assistant Surgeon Edward

Gilchrist had been warned about the rampant venereal disease among the islanders. Instead he found it to be less than "among the lower orders of any American city."[48] Even that paragon of primness and propriety, Charles Wilkes, saw no appreciable difference in the morals of these people than those of any other nation. In fact, he was convinced that the Tahitians might have an edge. "When compared with many parts of the world that arrogate a superior civilization, it [Tahitian society] appears almost in an advantageous light. Vice, at any rate, does not stalk abroad in the open day as it did in some places we had lately visited upon the American continent."[49] Pickering agreed, finding "the difference from the rest of the world" to be "not so striking." While still laboring within a scientific and societal frame of reference that mandated clearly marked barriers between "savage" and "civilized," Pickering made observations that indicated he was adopting a more relativistic perspective concerning culture. "Besides," he argued, "these people are not to be judged precisely by the same rule as ourselves—their Social institutions are in some respects different.—They are a plain-spoken set, who call things by their right names—and it seems their conversation among themselves is often of the broadest cast, without any body supposing any harm—as though, we are tempted to say, they had not the *refinement* of indecent *ideas*."[50] These conclusions emanated not from a misty-eyed romantic common in that era. Nor were they wistful theories expounded by a stay-at-home intellectual. Instead, they were the property of an energetic field observer taking great pains to come up with some valid structures with which to classify the various families of humankind.

Others testified to the positive attributes of Tahitian character and society. Lieutenant Henry Eld noted that during their entire stay, "never such a thing was seen or heard as a quarrel among them, although they were all sorts mixed together of Every . . . rank and disposition, still Everything was harmony and playfulness and good humour. . . . What an example these people set to us who pretend to call ourselves civilized."[51]

Not all the members of the expedition considered the "licentiousness" of the natives as such an unwelcome occurrence, of course. Many, if not most, had anxiously awaited the appearance of the celebrated Tahitian women— their mariners' libidos titillated by the now legendary accounts of Cook's voyages and Captain Bligh's mutineers. Indeed, it seems that the expedition found its share of both beauty and enticement while in Tahiti, if one reads between the lines. "The ladies," Erskine gushed, "may God bless them all, old and young, are pretty . . . of a light olive complexion . . . with handsome, round, full faces, jet black hair, round, piercing eyes, and large white teeth."[52]

Nor were the women particularly shy. Nearly every evening, those confined to the ships were awakened by what Erskine dubbed a "Tahitian Opera." "Nearly every night, about three bells, we were roused from our peaceful slumbers by the fair Tahitian mermaids, who would launch forth from their coral caves with comb and glass in hand, their long hair floating in the breeze. When they reached the beach just ahead of the ship, they would commence to sing. Richer, clearer, softer, or sweeter voices I have never listened to in any part of the world."[53] After serenading the sailors until two or three in the morning with a medley of whalers' chanteys, hymns, and native songs, the performers slipped into the water, surrounded the vessels, and begged to come on board, only to be refused, according to Erskine.

Such Tahitian "hospitality" became somewhat tainted and cheapened by the light of day, however. Their culture was slowly crumbling under the extended siege of European civilization and its Christian soldiers. Faced with the inevitable, the islanders attempted to parry these righteous thrusts through adaptation and evasion. The zealous observance of the Sabbath that was so pleasing to the missionaries was largely accomplished by incorporating the concept of the Tahitian taboo and reinforcing this with a mortal fear of punishment at the hands of the Christians. Thus, while at night young girls alluringly serenaded the expedition, women by day dutifully trod the paths cowled in broad bonnets and draped in "Mother Hubbards," the formless gowns introduced by the missionaries to keep Polynesian flesh out of sight and out of mind. Native songs, dances, and theater—vividly described in detail in the English narratives—had long ago gone underground, replaced by hymns, prayer meetings, and needlework. Ancient sports such as surfing were deemed corrupt and immoderate and were interdicted. Even the Tahitian love affair with flowers was frowned upon—no more were they allowed to lace them through their dark locks.[54]

The expedition observed that the introduction of Western capitalism and money had been equally unsettling to Tahitian culture. Stuart's experiences here taught him that native kindness now most often came with a catch, as favors were dispensed only in exchange for rewards—expected in cash— "sacrificing all for money," he called it.[55] Pickering, when in search of guides to lead about the island, found that "the present generation" was "very keen after the dollar, and understood perfectly the distribution between the 'big and the little one.' "[56] Meanwhile, the missionaries continued to fill the heads of many an officer with pie-in-the-sky accounts of their "progress" in "civilizing" the natives. But at least one man found the chasm between propaganda too great not to comment upon.

"Mode of carrying child by woman of Metia Island." Sketch by Alfred Agate. Protestant missionary influence became more evident as the expedition sailed closer to Tahiti. Agate's color sketch is interesting for the "Madonnaesque" convention of draping the mother in garments of red and blue. I have found that this interesting artistic motif was used in colored woodcuts and engravings of American Indian mother and child depictions in this period as well.

> For my own part I was much astonished when contrasting the difference between the missionary accounts and the actual state of the morals of these people. It is not uncommon for a father to prostitute his daughter for a dollar, and even his own wife has frequently been disposed of in the same manner. There is but few exceptions to these libidinous practices. And still you hear the missionary preaching up the great change they have wrought in their morals; if there is any change it certainly must be for the worst—for they have learnt them the use of money, and they will go to most any length to obtain it.[57]

Traditional commerce had existed between Tahiti, the eastern Paumotus, and Samoa prior to the European invasion. This was now terminated and replaced by a reliance upon goods introduced by British, French, and, if the expedition was a success, American merchants.[58] This perhaps was the whites' "greatest" accomplishment. Christianity, commerce, and coin had indeed brought change to Tahiti.

Early in the expedition's stay, Pickering, as was his wont, set forth on a lengthy excursion into the interior of Matahevi in search of a more pristine sector of the island. Little native vegetation remained along the coast as a result of the introduction of exotic plant and animal species by Europeans—a sad parallel to the rapidly receding island culture. Pickering hoped that such a trip would offer him and his companions an opportunity to glimpse what once was and what still remained of Tahitian environment and culture.

First, Pickering turned to his native guides and pointed to Oroena, the island's most prominent peak, as their ultimate destination. The leader replied that "no Tahieti [sic] man had ever been able to get there, and therefore a white man could not go."[59] The others merely shrugged and answered that they did not know the way. Undaunted, the doctor set out at a brisk pace up and through a mountain torrent, his guides literally following in his wake. Pickering spent these days moving forever upward through the canyon, fording and refording the rushing river while keeping an eye out for unusual specimens, conversing with the natives and observing their habits. He observed that as the distance increased between them and the coast, the thin veneer of "civilization" that had been so piously applied to the natives by the missionaries began to melt away in the natural tropical environment. What remained was a unique civilization in its own right, one in which Pickering came to consider in many ways equal to and even superior to his own. Certainly the Tahitians were more practical and logical when it came to the basic necessities. The doctor found that his bulky clothing was as great an anomaly in the unremitting showers and intense humidity as Mother

Hubbards were on Tahitian girls. Having cold and clammy wools and cottons clinging to his already traumatized skin led him to confess that "if I lived in such a climate and had much of such travelling I should feel strongly tempted to dispense with it [clothing]"—quite a concession for his day and age. The natives remarked to the doctor that, until they were persuaded to don clothes as a moral prophylactic, they had never known anyone to catch a cold.[60] Each evening, slumping down to a sumptuous repast of pit-baked pig and taro, a weary Pickering again found himself envying the islanders: "Here again we were obliged to acknowledge our inferiority. The Savage, owing to the greater use of his limbs, will rest easily in positions (not always according to our ideas of grace) but which we, who have been used to chairs, find it impossible to imitate."[61] Nor did Pickering's admiration extend merely to the basics. Their navigational skills were already common knowledge to white observers. As a naturalist, Pickering was impressed with the Tahitians' wealth of knowledge concerning their natural environment. He was surprised at the "intimate acquaintance which everyone seemed to possess of the *plants* and other productions of the islands." He was astonished by the complexity with which they could describe the human anatomy, finding that "they were much more particular in their names they give to the different parts of the *human frame* than we ourselves."[62]

While his exploratory trek turned up few botanical rewards, it did much to bolster his notion of the Polynesians as a "noble race." "On the whole," he concluded, "taking these people and their institutions, as well as I was able to understand them,—though I would not by any means be understood to recommend them—I am satisfied that there is less to corrupt the heart, than in our 'Civilized Communities.'"[63] If his Tahitians were neither the "Edenic" savages of Cook nor the indolent and lascivious sinners depicted in missionary tracts, then who or what were they? Where did they fit in the grand classificatory systems of ethnological science? In a telling slip of his pen, perhaps Pickering reveals both what he had traveled half the globe to find and what he was looking for: "These people," Pickering decided, "are the least helpless of any I have ever read of." Then, in a classic catachresis, he continues:

> Strip *an Indian* entirely in the morning, and without an implement in his hand, turn him into *the woods*; then pay him a visit at night—we shall find him clothed from the lace of the Cocoa-nut tree, a garland on his head; a house over him, made of the wild Bananas; thongs and Cordage of all sorts from the back of the Poorow tree, baskets made by plaiting the segments of a Cocoa-nut leaf; perhaps a mat to sleep on; Cups or wash-bowls of Cocoa-

nut shell, or even tumblers and casks of the joints of the large Bamboo; a Cape or an Umbrella if it is wanted of the Banana leaf; a fire kindled . . . provisions enough for a week—all this is quite possible [italics mine].[64]

We can assume that Pickering had not witnessed Indians frolicking among the coconut groves, nor had any of the scientists before referred to the interior of Tahiti as "the woods." Pickering's wise, self-reliant Tahitian native indeed echoes the classic depiction of the "noble savage" of American lore. Throughout the expedition's voyage, Pickering and the others continually employed the image and supposed traits of the North American Indian as a yardstick for which to gauge the "savageness" of the people they met. Here in Tahiti, it seems, Pickering discovered a society that was everything America's "noble savage" should have been but was not, in their eyes. Nevertheless, the *image* proved invaluable in gauging cultures.

As a whole, the expedition's month-long stay in Tahiti persuaded them that little good had come from more than a half-century of European contact. Missionary work, particularly in secular matters, was held in somewhat low esteem. Even Wilkes, who often parroted missionary claims in his narrative, admitted that many of their methods were rather hypocritical. At Eimeo, an island ten miles from Tahiti, the officers were greeted by the Reverend and Mrs. Simpson, who provided a tour of their establishment. All along the way they were surrounded by nearly the entire native population, who hoped for a close inspection of these uniformed foreigners. Uncomfortable, Wilkes remarked that he now knew what it must be like for an Indian chief walking through an American city.[65] They left the throng behind, crossing through a well-built stone wall and into an immense sugar plantation belonging to the Simpsons. In between their duties as sugar barons and savers of lost souls, the Simpsons found time to run a missionary school, with a twist: this school was segregated—for children of white missionaries and other "respectable white parents" only. According to the Simpsons, this was a proper precaution taken to protect the white children from "receiving improper ideas from the natives."[66] Such a system offended Wilkes's republican sensibilities, though segregation according to race was as popular in New York City as it was among the whites at Eimeo. Whether he made any such connection is not known. However, he did point out the inherent dangers of the Eimeo education system, condemning it as the "worst feature" of the missionary establishment. He lamented the fact that the whites would choose to "bring up their own children to look down upon them [natives] as beings of an inferior order" while professing to be so concerned for "the conversion and moral improvement" of the native children.[67] Pickering was another one who was appalled by such hypocrisy, tersely jotting off that "I have no comment to make on these proceedings," perhaps secretly glad that the *native* youth would be spared from such intermingling![68]

Shortly before departing the Society Islands, the crew of *Peacock* obtained permission to stage a "theatrical entertainment" for the natives, a cultural recompense or exchange designed to entertain the natives as well as to amuse themselves. The play chosen for the edification of the islanders was Schiller's *Robbers* (a comment on purported island thievery, perhaps?). While the acting was accorded generally good reviews by the officers, the Tahitians at first proved to be a tough crowd. They grew restless, squirming through the lengthy and loquacious Germanic dialogue. Soon, grumbling from the indigenous audience that there was too much *parau* (talk) threatened to close the show. However, the day was saved when several sailors portraying the heroine and her entourage appeared, appropriately dressed for their roles. The Tahitians ranked this bit of novelty even higher than the juggling they had witnessed aboard French vessels. The coup de grace à l'Américain, however, was the next act—the performance of stylistic "comic songs" then currently in vogue in America. The Tahitians were treated to a real taste of Americana as blackfaced sailors "in character" shuffled on stage and performed the songs and dances of "Jim Crow" to the hearty laughter and ultimate delight of the islanders. Wilkes recorded that the Tahitians came away convinced that the rendition of this slow-talking and quick-footed caricature of American blacks was the real thing—a misconception they shared with their contemporary North American theatergoers.[69] It is not recorded whether any of the handful of black stevedores and cooks assigned to the expedition were granted the privilege of seeing themselves caricatured on shore that evening. Most likely not.[70] Surely their attendance would have ruined the humorous image that was being conveyed about Americans with dark skin. Scenes such as these were to be repeated, not only by the United States Exploring Expedition in its travels throughout the Pacific but by future expeditions as well, as Americans spread their culture and racial attitudes throughout the world.[71]

As the expedition prepared to leave the Society Islands, observers paused to ponder the impact of their civilization on the Tahitians. Pickering, who had already formulated some rather startling deductions for his day and age, wrapped up a journal entry by rejecting the reasoning that white dominance had resulted from superior physical or mental endowments. Attempting to explain the process and apparent ease by which Europeans had nonetheless infected and overwhelmed island culture, he finally concluded that "it is not the superiority of our Natural faculties, whether Intellectual or Physical, that is giving *our* race the advantage in some parts of the world, but our *System* of Civilization."[72] Such insight had come not from measuring crania or surveying the bumps on a human skull. Instead, it emanated from field observation and comparative analysis without seeking to classify culture and people in terms of hierarchy. While the above methods did not ensure objectivity—an impossible task for the scientist of any era— his investigations into race and culture was certainly more holistic and less predetermined than Morton's methods. Though Pickering employed the methods of the naturalist in grouping and classifying what he perceived as the various races, or even species, of humankind, his appreciation of cultures like the Tahitians' was such that never did he succumb to ranking them in terms of superiority and inferiority.

Upon leaving the Society Islands the expedition made due west for the next island group on their itinerary—the Navigator Islands, also known as Samoa. It was here that the Frenchman La Pérouse met a gruesome fate at the hands of the natives in 1778. In recent years, however, since the arrival of Christian missionaries, great changes had come over these isles. The principal result was that Samoan society had been reshuffled into two opposing camps. Those who followed the missionaries were naturally called the "Christians." Those who did not were dubbed the "devils," the latter being named by the former.[73] The Christian villages were equipped with standard "civilizing" fixtures: churches, schoolhouses, and presses for printing translations of the Bible. They lived under missionary rules and dictates. Loose gingham or calico frocks for females and shirt and/or trousers for males were acceptable apparel. The hair of both sexes was cropped short, a severe hairstyle reminiscent of the zealous Roundheads of English history. Shearing the natives' locks proved an effective method of discriminating between heathen and Christian and also removed the chronic temptation to adorn their hair with flowers. This regulation was a boon to the phrenologist Stuart, facilitating his investigations into the Samoan character. Judging from his unobstructed view of those cranial contours, his prognosis was discouraging: "According to Phrenology, I should think they might be guilty of many foul actions—acquisitiveness, Caution, Secretiveness and Combativeness and Contracted perceptive and Reflective faculties."[74]

Stuart's judgments concerning the Samoans, though backed by "science," found few adherents among the members of the expedition. If they had been generally impressed by the Tahitians, then the expedition fairly gushed

War chief Matetau of Manono, Samoa. The expedition arrived in the midst of a war between the "Christians" and "devils"; a war egged on by Protestant missionaries on the islands. Pencil sketch by Alfred Agate.

over the Samoans. Wilkes was certainly no exception. He was awed by the "manliness and intelligence" of the inhabitants of Tutuilla, the first island visited by the squadron. In contrast to the "indolent" Tahitians, "laziness" was "not a part of their national character." In fact, he considered the Samoans particularly "disposed to exertion and willing to be employed." Naturally, the commander foresaw a promising future for these islanders.[75] Again, in vivid contrast to the Tahitians, whose "salaciousness" Christianity had not yet totally expunged, Samoan women were considered paragons of faithfulness and constancy, "domestic and virtuous" creatures seemingly beyond moral reproach and above temptation.[76] According to Wilkes, during a visit to his ship a Samoan woman was forced to tactfully rebuff a sexual proposition by one of the crew members. When told that she need not fear detection by the missionaries, the woman shook her head, pointed skyward, and rebuked her tempter with a reminder that "there missionary see."[77]

Of course, these were the "Christians": those who renounced such sins as dancing, surfing, and similar "lascivious" activities, sheared their hair, and at the instigation of the missionaries, carried on a bloody feud with the "devils." In time, however, many members of the expedition found the heathens in fact more hospitable and certainly more interesting than the other camp. George Sinclair, for instance, thought the men of Savaii "the very finest race . . . I ever saw." He found that the beauty and manners of the women quaked his American sense of propriety in a way that left him groping for words to describe their charms. "It is impossible to describe them in sufficiently pleasing colours. . . . [S]everal beautiful young girls played round the boats like so many Fawns and sorely tempted our virtue. The only clothing they wore was a slight fringe of grass in front and another behind which only half concealed their charms and in their wild and lascivious gamboling around us, they would frequently flirt this slight screen aside, but with such artful dexterity that, so far as exposure went, its object was but little impaired."[78] While some such as Sinclair ogled and squirmed aboard ship, other crew members were not as hesitant about mingling with the Samoans. William Reynolds spent his precious days ashore strolling through the villages hand in hand with "my two sweethearts," Samoan girls in their early teens, causing him to contemplate seriously the relative merits of Samoan versus American lifestyles. Reynolds deferred to much that was Samoan. But, pleasing as they were, he found a "wide difference between them and my own race," which, he felt, would lead inevitably to their demise. Reynolds feared for the survival of Samoan culture. "I could not help thinking," he pondered, "how much better it would be to let them go on their own old way—but No!, No! We must have all the world like us, if we can!"[79] Such magnanimity on the part of Reynolds did not obscure the fact that he apparently assessed Samoan and other native cultures encountered during the voyage positively or negatively according to the accessibility of their women. Thus, "good" (or "tamed") cultures, such as the Tahitians, Samoans, and Hawaiians, bestowed sexual favors to whites; "bad" (or "savage") ones, such as the Yahgans, Maoris, and the Fijians, did not.

The scientists were charmed by the intelligence, good humor, and in-quisitiveness of the heathen camp of Samoans. Pickering was particularly delighted with these people. Thickly tattooed from the hips down (at first thought to be breeches!), concealed only with a slip of *ti* (*Drucana*) leaves, they could have been taken for the earliest inhabitants of God's Paradise, in the eyes of the doctor. He mused that perhaps such apparel matched the "Fig leaves worn of Old by Adam and Eve."[80] The scientists hastened to collect

"Emma Malietoa." Source: *Narrative*, 2:88, facing page. From a drawing by Alfred Agate. "It is impossible to describe them in sufficiently pleasing colors. . . . [They] played round the boats like so many Fawns and sorely tempted our virtue." George Sinclair, Journal.

information on Samoan amusements; fortunately, the "devils," unlike their pious rivals, held no interdictions on traditional music and games. They sat up at night and feasted with the natives, listening to songs that sometimes lasted until dawn, occasionally discovering themselves incorporated into the extemporaneous lyrics. Games of chance and skill still abounded on the heathen side of the islands, from the simplest guessing games (*lupe*) to elaborate spear-throwing competitions (*litia*) held between neighboring villages. They witnessed organized wrestling matches that rivaled the American frontier's "gouge-fests" for ferocity. The oddest amusement, however, was discovered in the interior—a mockup of a *papalangi* (white man's) sailing ship. Constructing a "hull" by fastening timbers around a pruned coconut tree that served as a ship's mast, Samoans swung from the vine "rigging," manned the "rudder," and heaved the coral "ballast" for hours, imitating a bellowing captain and his salty crew.[81]

Questions abounded for those interested in ethnology. Where could such a people have originated? To whom were they related? There were clues— tantalizing tidbits of traditions that seemed to point to an eastward migration from Asia or even farther west, toward the Nile Valley. Peale found that the "devils" still practiced circumcision, which he considered "a pretty strong proof of Asiatic origin."[82] Others found the similarities between Samoan and Jewish marriage ceremonies quite remarkable.[83] Pickering could not help but ponder the possibility of a great ancient diaspora emanating from the Nile River after hearing of the existence of a crocodile thrashing about the interior of Upolu.

> I am confidently informed of the existence of a *crocodile* in one of the streams at Upolu, which is known to have been there at least 50 years. . . . Again we call to mind the "Image of the large Lizard" . . . at Tahiti. I would not infer from this that these Old Egyptians had brought Crocodiles with them all the way from the Nile, but it certainly looks like some traces of their ancient veneration for these Animals—Crocodiles are also held in veneration at Timor and a species, *C. biporcatus*, exists as far to the Eastward as New Ireland. Though the latter may take to the Salt water when pursued, it is difficult to suppose that it could have transported itself over so great an extent of Ocean, to these islands.[84]

The philologist Hale, who continued laboriously collecting native grammars and other ethnological data, had not traveled far enough westward to come to any definitive conclusions concerning dispersion. Eventually he, too, proposed a general west-to-east Polynesian dispersion, though based on a bit sounder evidence than Pickering's "crocodile theory."

About the only Samoan characteristic that continued to rankle Europeans and Americans was their rejection of money as a medium of exchange. It seemed to visitors that Samoans had not developed any "standard of value

"Trading Scene at Apia, Samoa." Sketch by Alfred Agate. The Samoan's insistence on basing prices for their foodstuffs on the laws of supply and demand continually frustrated naval pursers who preferred fixed rates of exchange.

for European Commodities, and are likely to require too much as too little" in trade.[85] However, there was evidence that the natives of the Navigator Islands were not as commercially naive as they were usually considered to be. Frustrated naval pursers who ventured on shore to acquire foodstuffs found that standards of value could not be fixed for pigs, coconuts, and taro; instead, exchange varied according to the islander's immediate needs and—that lubricant of Western capitalism—supply and demand. Price lists compiled prior to the expedition's departure from America proved to be of little value here. After witnessing the monetary obsessions of the Tahitians, Pickering fretted about the inevitable use of coin in Samoa. What will happen, he wondered, "after the secret shall be made known, that it is possible to hoard property, or to change its form at will?"[86]

Most expedition members considered the Samoan commitment to Christianity to be deeper than that of the Tahitians. Nevertheless, missionaries in the Navigator Islands had their hands full keeping apart the two island factions while maintaining strict control of their "Christian" allies. A third challenge came from apostatizing Samoans. Hybrid Christianity had sprung up among the Samoans, a phenomenon that threatened the social and spiritual monopoly that the white Protestant denominations insisted was essential to civilizing the population. The most popular of the native Christian "heresies"—the "Gimblet" religion—disdained white missionary input, its adherents preferring to be led by their own insights and revealed inspiration. Peale, on an excursion around one of the islands, watched as a sick native was brought in from the coast to the village where he was staying. A Gimblet priest was immediately called on to come and pray over the ailing man.

> This gave me an opportunity of learning some matters connected with their faith which otherwise I should not have understood: The priest is supposed to hold converse with the Deity, and by this means learns the fates of his fellows. On this occasion the prayer was to all intents and purposes Christian. The priest stood on the stone platform fronting the house, with his face west. He opened a book which had previously been carefully enveloped in tapa, and calling on *Jehovah* he returned thanks for the many blessings which had been conferred on his people and asked a continuance of the same, invoking the aid of *Jesus*, and ended by asking the divine will concerning the sick man, asking mercy for himself. I could not see distinctly what the book was, but believe it was a *blank note book*.[87]

Blank book notwithstanding (Peale later discovered it to be a copy of the *Rambler*, which he acquired for the expedition), the practicing of this faith as witnessed by Peale would have raised few eyebrows if transported to the camp meetings of Cane Ridge and had its followers been "civilized" or of a different hue. Jacksonian America continually sprouted Mormons, Millerites, and Owenites, hybrids all who were responding to the spiritual, social, and economic pressures of Western religion and society. With the possible exception of the Mormons, most were allowed enough religious and social space in America to plant and till the soil of their new communities or beliefs and practices. A similar response to the Word among dark-skinned natives of the Pacific was not acceptable, written off as "mongrel Christianity," an apt phrase that revealed a confluence of race and religion that was developing in this period.[88]

Pickering, for one, felt that in fact the white missionaries of these islands should count their blessings in being so providentially placed among so enlightened a population, especially when compared to their poor brethren back home in the wilds of the American continent. "I had frequent occasions during my stay, to remark how different was the task of the missionaries among these islands, and in North America. Here was a people extremely eager to learn, and ready at all times to adopt anything new. I was sometimes amused at the inveterate pains taken by grown people to learn to read;

Inhabitants of Manono, Samoa. "These people are not savages, unless the wearing of a dress suited to the climate, and ignorance of money makes them so." Charles Pickering, Journal, 22 October 1839. Pen and pencil sketch by Alfred Agate.

although the Literature as yet furnished them is amazingly scant. . . . *These people are not savages, unless the wearing of a dress suited to the climate, and ignorance of money makes them so* [italics mine]."[89]

Pickering's experiences on the Exploring Expedition had led him to reflect upon the nature and identity of "savagery" versus "civilization." He rejected the latter as a static term, opting for a more flexible and relative definition. Such conclusions are not to be trivialized or underplayed; most if not all of his eminent contemporaries back home never approached these insights. Then again, we can see that in fact he is not so much proclaiming the Samoans as civilized as he is confirming their "unsavagery." If the Samoans are not savages, then who are? His frequent comparisons and allusions to the Indians of North America indicate that Pickering considered the physical and cultural traits of American Indians the most reliable yardstick by which each native culture can be measured and classified. In essence, white perceptions of Indians served as the litmus test of savagery in aboriginal society.

As they had done at Tahiti, before the expedition left Samoa they presented a commercial and "diplomatic" treaty to the local leaders for their approval, although here, unlike in the Kingdom of Tahiti, the process was muddied by the republican nature of Samoan society: too many "chiefs" with too little power governing too many factions. Through these treaties, documents which were drawn up unilaterally prior to the expedition's departure from America, the United States government sought the same commercial and legal rights and privileges granted previously to English and French consuls. Wilkes procured the proper X's and immediately set out to enforce its edicts. In a trial before a council of his peers, presided over by Captains Hudson and Wilkes, an islander was tried and found guilty of murdering a white sailor. Protesting Hudson's demand for the death penalty, the islanders (which Wilkes felt greatly resembled the Indian councils in America) argued that the alleged offense should have "no ex post facto" bearing, since it happened years before the signing of the treaty, "when they were still in darkness."[90] In a grand show of magnanimity, Wilkes commuted the death penalty imposed by Hudson to banishment to a deserted island.[91] This episode was the first, though not the last, instance of American police action in the course of the voyage.

The expedition bid Samoa farewell on 10 November 1839 and set a course southwest through the Fiji Islands, making its way toward Australia. On 29 November the lighthouse of Port Jackson, New South Wales, shone through the dusk of early evening. Soon *Vincennes* and *Peacock* were anchored off Sydney Cove, awaiting the morning.

Wilkes planned to tarry in Sydney until just after Christmas, then lead the main body of the squadron south in hopes of beating the French and English to the honor of discovering a landmass in Antarctica.[92] The captain decided that scientists—particularly the naturalists—were excess ballast on such a quest to the barren and uninhabited polar regions. Thus they were to remain behind, keeping themselves occupied in New South Wales and New Zealand until the squadron's return. Most seemed heartily glad for the opportunity to work unsupervised and, no doubt, the respite from shipboard life and the overbearing Wilkes.

The morning of 30 November found the expedition joyfully back in the bosom of "civilization." Before them lay Sydney, a city of thirty thousand inhabitants, most of whom were of their own Anglo-American culture. Again they were among the familiar. In the distance, the spire of the church of Saint James projected upward like a sturdy mooring post in the midst of a sea of neat greystone structures—a stark contrast to the low, thatched dwellings of the coral islands and so much like home. Here, they felt, was truly a "terrestrial paradise" in a sea of savagery. Pickering, like the others, fairly gushed at the prospect of reentering "civilization." "The transition from Savage to Civilized life was very striking this morning and was sensibly felt, as well as seen. The town in the distance seemed almost a Terrestrial Paradise. The neat and substantial appearance of the dwellings which we had so long been unused to, reminded us of home—We had even been long strangers to a feeling of entire personal security in our intercourse with our fellows—Society, the pleasures of intellectual communion, had been long foregone."[93] Upon landing, the men ventured down along George Street, the main thoroughfare. The officers noted the "well built and commodious" businesses and homes on one side, while the crew marked out for future reference the numerous brothels and grog shops on the far end. Everywhere it seemed there was something to remind them of home: finely dressed ladies promenading by, accompanied by well-heeled gentlemen; familiar aromas emanating from the shops; the mother tongue wafting in the air, filling the streets.

Along the wharves they witnessed the arrival and unloading of the latest batch of "immigrants" from England and Ireland, the true builders of this paradise among savagery. Wilkes stood and watched as the long train of shackled convicts trudged past, bringing back memories of the African chain gangs he had seen in Rio de Janeiro; the only difference was that these wretches were white-skinned and lacked the "cheerful song and . . . apparent merriment" of the Brazilian slaves.[94] Pickering, on the other hand, was reminded of home and "the slaves in our Southern States."[95]

The officers and scientists found the hospitality of the Australian gentry very gracious. The sailors, of course, preferred the low road to the cove. There they found the debauchery of Sydney fully equal to—and possibly unsurpassed by—that of any other "civilized" city in the world, according to Erskine, a seasoned salt who spoke from experience. "I have never been in a place where there existed such a low state of society, and where so much drunkenness was to be seen. There was not only half-dressed, dirty soldiers, but dirty and drunken women, staggering along the public streets, brawling and fighting, or being carried off by the police, who, by the way, were the proprietors of many of the rum shops."[96] Such licentiousness and dissipation could just as easily be found almost anywhere sailors congregated, whether it be Old Ann Street of Boston or Philadelphia's infamous South Street. What truly shocked his sensibilities was a peculiar but common occurrence, even on the finer avenues of the town, that left Erskine and his shipmates gaping at the incongruity of "so unnatural" a sight. "Although seeming to be rude," Erskine explained, "one could not help stopping and staring" when "a big, burly, thick lipped negro, black as coal," would casually stroll down George Street, "walking . . . arm in arm with a beautiful English lady, both neatly dressed."[97]

Sydney, though infinitely interesting with its contrasts of virtue and vice, genteel hospitality and raucousness, individualism and shackled servitude, afforded little in the way of scientific study for the marooned naturalists. Most of the plant life in the surrounding areas were introduced species: horses, sheep, pigs, and dogs were now the predominant quadrupeds. And there were few Aborigines to be found—they had been driven into the barren interior and hunted to near extinction by bushrangers and cattlemen. Many of the expedition probably never came face to face with an Aborigine "in the wild." Consequently, Wilkes drew much of his ethnological conclusions from secondhand sources, most notably the English botanist F. Armstrong. Those who did happen to come across the few natives wandering about near Sydney were not impressed. Some considered them "the most miserable beings I ever saw, more resembling baboons than human beings" or "the most miserable beings in the world," a title previously held by the natives of Tierra del Fuego.[98] They appeared to be an odd amalgam of racial types—the skin tone and general features of an African capped with the long, smooth (though occasionally blond) hair of the Polynesian.

Hale and Pickering, not wishing to depend upon such a small sample to study, left the city in order to gather more data on the language and habits of the natives. Contact was quite difficult, owing to the understandable aversion the Aborigines had toward meeting up with whites. Only about thirty full-blooded natives were observed at any length. The young philologist, however, managed to continue his diligent work recording vocabularies and grammars. He found the Aborigine language to be totally divorced from either African or Polynesian tongues. He likened their polysyllabic speech to that of the Indians of North America.[99] Pickering was a bit too anxious to form definitive conclusions based on such a small cultural sample. However, it is significant that he was able from these observations to dispel with some confidence several misconceptions concerning these people. He discovered that the majority of portraits drawn of the Aborigines, particularly the well-known works by French and English artists, "were for the most part caricatures . . . rather calculated to deceive."[100] He also found that while the general depiction of the Australian as an African-Malay may hold from a distance, closer contact revealed considerable diversity of physical features

"King Teapot and His Two
Gins—New South Wales" and
"Buncaree—Chief of the Broken Bay
Tribe." These are two 1830s British
lithographs collected by George
Emmons during the expedition's stay
in Sydney. Charles Pickering
commented that the majority of
portraits drawn of the Aborigines,
particularly the well-known works
by French and English artists, "were
for the most part caricatures . . .
rather calculated to deceive." Source:
George Emmons Journals.

Bamboo Kain (Newcastle Tribe) and Cungara, wife of Charcoal. Sketches by Alfred Agate. In an era before the advent of photography, artists played a crucial role in creating a popular image of a people, particularly those of an "exotic" or unknown nature. Fortunately, the Wilkes Expedition included three excellent artists: Titian Peale, Joseph Drayton, and especially Alfred Agate. Dana, in a letter to Asa Gray, assured his fellow scientist that Agate was compiling "an admirable series of portraits—Unlike those of the French voyages, they may be trusted not only as characteristic, but as accurate likenesses of the *individuals.*"

(more so than the Negro, he felt). Certainly, he agreed, "some were ugly enough." But others, "contrary to all anticipation, had very fine faces."[101] Rebutting the stereotypical ill-shapen beast of European imagination, he found the physique of one particular individual to be "the finest model of the human proportions I have ever met with; in muscular development, combining perfect symmetry, activity, and strength; while his head might have compared with an antique bust . . . of the Grecian Philosophers."[102]

How to categorize such a unique people? Were they a separate race? Pickering thought so. Were they less than human, or at least did they occupy an inferior version of humanity? Not according to Pickering. A letter sent back to his friend and colleague Samuel Morton warned against formulating just such base generalizations about these people. "It has been," he informed Morton, "very much the fashion to caricature these people." While it was true, he went on, that "this race" in its "Savage State, is not known to 'reap or to sow' " and "is naked, 'without knowing it,' yet in its practices and pursuits has shown the most singular ingenuity. The White Man, placed in the same circumstances in the interior of New Holland, could have hardly maintained his existence."[103] It was obvious to Pickering that their primitive state was not due to any intellectual deficiency. English missionaries had assured him that when given the chance to attend school with whites, Aborigine children "have shown intellectual powers fully *equal*" to their classmates.[104] It took only a walk into the barren interior of New South Wales to appreciate why the natives did not cultivate the soil. "It should be borne in mind that this Continent does not possess naturally a single esculent plant" amenable to intensive cultivation.[105]

The natives of Australia had routinely been placed "at the bottom of the scale of civilization," yet aspects of their culture seemed to defy explanation and categorization.[106] Nothing so defied whites' denigration of Aborigine physical culture as the native development and skillful use of that aerodynamic masterpiece, the boomerang. According to Pickering, the boomerang was a weapon "whose devious course remained so long the subject of incredulity" among the " 'Professors' " who had heard of this unique device.[107] Once its performance had been verified, however, the same people could not bring themselves to give the Aborigines credit for manufacturing the boomerang; either it had been introduced to Australia by a "superior" culture, or its discovery was merely some freak accident of nature that placed such a remarkable piece in the hands of such abject savages.[108] No one in the Exploring Expedition who witnessed the natives artfully curl their boomerangs around trees and other obstacles to score a

Corrobory (dance). This ceremony was performed following combat between groups of aborigines. According to Wilkes, "the effect of one of these exhibitions almost equals that of a tragic melodrama." Source: *Narrative,* 2:188, facing page.

direct and debilitating hit on their target doubted their mastery over this seeming anomalous bit of technology. But Horatio Hale, after inspecting one of those handcrafted "accidents," concluded that "though the curve thus described is one which might unquestionably be determined by mathematical calculation, we must suppose that it was an accident which first taught the use of this extraordinary weapon."[109]

Even more perplexing to the members of the expedition were the attitudes and beliefs of the Aborigines. They were described as "superstitious" but "devoid of religious (or devotional) feelings." When the concept of one God or Supreme Being and the prospect of an afterlife of heaven or hell was broached, it was the natives' turn to be incredulous. When missionaries pointed upward to "Him in the sky" and described the heavenly city, the Aborigines retorted with "But how will God get us up to him in the sky: will he let down a rope for us?"[110] Hale saw this as an example of the natives' "mental obtuseness" bordering on "almost brutal stupidity." Hale was likewise not impressed when the Aborigines attempted to explain to the philologist their belief system, dismissing their explanations as "silliness" that bespoke "downright childishness and imbecility."[111]

Hale and others found it most "remarkable" that such a "degraded" people could dare to be so fiercely independent and "extravagantly proud"—to the point of "haughtiness and even insolence." Wilkes called them a "proud, high-tempered race: each man is independent of his neighbor, owning no superior, and exacting no deference."[112] The Aborigines declined to refer to any white as "Mister," as they were aware of what this title implied. The scientists found that the Aborigines viewed them "with a mixture of distrust and contempt."[113] Any attempts to "amuse themselves" by teasing or ridiculing the natives was met by anger and physical violence.[114] According to Hale, "They appear to have a sense—or it may almost be termed an instinct—of independence, which disposes them on all occasions to assert their equality with the highest. They frequently observe, on being asked to work, "white fellow works, not black fellow; black fellow gentleman." On entering a room, they will not remain standing, out of respect, but generally seat themselves immediately."[115]

One can imagine the negative impact that such an attitude had upon the British, and it no doubt contributed to the attempted extermination of such an obstinate population. It is not as clear why such independent airs would have irritated Americans so. Similar attitudes had been attributed to Americans by Europeans visiting the United States. Indeed, these depictions of the Australian Aborigine matched well Alexis de Tocqueville's definition of the archetypical American citizen. Wilkes characterized the natives as "difficult to manage," a complaint often voiced by the British about American colonists in the eighteenth century. No one in the expedition rushed to embrace the Aborigine in a bond of republicanism, however.

Wilkes quoted the native population at that time to be sixty to seventy-five thousand, which was a four- to fivefold drop from that on the date of the first European contact. Accordingly, he predicted their imminent extinction.[116] It was ironic that, for all the cultural and physical allusions and comparisons to Native Americans, it was this statistic that was most "precisely according to our American Indians."[117] It was left to Pickering to contemplate the implications for native cultures facing white encroachment. After visiting Australia, where the natives had been evicted from favorable coastal land, then hunted down and shot along with their major food source by settlers and bushrangers—such acts permitted if not condoned by a home government that prided itself in the preservation of individual freedoms—his judgment on Britain and its Australian colony was harsh. "Here," he wrote to Morton, "is where Britain determined to let loose her hellhounds! to found a centre of dis-humanizing principles. . . . The Native offered no resistance to the newcomers, neither did he shrink from them. He still wanders through his ancient grounds, ever unconscious of any ownership in the soil, and only mourns the loss of his kangaroo—If he has been sometimes troublesome, his wrongs have been greater, aye!"[118]

Perhaps Pickering did draw parallels to the plight of "his Indians" back home. Perhaps not. But it is evident that what he had witnessed thus far on the voyage led him to question the justifications for eradicating or even encroaching upon another's culture. He had already seen enough to conclude that "the exploits performed not only in Australia, but New Zealand, the far scattered islands of the Pacific, etc., etc., if shown to the world, form a dark chapter in our history. The right one part of the world has thus to inflict a nuisance upon another, it is useless to question."[119]

Thus ended their stay at New South Wales, a land that Wilkes, shortly before he sailed for Antarctica, described as "a glorious colony which the mother country, and the whole Anglo Saxon race, may well be proud of."[120]

In early February 1840 the scientists ferried to the rock-studded harbor of Bay of Islands, New Zealand, to continue their work. This port had been nominally under British jurisdiction for decades, though in reality it was an "open town," a favored port of call for whalers and sealers of all nationalities hoping to evade British levies and surveillance. This was soon to change.

New Zealand offered the naturalists, and briefly the remainder of the expedition, a real change of pace from either populous Sydney or the little atolls of the Pacific. The topography was multiform—fine-grained beaches led upward through verdant, grassy valleys to lofty, rugged peaks. There geysers, volcanos, and earthquakes rumbled and bubbled in a constant metamorphosis of earth and water. The inhabitants of New Zealand, the Maoris, were as different as night and day from their nearest neighbors, the Australian Aborigines. They were obvious relatives of the Samoans and Tahitians, with like customs and language. Though altered somewhat, all was readily identifiable as Polynesian in nature.

Pickering, much to his chagrin, was thwarted in his efforts to secure a guide in order to explore the rich interior. Stranded at Bay of Islands, he turned his attention to the Maoris. Again he found that he had been deceived as to the general features of the New Zealanders. Portraitists had attempted to differentiate the Maoris from other Polynesians by creating artificial distinctions: for instance, drawing exaggeratedly large noses on their subjects. Pickering, on the other hand, saw no basis for such distinctions. Traveling among the Maoris, he "saw every variety of feature and could make out no difference in this respect from the Taheitians and Samoans."[121] The Maori physiognomy was distinct, but that was a result of tattooing, pervasive on the men and framing the mouth and "labia pudendi" of the women.[122]

The Maoris were described as a "fine looking set of men" of varying skin hues, with round, well-proportioned faces and bodies, wide eyes, and fine white teeth. They possessed a "beauty and symmetry" and a "vigor of body and mind, which gives them a preëminence over many of their savage neighbors." Clark appraised them as "the antipodes of those [savages?] of New Holland [Australia]. . . . Both are savages, but one is intellectual, active, and *man-like*, the other corrupt, deformed, physically and mentally degraded and *brutal*."[123] While some members of the expedition found the natives aggressive and lacking in the expected Polynesian arts of hospitality, neither were they able to verify the reputed warlike and cannibalistic nature traditionally attributed to the Maoris—a failure they attributed to missionary influence.

For some, the Maori seemed more like American Indians than Polynesians. Hale, while acknowledging the linguistic and cultural evidence that pointed to a Polynesian migration, still found the Maoris and the North American Indians a close match. In "complexion, form, and profile," he felt the two were quite alike. In "character" they were interchangeable: both were "exceedingly proud, often sullen, and always quick tempered," rendered furious by the most "innocent" teasing.[124] Wilkes in his narrative related several examples to sustain this point, such as the time when an unidentified white visitor sought to amuse himself by touching his lit cigar to the nose of a Maori leader.

> An untoward circumstance occurred, which had well-nigh ended in an open affront. As they were seated in the porch of Tibbey's house, one of their thoughtless visiters, by way of affording amusement to the company, played off upon Ko-towatowa a boyish trick, by burning him on the nose with a cigar. This produced great anger in the chief, who would have at once punished the rudeness, but through the timely interference of the bystanders, he became appeased, but required some atonement for the insult offered him; a half-dollar was given him, but he said he would only accept half, as he did not want to be paid for it, but merely desired a token that it had been atoned for. In the opinion of all, he rose above the silly trifler who had been the perpetrator of the joke.[125]

Wilkes, too, perceived a similarity between the Maoris and American Indians. Overall, however, he felt that the New Zealanders lacked that "dignity which is sometimes seen in a savage of our country."[126] There were others on the expedition who, halfway through the voyage, had seen enough to venture some even broader generalizations concerning the Maoris in particular and "savagery" everywhere. "With regards to the Inhabitants of New Zealand, it is sufficient to say *they are Indians and Indians will be Indians all over the world* [italics mine]. These may perhaps be a little more industrious than some of the inhabitants of the South Sea Islands, granting this to be true, which is all that can be said of them. They are a poor miserable set of *Devils* not fit to control themselves, or worthy of the Land which they occupy."[127]

With this statement, in particular the closing remark, the English government heartily concurred. While Wilkes was in Antarctica, the scientists had the opportunity to witness colonialism and conquest, British style. During their stay the English consummated the Treaty of Waitangi, formally annexing New Zealand and making Victoria "Queen of the Canibals," according to Peale.[128] On 5 February Captain (and soon to be Governor) Hobson called a meeting of all the Maori leaders at Bay of Islands in order to induce them to cede their "lands, authority, and persons to Queen Victoria." After five hours of "negotiations" the meeting dissolved with every Maori representative refusing to sign. Several days later, following intensive lobbying by missionaries and other "interested persons," approximately forty Maori leaders were rounded up—according to Wilkes, "a very small representation of the proprietors of the soil"—and dutifully placed their mark upon the treaty.

When Wilkes arrived from the frozen south over a month later, he asked Pomare, one of the most powerful Maori leaders, what he understood the implications of the treaty to be. The captain found that Pomare "was not under the impression that he had given up his authority, or any part of his land permanently; the latter, he said, he could not do, as it belonged to all his tribe." His acquiescence took the form of a personal land grant to the queen, nontransferable and for her use only.[129] Pickering was told that though "the soil was said to be held by the chiefs, the consent of each member of the tribe was necessary to a sale."[130]

The British justified annexation by insisting "that it was necessary to extend the laws of New South Wales over the island in order to protect the natives," an excuse Wilkes dismissed as fallacious.[131] It was also considered their duty to provide more land for the ever-arriving surplus English population and to promote and protect British commercial interests. It might be expected that such reasoning would have struck a familiar chord among the Americans. Three years prior to the expedition's departure from the United States, Andrew Jackson had uttered similar justifications for depriving the Cherokee Nation of their Georgia homeland and had utilized precisely the same methods to secure the Treaty of New Echota that "legitimized" the act. In 1838, even as the ships of the United States Exploring Expedition were sailing out of Norfolk harbor, the Cherokees were being rounded up and placed in internment camps preparatory to the one-thousand-mile march to Oklahoma.[132] But despite the continual allusions to the supposed "Indianness" of the Maoris, no one contemplated—at least in writing—their comparative plights.

Wilkes seemed to draw from his perception of the Indian experience when forecasting the future of the Maoris. The treaty was in hand,

> and the country will now be retained by England, even if a military power should be necessary. Should the New Zealanders resist, and they are a warlike race, yet acting against European discipline, they will be readily overcome. They are not unlike grown children, and may be more easily ruled by kindness, and by satisfying the wants of the chiefs, than by force. The population will soon disappear before the whites, for the causes that have operated elsewhere are to be seen in action here, where the savage is already sinking imperceptibly before the advances of civilization.[133]

Like many Americans, he may have resented British criticism of the perpetuation of slavery and American Indian policies. Thus he found it hypocritical that while English "philanthropy, real or pretended, is ransacking the globe to find subjects for its benevolence, it seems a little surprising that scarcely a voice has been raised in Parliament against this act of usurpation."[134]

The expedition was reunited at the end of March, which gave the still-shivering crew members who had returned from Antarctica little more than a week to spend in New Zealand.[135] The happiest man on the expedition had to be John Sac, the Maori sailor who had been absent from his native land for nearly a decade. Sac was very popular with his shipmates, in their eyes "every inch a man, an excellent sailor, and a jolly good fellow."[136] The fully tattooed, robust Maori, though eminently content on the high seas, was anxious to visit his home, longing, as Erskine put it, "to return to his wigwam."[137]

The scientists who had been staying at Bay of Islands found Maori hospitality tempered (like that of the Tahitians) by the recently introduced money economy: there were charges of one shilling each for the right to pick up shells on the beach; admissions fees were demanded to witness Maori ceremonies. Sac, when informed of such penuriousness, was angry. It appeared that much had changed over the past ten years. Seeking to atone for the actions of his countrymen, Sac (a man of noble lineage whose real name was Puatti), invited his friends on the expedition to visit his village for an evening of dining and dancing. While they feasted on a spread of fresh pork, boiled fish, sweet potatoes, and peaches, they were treated to a trilogy of Maori dances—the *War Dance*, led by their shipmate Sac, the *Peace Dance* or *Entertaining Strangers*, and finally the *Love Dance*. For Clark, viewing these performances evoked memories of Mother Ann Lee and the Shakers.[138]

During an interlude, the sailors rose from the banquet spread and returned the favor with some salty sailor jigs, dancing "several fore-and-afters, all-fours, and the Sailors Hornpipe." Then it was "all partners on the dance floor" for the *Love Dance*—which continued till morning.[139]

Throughout their stay in New Zealand, the expedition found it difficult to obtain Maori artifacts for its collections. Particularly precious was that most prized Maori curiosity—tattooed shrunken heads—the sale of which had been prohibited by law since 1831. Wilkes discovered that even if the Maoris were no longer ready sources of cultural paraphernalia, others stood ready to supply their needs—for a price. Lying at Bay of Islands was a missionary brig that doubled as a floating curio shop of native artifacts. Hence it was from this rather unlikely source that the expedition rounded out their Maori collection, clandestinely securing two preserved heads—both dubiously identified by the proprietor of the vessel as "New Zealand Chiefs"—for £10 sterling.[140]

The second week of April found the Exploring Expedition again moving out across the Pacific, backtracking toward the Friendly and Fiji Islands. For a bored Titian Peale, it was not a moment too soon. He wrote to his father concerning New Zealand: "We gather all the plants, shot all the Birds, caught all the fish, and got heartily sick of the natives, in spite of their tattooing and carving; they won't bear a comparison for good qualities with the worst of the Polynesians."[141]

The ensuing northeastward track turned out to be quite tedious. The squadron was forced to spend nearly a month sailing around contrary winds, an aggravation increased by frequent calms that often left them dead in the water. Finally, on 24 April *Vincennes* entered the harbor at Nukualofa on the island of Tongataboo, the largest of the Friendly Islands. Tonga was one of some fifteen hundred islands dubbed "Friendly" by Cook during his three visits in the 1770s.[142] This level and lushly verdant limestone outcropping had been the home of English Wesleyan missionaries for over a decade. To no one's surprise, Wesleyan modes of "civilizing" the natives were nearly

identical to those of the missionaries at Samoa and Tahiti: the same prescribed neat and orderly rows of native dwellings, the same proscriptions on
native popular culture. The result was as in Samoa—the islanders polarizing
into "heathen" and "Christian" camps. The Wesleyans, however, carried
their commission to propagate the gospel and destroy "heathen" culture to
the extreme. They actually encouraged war between the two factions that
they in fact had created.[143] Wilkes, coming ashore, was dismayed by what
seemed to be imminent bloodshed between the adversaries. He called for a
summit, hoping to mediate a settlement or at least an armistice. Somehow
he managed to coerce the opposing leaders to attend but quickly realized the
futility of his plan, as it became clear to him who the aggressors were. The
Christian party had been recently reinforced by warriors from the neighboring islands whose leaders hoped to benefit from the turmoil on Tonga.[144]
They were itching for a fight. The heathens were much less so, insisting
only that their customs be respected. Whenever Wilkes sensed that he was
making some headway in breaking the resolve of the Christians to make war,
he found that their ardor was rekindled by their "ghostly advisors"—the
missionaries—lurking in the background. The Wesleyans envisioned only
one final solution to the conflict. As one missionary remarked to George
Sinclair, "the only way to settle the differences of the Island would be to
exterminate the Heathen Party," a solution Sinclair considered "a most cruel
doctrine to advance."[145] He had seen enough of the missionaries during the
expedition to conclude that "the most damnable and blood thirsty Tyranny
that a nation can be subjected to, is that of a Bigoted religious sect."[146] At
least one officer concurred with the missionaries as to how to resolve the
problem, only he did not draw any distinctions between the Tongans—or
any other natives, for that matter. "They are at it again," he shrugged. "I
believe there is no way of satisfying an *Indian* [italics mine] when he is for
war but to kill him."[147]

Nearly everyone on the expedition, from Wilkes on down, genuinely liked
the people of Tonga—especially the "heathens," Polynesians whose "sin"
seemed to be that they were more "attach[ed] to their ancient customs than
others."[148] They considered the Tongans particularly handsome, with their
full cheeks, well-turned limbs, and prominent stature.[149] Wilkes thought
them a "fine race of men and by far the most prepossessing of any of the
Polynesians we have yet visited."[150] Among other things, the men of the
expedition found that the "civilizing" influence among the "Christians"
was not quite as pervasive as the white missionaries would have liked.
While tobacco was effectively banned among the Christians, both parties

indulged in the traditional sharing of kava, an intoxicating beverage made by masticating and spewing the dried roots and lower parts of the *Piper methysticum* plant into a large communal bowl. Nor was alcohol eradicated among the Christians. When John W. W. Dyes rebuked a native for soliciting a bottle of rum, asking him "if the missionaries had not learned him better," the Tongan "shrugged up his shoulders in reply and said, 'I *am* missionary.' "[151]

Whenever they came on shore the voyagers were immediately surrounded by children—a joyful occurrence not previously experienced thus far during their travels. Pickering could not help but contrast their "cheerful and good humoured" dispositions with the "moroseness and covetousness so apparent in New Zealand."[152] The women, whom Wilkes found "intelligent looking," were dressed only in a tapa loincloth; many were missing the little finger of one hand, though this custom had been curtailed by the missionaries.[153]

Sailors and scientists alike were impressed with the Tongans' finely crafted and graceful double canoes.[154] By unfurling a large triangular sail, they could catch the wind to either the Fijis or Samoa whenever they chose. Pickering likened them to the ferryboats found in America.[155] In years past, Tongans had brought back Samoans to serve as slaves. The interaction between Tonga and the Fijis was more symbiotic. Many boys served an apprenticeship among the Fijians, partaking of their knowledge while serving as scullers for the elite. The amorous trysts that often occurred from this tradition the scientists humorously equated "to the advantages accruing to our own young men from a visit to Europe."[156]

Especially delightful to all was the sonorous singing of the Tongans. The most rhythmic were the scullers, whose voices blended into perfect, intricate four-part harmonies while plying the oars of their double canoes. Most remarkable about the native music was its lack of a minor mode. Drayton, the amateur musicologist of the expedition, remarked that "he did not hear a single strain in the minor mood in singing, nor even in their natural sounds in speaking."[157] Their "wild but agreeable" singing prompted Dyes to "confess I never heard anything that sounded better."[158] Opportunities to listen to the Tongans were few, as the natives were continually fearful that the missionaries would overhear them; singing, too, was banned.

Probably the only feature of Tonga that did not endear itself to the expedition was the insufferable mosquitos that feasted on the blood of their pale and sensitive white bodies. "The mosquitos! Good Heavens!," James Alden wrote after a particularly bad bout with the insects. "Never in my life did I ever see such quantities. The Air was literally *thickened* by them—so soon as the sun set, when they usurped the solace of flies who were most actively engaged during the day annoying us poor unoffending mortals almost past endurance."[159]

During their stay in Tonga, the naturalists took several walks around the island, but owing to the unstable state of affairs, explorations into the interior were kept brief. Pickering made one such excursion by canoe to the "heathen" village of Moo. He was received "with a good deal of dignity and politeness" by its inhabitants, who allowed him to roam about the town and beyond. Outside the village, Pickering fell in with an English-speaking native who guided him through the extensive tracts of cultivated land. Tongans, he discovered, were quite knowledgeable tillers of a rich volcanic soil that ran as much as ten feet deep. In his inquiries, he found them "as discriminating in the qualities of the soil as our farmers at home." As he followed his guide around the island, "land was pointed out to me as good for bananas and other tracts that were unfit for their culture, though I should myself have been puzzled to find the difference."[160]

While roaming about the island, he was surprised to meet up with a boy from New Guinea, "an Arramanga Lad" who was living among the Tongans. Observing the boy, Pickering noted incongruities in the physical features that failed to correlate with the accumulated evidence depicting this type as being Negroid. There were the commonly denoted "Orang" features— his hair was "unequivocally *woolly!*, precisely as in the Negro" and the lips thick. The nose, however, was "hardly as broad as in the Negro." Significantly, according to the doctor, "the countenance was very pleasing, and he seemed unusually active and intelligent, and withal good humoured." There seemed to be no doubt that "this individual was unquestionably of a different race from the New Hollanders, and may probably constitute a 6th race."[161]

And so it was at this juncture that Pickering made a crucial break and abandoned the traditional enumeration of the five races of mankind, broadening the model to include the possibility of one or even more additions to the prevailing racial paradigm. Such a radical hypothesis based on the external features and actions of a single "specimen" was certainly not beyond Pickering, or indeed most any other scientist of his day. Such was, and is, the methodology of science. It does, however, seem unlikely that this solitary encounter alone triggered an ethnological epiphany. During the course of the voyage, the wide variations of countenance and culture that Pickering had observed had strained his concept of the races of mankind, until at Tonga he surrendered to the naturalist's bent for boxing and splitting. From now on, Pickering, though still saddled with the prevailing notion of distinct races, would henceforth explain human variation not by stuffing each group encountered into one of the five existing conceptual racial receptacles; instead, he simply made new boxes. As a result, by the next time he corresponded with Morton (August 1840), he had added two more races to his list. Five years later, he declared for at least eleven, and so forth. Such packaging allowed Pickering to retain and expand the prevailing racial model without disassembling it.

Returning from his visit to Moo, Pickering spied two more dark-skinned natives lounging on the beach. These, he was told, were neither Arramangans nor Tongans but natives of Fiji. In this instance he considered himself "not yet prepared to draw general conclusions from such scanty material."[162] At first pass he leaned toward classifying them as Australians. However, Pickering's and the entire expedition's experience over the next two-and-a-half months was to prove that cataloging Fijian culture within any system known to Americans would prove frustratingly futile, even deadly.

The Fiji group they have surveyed
    With well-instructed hearts;
And all those islands, reefs, and bays,
    See pictured on their charts.
She paused; and lo! from Freedom's eye
    There fell a crystal tear.
"Two sons I've lost," the goddess cried;
    "Two sons I loved most dear."

Nay, Freedom, quiet each mournful sigh;
    Those crystal drops restrain;
The sequel shall relight thine eye
    With pleasure's beam again.
We are the men our chieftain led
    O'er dark Malolo's plain;
Before us hosts of Indians fled,
    And left two hundred slain.

We are the men who burned their town,
    Well fortified and new;
Destroyed their cattle, fruits cut down,
    Because thy sons they slew.
On hands and knees that murd'rous host
    Did crawl our chief to meet—
They owned 'twas retribution just—
    Begged pardon at his feet. . . .
—By one of the crew, as quoted in Erskine,
        Twenty Years Before the Mast

The expedition left Nukualofa for the Fiji Islands on 4 May. Four days later they entered the harbor of Levuka, on the eastern end of the island of Ovolau.

The over eight hundred islands of the Fijian group seemed unsurpassed in beauty and variety. For every cluster of coral atoll peeking above the blue Pacific that they passed, there were forest-covered, mountainous volcanic islands. Other islands were laden with dense jungle or blanketed with savanna. Such an enchanting scenic cornucopia stood in vivid contrast to the revolting reputation of the inhabitants of these islands, for they had entered the realm of cannibals. Everyone had heard or read about the man-eating propensities of these people, the daily, deadly offhand violence, the inhumane cruelty—especially toward their own. The handful of missionaries who were attempting without success to convert the natives wasted no time giving the expedition an earful concerning the Fijians, adding to the lore of atrocities. They told of the Fiji custom of strangling the wives of recently deceased chiefs, and taking pains to perform this within view of the missionary house. Parricide, as well, was the custom here. Then there were the great feasts where, it was said, to ensure sufficient repast for the party, children were bound and heaved into the glowing coals when the supply of pigs had run short.[1] Prompted by these graphic accounts, some officers hurriedly made out their wills. The pervading notion, however, was not one of fear but of a determination to keep an open mind during their stay. It was not that they discounted the dangers, but they had just been misinformed too many times during the course of the voyage about the habits of native peoples to accept such stories at face value. They had been warned to beware of cannibals at other stops along the way, only to find that such practices no longer, if ever, took place. It certainly did not inspire faith in such information when it emanated from the mouths and pens of missionaries: the expedition members had become increasingly incredulous of their reports. As a result, most took a wait-and-see attitude toward the Fijians and their notorious practices.

American and European merchants had plied these waters on a limited basis since Bligh had literally drifted through this group in 1789. They first took aim at the plentiful sandalwood so prized by the Chinese as altar incense, gathering such a prodigious amount that within just a few years the islands were stripped of this fragrant wood. In the 1830s merchants braved the ferocious reputation of the Fijians to harvest a foot-long sea cucumber— *bêche-de-mer*—that was a mainstay of Chinese soups and various delicacies.[2] So whether they approved or not, the natives of these islands found themselves at the crossroads of seagoing trade and they made the best of it. They willingly exchanged *bêche-de-mer* and various provisions not for the usual "useful" handicrafts of European and American technology—iron pots, tobacco, or alcohol—but for items to render their frequent interisland wars more efficient: muskets, ammunition, even a cannon!

Considering the recent history of commerce with white civilization, surprisingly little was known about the natural history and customs of the islands and their inhabitants, no doubt owing to their nefarious reputation. Pickering noted that only D'Urville had conducted any scientific work there. Still, if one read past the sensational tales of Fijian atrocities, glints of a rather remarkable civilization filtered through. Pickering had uncovered an English account that depicted the Fijians as "the only 'savage people' he had ever met with, who could give reasons [for their actions], and with whom it was possible to hold a connected conversation."[3] Reasoning or intelligent "savages": a concept sure to intrigue some and terrify others. Even the missionaries conceded the exceeding intellect and ingenuity of the Fijians—so much more reason to fear them. The scientists on the expedition were anxious to discover for themselves the truth of the matter by making acquaintance "with this remarkable people—one of the least known of any of the branch of the human family."[4]

The voyagers were welcomed into Levuka Harbor by a thunderous roar from the natives on shore. Wilkes even imagined that they were applauding. The islanders then manned their graceful canoes and, weighted down with yams and taro, made for *Vincennes*. As soon as the first native climbed on deck, Pickering was forced to revise completely the earlier notion he had formed at Tonga, that these people were akin to Australians. He listened to the African American crew members marvel at the similarities between themselves and the natives, remarking that "people at home would hardly believe that these were natives."[5] George Emmons later observed that "excepting the natives of Clermont Tonnere, I have seen none so dark as these."[6]

Soon, however, Pickering felt sufficiently able to discern significant physical differences between the Fijians and his black shipmates, once they had drawn side by side. Indeed, the doctor and others in the expedition came to perceive more variation in skin color and physical features in these people than they allowed for American blacks. Hale concluded that rather than a universal pigmentation, the Fijians possessed "two shades, very distinctly marked, like the blonde and brunette complexions in the white race."[7] Sinclair's description was more graphic and succinct: "while you meet many who are full blooded wooly headed, thicklipped negro, there are others who tho' black, yet cannot be called negro of the African kind. Their features are rather of the European."[8] While the Fijians had a specific name for those of a lighter complexion—*viti ndamundamu*, or "red Fijian"—Hale found that this distinction was not a factor in determining caste or class in the highly structured Fijian social order—a novel concept for American observers prior to this voyage. For Fijians, differences in skin color was merely a phenomenon, observed and noted to be sure, but with no social significance.

This was not to say that the social organization of these people approached in any way the "republican" tendencies of the Society and Navigator Islanders, where "chiefs" and "kings" seemed to be merely "first among equals." Instead, the members of the expedition uncovered a bewildering (to them) web of hierarchical relationships that had no peer even in aristocratic Europe. Indeed, the Fijian devotion to their rulers and the absolute power that the leaders held over those below them was enough to make any European or Asian despot envious. "As to *loyalty*," Pickering explained in a letter to Morton, "all that you can find in history is a fool to what these people are capable of." He found that those lower in the pecking order willingly consigned the power of life and death to those above them—a prerogative frequently invoked in a seemingly arbitrary and ferocious fashion.[9] Some, like Pickering, saw this social system as evidence of Fijian sophistication, while others as proof of their savagery. One officer attempted to explain Fijian deference—and saw American Indians. In his eyes deference was synonymous with savagery. Indeed, the two words seemed interchangeable. "If one Chief comes into the presence of another who is his superior, he immediately squats on his hams, until the superior has passed, or bids him rise. This is invariably observed when one Indian meets another, that is, when they belong to different tribes, that is, if they are at peace with one another."[10] The "Indians of the Feejees," he went on, are always armed and on guard, carrying their war club "over the shoulder in the manner a sportsman carries his fowling piece. If he meets another Indian in his path, [his club] is immediately lowered in a kind of salute."[11]

Like the Polynesians, the Fijians wore little more than a fringe of tapa about the waist. However, one risked death if caught without this covering—a custom that predated the arrival of the missionaries. Jewelry and other ornaments were popular but strictly prescribed by the wearer's social standing. Nearly all had their ear lobes bored, some so radically that Wilkes imagined that he could put his hand through the openings. Nothing, however, so physically distinguished these people from any other group as their great preoccupation with maintaining their huge bulk of frizzled hair, the pride and joy of all Fijians. Barbers and stylists conducted a brisk business coifing the hair of the well-to-do. The expedition encountered one head of hair that had been frizzed out to a circumference of sixty-two inches. Great care was taken to protect such a styled bulk while sleeping. The Fijians had designed bamboo "pillows" to carefully cradle the slumbering head. They loved to dye their hair: flaxen and vermilion were particularly popular. Even the natural black was often intensified to achieve a heightened affect. Those who felt themselves deficient in locks resorted to wigs. The Fijian custom of frequent bathing did not extend to the upkeep of their hair, however, as washing or even combing was nearly impossible under the circumstances. As a result, their hair was teeming with life, a not unwelcome occurrence for these islanders. Their solution, according to Wilkes, was the "disgusting custom" of picking out the vermin and "sharing in the banquet that results in the hunt." He noted that even this activity was strictly regulated, with one-third of the vermin "awarded to the searcher." He was told that "no greater insult . . . could be offered a native than to appropriate more of these spoils than the allotted share. It is also considered a great insult to search a child's head, as that is considered entirely the father and mother's perquisite."[12]

Without a doubt many found the Fijian appearance to be disgusting. John Dyes remarked that "if there is a race of beings on God's earth resembling the Baboon, it is these."[13] Of course, such conclusions coincided well with the ferocious reputation of the islanders. The Americans saw little of the bodily symmetry and imposing physique characteristic of the Polynesians they had encountered. This contrast was made all the more evident by the number of Tongans that resided in the Fijis. Still, there was something about these people that made them eminently more interesting than their Polynesian neighbors, despite their unprepossessing appearance. Soon the members of the scientific corps began to appreciate and take note of a culture that even the rebuffed missionaries considered "far more ingenuous . . . than the Polynesians."[14] Pickering, after studying the Fijians, theorized that this group was the wellspring of all that was "advanced" in Pacific Island culture, going so far as to depict the Fijians as the innovative "Greeks" to the imitative Polynesian "Romans."[15] Nor did anyone accuse them of being indolent— a favorite adjective attached to people considered "savage." Hale found them fully in possession of those traits formerly considered the exclusive possession of those of "European stock"—an intense industriousness and acquisitiveness, the Fijian version of the Protestant ethic. Nor were the arts ignored by these amazing people. Hale was intrigued by their propensity for "verse-making," composed in a variety of "peculiar and different" rhyme schemes.[16] Even the hard-to-impress Titian Peale, who, apart from being an expert marksman, was a member of a prestigious bowmen's society back in

Philadelphia, took time to comment favorably upon their handiwork and abilities in archery.[17]

Nothing impressed the expedition members more than when they had the opportunity to sample the great culinary fare of the Fijians. Man after man waxed eloquent over the variety and excellence of Fijian cuisine. For those too long sustained by dried beef and weevily hardtack, the art of cooking, of which the Fijians apparently were considered unrivaled, took on an even greater significance. The islanders had mastered the techniques of roasting, steaming, baking, and parboiling, utilizing a variety of pots, pits, and barbecues. Especially savored was *okalolos*, a baked pudding consisting of coconut milk, bananas, and other fruits. Charles Erskine gave a mouth-watering rundown of the recipe:

> Half a calabash was first lined with a few plantain leaves. A layer of the golden banana cut in slices was placed on the bottom, and on this was laid another layer of a different flavor, and so on. The meat of the cocoanut, which is, when ripe and freshly gathered, as soft as jelly, was placed between the alternate layers, which were continued until the dish was filled. The milk of the cocoanuts was then poured over the whole, and then the ends of the plantain leaves, with which the dish was lined and which had projected above the top of the dish, were gathered up and tied around with a string taken from the bark of a tree, after which the jar was placed in the trench, under the leaves, to steam. . . . I can testify that they far excelled all the cakes, pies, and puddings which I ever ate elsewhere. I have eaten suet and minute puddings, English plum duffs, Jennie's kisses, "my Mary Ann's cookies," angel cakes, Satan's best cakes, charlotte ruses, pies of all kinds, and many other dishes with euphonious names, but the Fiji okalolos, or fruit puddings, leave all of them far "astern."[18]

While Erskine and many of the others eagerly gorged themselves on such delicacies, others such as George Sinclair were unable to overcome the fear that one of the ingredients just might be of human ilk.[19]

Not only were the Fijians great gourmands, but each meal was, Wilkes noted, "attended with much ceremony and form . . . evinc[ing] a degree of politeness and good breeding that was unexpected and cannot but surprise all who witness it."[20] Pickering even observed that "a sort of grace was said before each meal." All of the above gave evidence of refinement and—so be it—"civilization" in what were considered "savage" people. And all of these customs and practices, unlike the Polynesians' adaptation of European ways, had their roots in Fijian culture. In other words, they were of "heathen" origin.[21]

The first several weeks of the expedition's stay in the Fiji Islands was marked by a felicity and cordiality on the part of both groups that, at the time as well as in retrospect, was both surprising and suspicious to the explorers. In fact, their entire three-month stay was characterized not by violence but by hospitality and friendly interaction. Dana wrote to Asa Gray that "in our intercourse with them we have always found them kindly disposed towards us, and at some of the parts [of the islands] I presume there would be no danger in the most familiar intercourse, even without the protection of arms."[22] The expedition attributed this phenomenon to a sort of cultural (or culinary) bias on the part of the Fijians: white flesh was simply unpalatable to these native epicures! The islanders informed an incredulous Pickering that "his [white] flesh is bitter and the fat not firm as in the Feejee."[23] To this Dana added: "A white man they say tastes bitter," reminding his friend that "tame animals you know, have never the flavor of wild game."[24] In fact, friendly relations between the two parties had little or nothing to do with white men being an inferior grade of meat. The Fijians had no intention of chasing away any whites that ventured to their islands, as long as they brought highly valued trade items with them. Even missionaries could be tolerated as long as they attracted additional vessels laden with muskets and ammunition to exchange for *bêche-de-mer* and various supplies. The expedition was indeed safe from molestation but only so long as it did not violate or impinge upon Fiji customs. In such a highly insular and structured society as this, laws were to be obeyed by all, including visitors.

Wilkes, representing a government and society no less dogmatically self-possessed in its views, was determined to conduct the expedition's business as usual. He would conclude treaties, conduct surveys, and firmly establish American power and presence just as they had done elsewhere in the Pacific without serious opposition. Granted, additional precautions were to be taken, particularly by those on the survey parties. But he saw no reason to doubt that his objectives of charting, exploring, and securing treaties in these islands would be achieved, just as it had been elsewhere in the Pacific. A key component in his strategy for securing these aims, and one that had been used with seeming success earlier, was to impress upon these "savages" the considerable might and authority of the United States, as embodied in the expedition and its leader. His dealings with Tanoa, "king" of Ambau and the first Fijian personage of note encountered, was indicative of Wilkes's strategy for securing his directives. Shortly after the squadron's arrival at Levuka, Wilkes made a point of summoning the aged leader to *Vincennes* in order to conclude a treaty. By taking the initiative, Wilkes hoped to impress

Two views of Tanoa, king of Ambau.

By Alfred Agate. Anthropologists have found the expedition's material collections and artwork concerning the Fiji Islanders invaluable for identifying aspects of Fijian culture that receded rapidly under British colonial rule later in the nineteenth-century. [Top] is a watercolor; [bottom] is from *Narrative*, 3:56, facing page.

upon the islanders his ability to impose his will upon such a great chief as Tanoa.[25] Though many expressed doubt that Tanoa would respond to such a beckoning, he indeed came two days later with an entourage of Tongan bodyguards and advisors, interpreters, and various members of the royal family in a fleet, opulent one-hundred-foot outrigger canoe. The king, whom Wilkes guessed was nearing seventy years of age, turned out to be a slender, stooped old man, whose "European" features belied his ebony skin. He had a peculiar way of speaking through his nose, "as if he had lost his palate." A huge turban "as big as a bushel" encompassed his immense head of hair. From his neck hung a large disc of made of mother-of-pearl, tortoiseshell, and ivory. A thick, equally bushy beard ran down to his navel. Most of the men on board were surprised by the unprepossessing appearance of so renowned a king. The great Tanoa, "king of the cannibal islands" reputed to have served up one hundred victims at a single feast, and who, for sport, delighted in running under the canoes of his own people with his royal outrigger, was merely "a meager, fleshless old man, black and hideous, his skin coarsely wrinkled over a dying looking skeleton." He was considered "nearer a monkey than a man."[26] While everything about him seemed to invite ridicule from the crewmen (he was immediately nicknamed "Old Snuff"), one disdainful look from Tanoa prompted them to ponder the inherent evil that they were convinced still lay burning in the heart of this old warrior. "In his small piercing eyes could be detected all the wicked fire of licentious power. They were the only visible feature in his face . . . the remarkable eyes—the prince of darkness himself, could not outvie in him."[27] Wilkes, however, saw in those eyes a measure of shrewdness and intelligence that made the old king eminently more interesting to deal with than the earlier Pacific islanders he had encountered. He was not to be disappointed.

Upon Tanoa's coming aboard *Vincennes*, Wilkes wasted no time in getting down to business. He laid down mats on the afterdeck and opened a council to gain assent to American rules and regulations regarding foreign vessels entering Fijian waters. As usual, these were not intended as negotiations. Wilkes merely sought assent for American concepts of trade, sovereignty, and justice. He achieved this purpose, but the process did not occur as he envisioned it. He found that, unlike prior councils held in Samoa and Tahiti, he was not able merely to hand a document to an interpreter, who then secured a quick confirmation of American rights from the island leader. Tanoa, as befitting the king of Ambau, insisted that all dialogue be conducted through proper channels—a concept that Wilkes, a career naval officer, should have been comfortable with. Therefore, when the commander had

David Whippy, a white castaway living among these islands (and a personal acquaintance of Tanoa), translate and explain the rules and regulations to the king, Tanoa ignored the recitative on the grounds that it was beneath his station to acknowledge and receive official communications from someone of Whippy's or, it was implied, Wilkes's rank. And so the commander was forced into following Fiji rules and regulations, and in consequence, losing the upper hand he felt he had gained by his summons to Tanoa earlier.[28]

Thereafter, the council proceeded thus: Whippy translated into Fijian Wilkes's missives to Tanoa's counselor, Malanivanua Vakanduna, who in turn repeated everything to the king—even though, of course, Tanoa had heard everything Whippy had said. While the translation was clear, the meaning and object of the regulations was not at first grasped by the king, which meant that further consultation was necessary. Tanoa, according to Wilkes, " 'could not take the idea' until one of his entourage, who had travelled among the whites, further explained the object of these regulations." Eventually Tanoa granted his assent, then placed his mark on the paper. Wilkes put the king's copy in a "bright round tin case" in an obvious ploy to impress upon Tanoa the importance of this document.[29]

Some considered such goings-on akin to concluding a pact with the devil. Wilkes himself had no illusions as to the immediate benefits of his efforts. But in some ways the actual stipulations of these agreements, which Wilkes stressed would acknowledge the rights of islanders as well as those of ships' masters, were of secondary importance. These "promises" would no doubt be broken by both parties. It was the *process* of holding such councils and the assertion of his and, by association, American interests and power in a land where they were interlopers, that Wilkes considered noteworthy. Having managed to induce the king to come to him aboard ship, then, though not as easily as he had planned, securing Tanoa's mark on paper, he next attempted to lecture the Fijian—through channels, of course—"of the necessity of protecting the whites, and of punishing those who molest and take from them their goods in case of shipwreck." Tanoa graciously listened "very patiently, and said, 'he had always done so; that my advice was very good, but he did not need it.' " He went on to warn Wilkes that, in effect, he had best save his lectures for other Fijians, such as his son.[30]

Documents such as these rules and regulations ostensibly were intended to protect both whites and islanders from being exploited. However, they also exhibited a total lack of understanding of the customs of the individual island groups, disregarding the existing rules and regulations of the native societies and ignoring the distinctiveness of the various cultures of the Pacific. For example, Fijian institutions, which were unlike any the expedition had encountered, were only dimly perceived by the voyagers. And few realized just how much their mere presence in these waters helped to further throw off kilter a highly volatile environment already injected with the deadly virus of European technology.

Fijian culture, for all its finery, rested upon a delicate balance of reciprocity, submission, and retribution that went beyond the obvious flashpoint practices of cannibalism or parricide. Such customs, whether rumored or actual, naturally put them at odds with missionaries and explorers alike. But it was the more subtle traditions of Fijian culture that ultimately proved incompatible with the presence of the expedition in these waters. For instance, the island's domestic economic system had long depended on the custom of *solevu*, in which the manufacture of certain articles was limited to specific regions, so that a healthy trade was ensured between the islands. *Solevu* also demanded a strict reciprocity of gift giving that, if not followed, could result in bloodshed.[31] What whites depicted as wanton cruelty and brutality was often the custom of *neitauvu*, a religious, political, and social institution that connected the villages of Fiji in a matrix of pairs that allowed one village to dominate another with impunity and likewise be dominated by another.[32]

Perhaps the most ominous rules in Fijian society, the ones that invariably guaranteed a collision with American values, were those concerning property and its possession. *Kere kere* enabled certain individuals to "borrow" items without obligation to return them.[33] The American term for this was "theft." Finally, Fijians believed strongly in their rights of salvage. Thus, any vessel, from the smallest dinghy to a man-of-war that happened to run aground on their shores or reefs, could be claimed—crew and all—as salvage by the leaders of the nearest village. This concept was not unknown elsewhere; the expedition had encountered the custom among the Samoans as well. Even in American waters some New Englanders were known to light false beacons in storms to entice merchant vessels onto the rocks, then stripping the wrecked holds of their goods. That a "savage" people would be so impudent as to insist upon such a right was incomprehensible to the members of the expedition, especially as the islanders considered the crew as part of the salvaged goods. In retrospect, given the copious opportunities for conflict between white and Fijian customs, it is a wonder that more blood was not shed during the expedition's three-month sojourn in these islands. Wilkes's "rules and regulations," obligingly *X*'d by Tanoa and other leaders, were destined to be enforced only by violence.

Following their talks, Wilkes conducted the entourage on a tour of the ship. He continued in his quest to impress upon Tanoa the might and power at his command, as well as the technical superiority of American civilization. Cannon boomed, munitions were inspected, and marines marched in close-order drill. "By a conceit of the musicians" on board ship, they were serenaded with the tune "King of the Cannibal Islands"—a gesture surely lost on the visitors.³⁴

Leaving Ambau, the expedition next proceeded to Rewa, a larger and more populous island in the group. Here the scientists began their work in earnest while the naval officers plied the waters conducting their painstaking surveys. Wilkes assigned Captain William Hudson the task of securing Rewan consent to the ubiquitous "rules and regulations." To Hudson also came the duty of capturing and prosecuting the culprits of a notorious incident involving an American schooner out of Salem, *Charles Doggett*. Seven years previous (there obviously being no statute of limitations where injuries against whites were involved), the ship had been cut off near Rewa and several of the crew murdered. In order to ascertain the identity and whereabouts of the Fijian perpetrators, Hudson obtained the services of a Fijian nobleman named Thokananto, known to American sailors as Phillips. This highly placed and gregarious member of the Rewan royal family made a habit of visiting every vessel that entered the island's waters. Intelligent and loquacious, he was a rich source of information concerning Fijian culture and customs. When questioned by Hudson aboard *Peacock*, he identified the instigator of the *Charles Doggett* affair as a fellow well-heeled Rewan named Vendovi.

While Hudson pondered his strategy for bringing in the culprit Vendovi, Pickering and William Rich left the ship and ventured up the creeks and through the wetlands of Rewa in search of botanical specimens. Everywhere they found the people hospitable and generous with both their food and lodging. The trip was a huge success as they came away with a plethora of plant specimens and ethnological information. During their return journey they were kindly guided back to the ship by three Rewans, "one of whom," Pickering recalled, "was taller than the others and from his appearance we should have taken for the fop of the village. His face was painted of a shiny black, except the lower part of the nose which was vermilion, carefully 'squared off,' and his hair from behind had much the appearance of an inverted iron pot."³⁵ Pickering gratefully offered the three men some recompense for their assistance, but it was refused. But when a little girl nearby asked for a Jew's harp that had been offered by Pickering, the tall "fop" requested the harp, then turned and tenderly gave it to the child.

Pickering was favorably impressed by this scene, as well as by the "civil and attentive behavior" exhibited by this man.[36]

The next morning, on 21 May, the king and queen of Rewa plus the entire royal family boarded *Peacock* as guests of the expedition. All, that is, except for the notorious Vendovi. Hudson was chagrined at this happenstance, as it was for this purpose that the invitation had been extended. Denied the opportunity to incarcerate Vendovi, the captain nevertheless entertained his guests throughout the day in hopes that the "fugitive" would presently arrive. As the sun shone into the late afternoon, Hudson finally abandoned this ploy. He ordered the drummers to beat to quarters and instructed armed guards to encircle the royal entourage. Hudson informed the frightened party— seventy to eighty in all—that they would be held hostage until Vendovi was brought to the ship, where he was to stand trial for murder. After a brief parlay the king acquiesced and agreed to send Ngaraningiou, a supposed rival of the fugitive, ashore to bring back Vendovi "alive, if possible."[37] In the meantime, no harm would come to the party so long as no one attempted to escape.

Hudson was true to his word and tensions eased as the evening wore on. The king, his inhibitions loosened by his evening draught of kava, ordered a series of dances performed for the enjoyment of his hosts. Those crewmen expecting the sort of suggestive frolics common to Polynesian dances were sorely disappointed by these performances. Many comments were heard concerning the distinct lack of lascivious or indecent movements in the Fijian dance, which to Pickering was additional evidence of the superior moral qualities of these people, especially when compared to the Polynesians. The Americans reciprocated, calling upon John Sac to perform one of his energetic Maori dances, a performance that "greatly astonished the Fiji natives," according to Erskine. Finally, the expedition's members continued their dissemination of American culture throughout the Pacific, concluding the evening with a "regular old-fashioned negro entertainment," featuring "Jim Crow" frolicking about the stage on a "braying ass" while "Juba and Zib Coon" set the audience wild with their rendition of the Virginia reel.

> Jim Crow's appearance, on the back of a jackass, was truly comical: the ass was enacted by two men in a kneeling posture, with their posteriors in contact; the body of the animal was formed of clothing; four iron belaying-pins served it for feet; a ship's swab for its tail, and a pair of old shoes for its ears, with a blanket as a covering. The walking of the mimic quadruped about the deck, with its comical-looking rider, and the audience, half civilized, half savage, gave the whole scene a remarkable effect. . . . The

dance of "Juba" came off well . . . but the braying ass of Godwin, with the Jim Crow of Oliver, will long be remembered by their savage as well as civilized spectators.[38]

What a strange web of images is brought forth by this scene! "Civilized" whites smearing grease on their faces, kneeling on hands and knees and making the most rude sounds in an attempt to entertain a group of interned "savages" by mocking the culture of erstwhile Africans—former "savages"— who had been kidnapped, enslaved, and "tamed" by white civilization.

Following the evening's entertainment, Hudson graciously gave up his cabin to the king and queen who, together with their small daughter, spent the night in comfort. The others stretched out and bedded down on large sails that had been laid across the gun deck. Phillips, that loquacious Rewan, had gathered an eager and rapt audience of scientists and officers about him. While they plied him with cigars, hardtack, and molasses, he waxed eloquent throughout the evening about Fijian philosophy and culture. Among those attending the lecture was Fred Stuart. He had put the day to good use observing the islanders "up close" and now felt ready to apply his phrenological insights to the people of Fiji.

> Conseeintiousness [*sic*] small.—Destructivness Secretivness and Cau-
> tiousness large, with Acquisitivness and Firmness rather large—without
> any further remark I may say, according to the best authors on this subject—
> the Existance alone of these propensities, connected together as they are—
> inclining toward the one disposition—there can be no manner of doubt—
> but what these people might be guilty of any act—Even should their own
> lives be in danger—for as before mentioned, they have no idea of its true
> value . . . an ordinary degree of the intellectual faculties and I might say
> all the animal propensities largely developed—with scarcely any Hope.[39]

Science, through the observations of Stuart, was utilized to reinforce the expedition's worst fears concerning the Fijians. It confirmed the notion that they were among the most dangerous of "savages," a people who "might be guilty of any act." Still, for others, more evidence—something even more tangible than bumps on the head—would be needed to convince them of the evil propensities of the Fiji islanders.

The next day Ngaraningiou, true to his word, returned with Vendovi. To Pickering's astonishment, Vendovi was the same tall "dandy" who had be-friended him during his island excursion. This time, however, Vendovi gave him no notice. The Rewan was immediately clamped in irons and brought to trial for murder. When allowed to speak in his own defense, Vendovi

Vendovi. Sketch by Alfred Agate. Source: *Narrative*, 3:136, facing page.

readily admitted his prominent role in the affair. He also claimed that he had been "deputed by a higher authority" to attack *Charles Doggett* and crew. Pickering, for one, considered this explanation "not at all unlikely."[40] The beleaguered islander continued on, echoing the words of those tried in a similar tribunal held earlier by Wilkes and Hudson at Samoa. After all, Vendovi insisted, "he had only followed the Feejee custom and done what his people had often done before."[41] His argument was to no avail. The verdict was guilty. Then came the surprising sentence: Hudson announced to the distraught gathering that no harm would come to Vendovi but that he would be taken to America to serve as an example to any native who in the future contemplated malice toward American sailors. This declaration was met by "much wailing and gnashing of teeth." Tearful friends and relatives of the convicted man grasped his legs until Hudson was finally forced to clear the decks of Fijians. Some, however, anticipated a happier ending to the affair. The irrepressible Phillips soon dispatched a Hawaiian barber to *Peacock* to ensure that Vendovi would be well coifed during his penitence. He included a ten-dollar gold piece, with instructions to bring back souvenirs from America.[42] Pickering remarked that the Rewan royal family, upon returning to their village, ordered that a large house be built "for the presents he [Vendovi] was to bring back from America."[43] This was not exactly the sort of reaction that Hudson and Wilkes had hoped for. Their worst fears were realized when another native, apparently jealous of Vendovi's good fortune, was overheard saying "that he would like to go to America and he supposed all he would have to do was to kill a white man."[44]

All in all, the punishment was a curious one. Perhaps Wilkes was borrowing a tactic used by Indian agents in the American interior. In the 1820s and 1830s Indian leaders regularly toured the major cities on the eastern seaboard at the expense of the federal government. These tours generally ended with an audience with the president. The aim was to awe, impress, and intimidate the leaders into obeying American law upon their return. Another motive was expressed by James Dana. He rejoiced that the expedition had just acquired a most prized "specimen." Sounding more like a member of the Peale family than a distinguished scientist, he notified Asa Gray that "we intend to bring him [Vendovi] with us to the United States to gratify the people at home with a sight of one of those man-eaters."[45] Vendovi remained in irons for nearly three months. Once the expedition had sailed out of Fijian waters, he was allowed to roam freely about the ship and became a very popular and, at times, valuable member of the expedition.[46]

The Fiji Islands were yielding a rich harvest of scientific material in nearly every branch of study. Ethnology was no exception. In late June Hale and Stuart—in a pairing of philologist and phrenologist—received permission to land on the island of Muthuata (or Mud-water, as some sailors pronounced it) to scour the local grave sites for intact skulls. Stuart had taken the rather unusual precaution of first asking permission from the local authorities to do so. The king voiced no objection, replying "with a smile: 'certainly, what good are they?' " according to Stuart.[47]

Muthuata was dotted with burial plots, the extravagant shrines of the highborn separated from the simple sites of the common people. Not surprisingly, they found the more opulent graves tabooed. The two men, accompanied by the artist Agate, ventured inland where, as the incredulous islanders watched on, they located and unearthed the complete skeletons of two men who had hailed from the neighboring island of Ambau. As was the wont of American scientists in this period, only the skulls were deemed worthy of retrieval. The two were bagged and the remaining bones, though in excellent condition, were discarded. These were the first skulls of Fiji origin to be added to the expedition collection. One week later, a third was added—gained, however, in a more unsettling and grisly manner.

After spending nearly two months among these islands, there seemed to be a growing tendency among the members of the expedition to question the vaunted reputation of the Fijians as cannibals. Some began to chalk up such stories as just another in the series of tall tales so often encountered concerning the people of the Pacific. Especially suspect were missionary accounts, likely of a secondhand nature, possibly drummed up to shock parishioners at home into keeping the financial pipeline primed and flowing. The expedition could offer no such evidence. In fact, few could find any fault in their treatment at the hands of the islanders, as Pickering attested to: "We had hithertoo been so well treated by the natives, had always found them so obliging, and so 'timid,' that many of us began to think they had been maligned. Some even doubted whether they were really *Cannibals*. . . . It so happened that though we had been nearly two months at these islands, no one could say that he had actually witnessed the fact, or name a person of credit who had."[48] There was a general agreement around the wardroom table on the evening of 2 July that, until hard evidence or a truly reliable witness was unearthed, they felt compelled to add "mud to the stream of knowledge" by reporting the fallacies of labeling the Fijians as cannibals.[49]

The very next morning following this discussion, a fortuitous opportunity arose to settle the issue to their satisfaction. *Peacock* was anchored in Naloa Bay, near the village of Fokasinga. For two days they had received reports of a battle going on between this village and one on a neighboring island. That morning, the islanders brought word that the fray had ended and the natives were said to be currently breakfasting upon the roasted body of a captive. Responding with skepticism, they dispatched the native canoes from alongside *Peacock* with a demand for tangible proof of the described event.[50] It was not long before three canoes returned from shore, bearing the usual fruits and vegetables that the islanders brought for daily barter. There, in one of the canoes, was their evidence. Spread out on a bed of plantain leaves like a display case at Delmonico's were the legs, arms, and other parts of a freshly roasted man. One native, acting as the *maître d'* of this ghoulish spread, picked up an appendage, brandished it in the air as if to flaunt the choice piece before the eyes of the gaping crew members, then bit off a chunk of cooked flesh, verifying its quality by exclaiming "*Vinaka!*" (good!).[51] Such "ocular proof" sent men scurrying to the ships rails, becoming sick at the sight and smell of cooked flesh being thus savored. "The smell! The smell!" Dyes recalled in disgust, "I shall never forget it!"[52]

Meanwhile, a few islanders had clambered aboard ship. In their hands was a human skull, charred and still warm, "still containing in many places the flesh and muscles . . . all the brains yet in it," covered with teeth marks from those who had earlier partaken of this Fijian repast.[53] His companion, "smacking his lips with unqualified relish," plucked an eye out of the head and, as a sickened crew watched in horror, bit off a piece and chewed it "with the greatest unconcern, saying that it was 'Vinaka.' "[54] Pickering had been below decks when he heard the initial commotion above. He rushed topside and, along with Dana, Stuart, William Spieden, and James Palmer, *Peacock's* doctor, fortified themselves sufficiently to proceed in a "scientific" manner. Spieden, as purser, was directed to purchase this new and fresh cranial specimen. He succeeded but not without some lively negotiation with its owners, who apparently had become aware of the rising and transcendent value of their merchandise.[55] Pickering secured the partially ingested eye; being technically a zoological specimen, he turned it over to Titian Peale. Bones and cooked flesh were examined to confirm its humanity. Perhaps disconcerted, Hudson immediately ordered *Peacock* out of the bay, leaving the puzzled though well-fed epicures of Fokasinga bobbing in their wake. The cause of American science had again been served but in a Fijian sort of way.[56]

Not surprisingly, talk at the dinner table was more subdued than that of the previous evening, as scientists and officers alike quietly picked up the pieces of their shattered theories and suppositions in order to make sense of what they had witnessed. A chastened Pickering summed it up: " 'There are none so blind as they that won't see,' but it turned out that these were even forced to see."[57] On the face of it, most by now were remarkably even-tempered about the incident. Cannibalism, after all, was just another custom to the objective scientist. Thoughtful minds formulated theories explaining why cannibalism thrived in these islands. Phillips, who was rumored to have been raised on human flesh during his childhood, was later questioned by Sinclair as to why his brethren continued such a revolting and inhumane (to whites, at least) practice. His reply reflected the cultural chasm that existed between the Fijians and the expedition members. "I [Sinclair] expressed my disgust at the practice, and Corydaudau [Phillips] asked, in a most sincere manner, why a man should not be good [to eat], as he was fed upon the very best of food, when a pig was [considered] good and eaten by us [whites], although it was fed on offal. It did not seem that he could imagine that any other motives than that of actual disrelish could operate to produce our disgust at this abominable practice."[58]

For all their attempts to deal with it in an objective and detached manner,

"Club Dance, Feejee." Oftentimes Wilkes would march and drill marines on the shore of various islands, partly to impress the natives with American precision and might. Tui Levuka, one of the many chiefs in the Fiji Islands, reciprocated with this regimented and awe-inspiring presentation of his own. This scene was strikingly captured by Joseph Drayton. Source: *Narrative*, 3:190, facing page.

the incident of 3 July had a much greater impact on the attitudes and perspectives of the expedition than they chose to admit. Subsequent events during the final month of their stay bore this out. The voyagers' perspectives on and relations with these people were altered, even skewed, once the Fijians were confirmed to be man-eaters. Not surprisingly, relations between the islanders and crew rapidly deteriorated from this point onward. A semblance of patience and forbearance for island culture gave way to shortened fuses and violent reprisals against the man-eating Fijians, even though the Americans had heretofore been treated most graciously. It was inevitable that, sooner or later, the expedition would run seriously afoul of Fijian customs and laws. The resulting clash of cultures, given the seriousness of which both groups held to their beliefs, boded ill for the participants. Unfortunately for both sides, they did not have to wait long for the first serious breach in peaceful relations.

After a review of the work thus far accomplished after eight weeks of surveying, Wilkes anticipated that it would take at least another month to satisfactorily chart these treacherous shores and waters. Accordingly, he felt it necessary to slash dwindling rations by one-third, while at the same time increasing the duty time for those manning the small survey craft. During the second week of July, one week after the affair in Naloa Bay, two such surveying vessels, commanded by Lieutenants Joseph Perry and Samuel Knox, were busy surveying the island of Sualib when a gale forced them to seek shelter in the bay. Later, when they tried to leave the inlet, Knox's cutter became grounded fast upon a reef. Immediately—and suspiciously— the inhabitants appeared, surrounded the cutter and made known that they considered it now their property. Knox's options were few. His powder and arms had been soaked by the storm, which left him in a decidedly poor position to negotiate in the usual fashion. He therefore retreated to Perry's boat to ponder his somewhat embarrassing situation.

What the islanders were doing was no more than acting upon their laws to claim what they felt was now theirs; the Americans quite naturally viewed the matter differently and no doubt were angered at the affront. The surveyors need not have taken it personally, however, as Pickering pointed out. "In order more fully to understand this matter it must be observed that it is *Feejee Custom* in cases of shipwreck (and touching the ground is sufficient), to seize the vessel and put all on board to death. In this respect their own people and strangers fare alike; and it is not from any particular hostility to the White man that he occasionally suffers."[59]

While Perry and Knox seethed helplessly in the remaining boat, two Fijian leaders swam out to them and, according to Wilkes's narrative, offered a typically Fijian compromise. They would personally guarantee the safety of the surveyors—an exemption of sorts—in exchange for the first rights of salvage.[60] Perry's response was to detain them as hostages. He then made for *Peacock* and informed Wilkes and Hudson of the incident. The prisoners were taken on board and put in irons, despite their offers of assistance. Upon receiving the report Wilkes immediately prepared a small armada of small sailing vessels, manned by over one hundred men, and set off for Sualib.

Contrary winds prevented them from entering the bay until the next morning, when Wilkes led a weary party of armed sailors ashore and demanded the return of the cutter and the property it had contained. What followed was a classic tug of war of cultural values and hegemony. Wilkes, ever insistent upon reinforcing and asserting his assumed superiority over the Fijians, decreed that if the boat and goods were promptly returned, he would, "for this time, forgive them."[61] If not, then he and his men would respond to this assault on United States government property by destroying their village. The "chief" whom Wilkes was threatening replied that, in essence, Wilkes should realize that the Americans were now under the jurisdiction of Sualib laws and "that it was a tradition among them that when a boat or canoe was cast away on their island, that they had a right to take possession of it in the name of their gods, to whom it belonged."

In vain, Wilkes strove to convince the Fijian of the "impropriety of such conduct," and attempted to "make him understand how he *should* [italics mine] act in such cases."[62] The chief countered that, be that as it may, it was no longer possible to reclaim the now-scattered goods from amongst the islanders. However, he would see to it—this time—that the boat, sails, and what few things he had acquired were returned, a quite generous offer considering the force of Fiji law. Wilkes, though, was not of a mind for compromise; neither was the crew. The commander ordered the weary men back to the ship for dinner but promised that they would return to shore that afternoon to burn the villages of Tye and Sualib to the ground. The men responded to this guarantee "with raptures" and "enthusiastic applause" that was disproportionate to the material wrongs inflicted upon the expedition by the incident. Such zeal was indicative of the change in attitude concerning the Fijians following the confirmation of their "true savagery" the week before. According to witnesses, this subsequent confrontation—cultural in origin—was viewed as an opportunity "to show their superiority to the savages."[63] Whether they succeeded is a matter of conjecture.

Captain Hudson landed two full divisions of men and marched in full view of the islanders to the first village. Although they had anticipated fierce resistance, none was forthcoming. An eyewitness recounted how the Americans set fire to the islanders' bamboo dwellings, "burning their yam houses, breaking up their war canoes, killing their hogs, and destroying everything that fell in our way." Sky rockets were fired among the frightened villagers, who scattered amidst cries of "*curlew! curlew!*" [spirits]. The same officer reported that any islander attempting to reenter the town was immediately felled by a volley of musket balls, declaring that "several met their fate in the like manner."[64] Wilkes later denied that any natives had been harmed. Perhaps finding such work infectious, the party paused on their return trek to the boats in order to torch another town in like manner.

Throughout the day, the men remaining aboard *Peacock* watched as the smoke wafted above the island, a sight that assured them that their comrades had done their job well. One of those, Fred Stuart, reported that during the entire afternoon "nothing was talked about but the burning . . . the slaughter of savages and quantity of plunder which might be taken on

"Burning of Tye," 13 July 1840. Fijians laid claim to an expedition surveying boat that had run aground. Wilkes attempted to negotiate a recovery of the government property. When that failed, he ordered the burning of the towns of Tye and Sualib. According to James Dana, however, "burning villages is of no avail as punishment. They only laugh at it." Source: George Emmons Journals.

such occasions."[65] At last, around ten o'clock in the evening, the exhausted but exhilarated punitive expedition returned to the mother ship with the "stolen" cutter in tow. The men were full of boisterous tales of their exploits. All marveled at the ease of their success and boasted that these "savages" were not so ferocious after all when confronted by determined Americans. "The cowardly devils, to suffer a handful of men (we were about 90), to spread waste and fire without a show of resistance. Our rockets threw them into a perfect panic . . . disappearing like frightened deer, when a rocket was lodged in the midst of them."[66] The men were empty-handed but well satisfied with their work. The towns had indeed been ransacked by the party. Hudson, however, had ordered them to leave behind both the bags of yams and taro and the pigs they had shouldered for the march back to the boats.

Wilkes was generally pleased with the results of the punitive foray, which he felt had been carried out "efficiently and promptly." He acknowledged that its lasting benefits were on the surface negligible, as it would take the islanders relatively little time or effort to rebuild their bamboo dwellings.

Most important, he believed that he had "taught these savages a salutary lesson" concerning the superiority of white civilization over savagery.[67] The expedition had also allowed his men to articulate violently their desire to establish their moral, cultural, and technological dominance over a people they now considered a "thieving and treacherous race of cannibals."[68]

Among the scientists, Dana was dubious about the effectiveness of inciner-ating Fijian towns, advocating even sterner "pedagogic" measures: "Burning villages is of no avail as punishment. They only laugh at it—A few weeks will repair all the damage. They have heretofore sneered at men of war. . . . [I]t is very important that some more effectual mode of exciting their fears should be adopted."[69]

Perhaps the only tangible lesson to be learned from this incident was that the Americans had no qualms about resorting to violence and destruction if one did not view things their way, native customs and laws be damned. No doubt the islanders took note. The Fijians, however, were also not a people easily given to compromise, as should have been evident in the expedition's dealings with Tanoa, the goings-on in Naloa Bay, and the incident at Sualib. Indeed, it was the perceived obstinence of the Fijians that seemed to anger the Americans most: the insistence of Tanoa to control the flow of negotiations, the flaunting of cannibalism, and the refusal of the Sualib leader to nullify the rights of his people to their booty. While the natives of Sualib might have been timid in meeting the expedition with force, there was no guarantee that other islands of the group would be so hesitant to meet violence with violence.

As the expedition's distrust of the Fijians grew, it was equally obvious that the islanders viewed the Americans with increasing distaste (pun, of course, fully intended). No doubt in the eyes of the Fijians, these interlopers possessed no respect for law and tradition, and except when it came to imposing military force, they could not be trusted to keep their word. The trickery and deceit employed by Captain Hudson to capture Vendovi was only one example. Another, peripheral to the same incident, came when Hudson had dispatched a shore party to hunt down the fugitive. The Americans had marched into the Rewan village of Vatia, a town renowned for the manufacture of pottery. Some of the men made it known that they wanted to purchase some specimens, which immediately drew "hundreds" of merchants "all pressing their wares on them." Only a few pots were bought, however, and the rest shunned, leaving the villagers feeling angry and deceived. They gave the Americans a rude escort out of their village, "hoot[ing] and shout[ing] many offensive epithets."[70]

Expedition parties venturing ashore often violated Fijian taboos. This was often accidental; however, some incidences were intentional. In one instance a party led by George Emmons was short of water. The lieutenant asked some nearby residents to "climb the trees & procure us some [cocoanuts], intending to pay them as we are always in the habit of doing." The Fijians refused, citing the fact that the trees were tabooed. Anyway, the trees belonged to the neighboring town of Bau; "it would cost them their lives if they complied with our wishes. We therefore removed the taboo & helped ourselves."[71]

Commerce between the two groups that had earlier gone smoothly was now racked by misunderstanding and mutual distrust as relations between the expedition and the islanders continued to deteriorate. If Wilkes had heretofore considered Fijian behavior "inconsistent," it was becoming clear that the islanders were coming to similar conclusions about the Americans.[72] Purser Spieden went ashore at Muthuata, where the expedition had earlier experienced a warm welcome, to purchase the yams, taro, papaws, and lemons that were more essential than ever to the health of the crew. As usual, he did not have to venture far, for the islanders were encouraged to supply so many foodstuffs that his launch was quickly filled to the brim. His marketing concluded—at least from his point of view—Spieden called a halt to the bartering and attempted to shove off for the ship, leaving the merchants and their excess goods standing on shore. Again, the islanders cried foul, and furiously raged at the deceit of the American who had summoned them to trade. In disgust they hurled their perishable goods into the river toward the departing boat, bitterly declaring that they had now learned their lesson concerning the Americans. They had always heard that "the white men never told lies," a reputation, of course, fostered by Wilkes throughout their stay. But now it was evident that the Americans instead "had two faces."[73]

Wilkes considered surveying to be the principal charge of the expedition during its stay in the Fijis. These activities as well became the source and scene of conflict between whites and islanders. Day after day, boats from the expedition surrounded the island coastlines, firing cannon, aiming their glistening theodolites toward shore, and planting flagstaffs along the beaches with neither permission of the islanders or thought regarding the possible implications of their actions.[74] Pickering recorded that, in fact, the Fijians subsequently complained of such actions—particularly the placing of staffs on their soil—as an official grievance.[75] But when the islanders began to remove the survey staffs from their shorelines, the reaction on board *Peacock* and *Vincennes* was predictable. At Muthuata, Hudson rushed ashore to threaten Tuemboooa, the same agreeable leader who had earlier assented to the expedition's request to gather skulls, that he would set fire to his town if the flags were not immediately given up. This threat, coming after the torching of the villages on Sualib, was taken as sincere by Tuemboooa, who no doubt wished to avoid a similar fate. He therefore promised their prompt return, or, failing that, he would pay double the "worth" of the wooden poles in foodstuffs, which he estimated to be ten pigs and four thousand yams.[76] This incident could easily have escalated into a confrontation similar to the one at Sualib, had it not been overshadowed by other events occurring around the same time. It was obvious that the tension between the two groups, with their respective cultures, was tightening. It was on another surveying jaunt that the taut nerves evident on both sides finally snapped, producing a tragedy that not only released violence and anger on both sides but soured the Americans for the remaining two years of the expedition.

To conduct both on- and offshore soundings and surveys, it was often necessary for the men to strike out in whaleboats and launches for weeks at a time. These were generally twenty-five to thirty feet in length, double-ended with a five-foot beam. Somehow, room was made for the mast, sails, oars, ground tackle, various firearms and other weapons, surveying equipment, and at least five cramped sailors. Out of necessity, provisions were kept to a minimum, salt pork and hardtack being the usual fare. Owing to the dangers on shore, crew members were ordered to sleep in the boat during overnight excursions lest they wake to discover themselves "breakfast guests" of the natives. In reality, the men often came ashore to stretch their legs and barter for fresh provisions.

At daylight on the morning of 22 July, Wilkes dispatched two boats under James Alden's command to survey the small islands of the Mamanuca group. Their orders were to rendezvous with the parent ship at sunset the next day off the eastern shores of the island of Malolo. By five o'clock on the afternoon of the twenty-third, Alden and crew had completed their surveys and were anchored in the harbor as planned. When *Peacock* did not appear, Lieutenant Joseph Underwood was ordered to go ashore where, according to Alden, "by ascending a slight eminence, he would have a view of her anchorage" in the event *Peacock* was delayed on the other side of the island.[77] Having only recently escaped a close encounter with the natives himself, Alden dispatched Underwood with some trepidation, "communicating to him my doubts of the good feeling of the natives with which I had been impressed in the short time I had had of observing their contact on my previous cruise . . . directing him at the same time to be well armed, and return before sunset."[78]

Underwood made for shore and, while scaling the slope in search of the brig, was kept under constant watch by the men in the launches. When natives appeared and moved suspiciously toward the lieutenant, Alden immediately signaled for Underwood to return to the launches, which he did promptly, reporting no boat on the horizon. So, with few provisions and no relief in sight, the men guardedly spent another night afloat in their cramped vessels.

On the morning of the twenty-fourth Alden awoke to find *Peacock* at anchor approximately eight miles eastward. By nine o'clock a cutter from the schooner, commanded by George Emmons, reached the stranded surveyors. Alden's request for supplies found *Peacock* in similar dire straits. According to George Colvocoresses, "the scarcity of provisions, and the distance of the schooner, whose own necessities were also pressing, now made it absolutely necessary to obtain supplies ashore."[79]

Alden had earlier sent John Sac into the village to ascertain the willingness of the natives to part with some food. Sensing their advantage, the villagers made it a point to display their goods along the shore. However, they could not be induced to deliver supplies to the launches. Lieutenant Underwood volunteered to take a party ashore to barter for meat and fruits, as his craft, the *Leopard*, was best suited to crossing the reef blocking the narrow channel separating Malolo and its smaller sister island, Malololie. He shoved off but was soon grounded on the reef, which was passable only at high tide. According to Fiji law, of course, the launch now belonged to the islanders. Alden watched as "a number of natives, perhaps fifteen or twenty, had collected about her, and joining their song with that of the boat's crew, were assisting to drag her through. As the number of natives appeared increasing, and impelled by apprehensions of some danger, I immediately attempted to follow him, but the cutter being much heavier, I was unable to do so."[80]

Alden was finally able to squeeze over the coral barrier with the rising tide and pulled up alongside *Leopard* twenty minutes later. He found that Underwood had procured a hostage—the son of a local chief—and had left him in the launch while he returned to the beach. This perhaps explains why the natives did not immediately move to claim their booty. Holding a native as hostage was a common security measure during the course of the expedition. In the Fijis it was relied upon heavily, revealing the deep distrust they had in the natives. One can imagine the message such a measure sent to the islanders.

Alden brought the hostage aboard his launch and, with the aid of his spyglass, observed the protracted negotiations taking place on shore. As the bargaining dragged on, Alden began to lose patience. A request for muskets or powder to exchange for provisions was denied. Alden then sent a message to Underwood "to hurry off, as I thought he had been quite long enough absent to purchase all we required, if the natives were disposed to trade."[81]

At this point, Midshipman Wilkes Henry, the commander's nephew, requested and received permission to go ashore to assist Underwood. Further negotiations were fruitless, however. Soon Alden spied a native canoe nearing the launch to exchange words with the hostage. When the young chief made an attempt to leap for the canoe, Alden forcibly "took him by the arm and directed him to sit down, giving him to understand as well as possible that he must keep quiet 'till the return of our party."[82]

As the minutes passed, Alden was able to inch the boat closer to shore with the rising tide. Underwood had been gone too long to expect positive results from his bartering. More natives were joining in on shore, bringing the number to nearly fifty. Alden now found his shipmates outmanned and undergunned in case of trouble. Weighing the facts, Alden decided that enough was enough and dispatched another messenger "to say to Mr. Underwood, that I desired to see him without delay; to come off with what he could get as soon as possible."[83]

It is at this point that the narrative bifurcates into at least two versions, the crucial difference turning on who fired the first shot. Considerable debate later ensued among the crew as to the answer to that question. Alden's version of what happened next came to be generally accepted among his crew members—with the important exception of Wilkes—and is as follows: Suddenly, as Emmons's cutter pulled up alongside the launch, the hostage broke free from his guard and leapt overboard, making for shore. Alden quickly reached for his rifle and leveled it at the fleeing young chief. He ordered him to halt. Briefly the hostage pulled up and the lieutenant held his fire "lest his death should bring destruction to our absent people."[84] According to Alden, it was only then that the men on board the boats heard the crackle of gunfire from shore. The hostage's escape was the cue for the natives—now outnumbering the whites by five to one—to proceed with their attack on the shore party. Wilkes's version, attested to by Joseph Clark, who was on shore, asserted that hostilities did not commence until someone in Alden's boat fired over the head of the escaping hostage. "The old chief," according to Clark, "immediately cried out that his son was killed, and ordered the natives to make fight."[85] Clark, in a fit of generalization, later wrote that at that moment "two *Indians* [italics mine] seized my rifle" and the attack commenced.[86] While the latter version of the incident would seem to place the weight of blame on Alden and the expedition for inciting the attack, both sides were convinced that, whoever fired first, the attack by the natives was premeditated.

The fray was over almost before it had begun. Amid cries of "*Turanga, turanga,*" the natives fell first upon Underwood, knocking him to the ground and piercing him in the shoulder with a hurled spear.[87] Heroically, the bleeding lieutenant rose to his feet to cover the retreat of his crew, discharging both his pistols, then using the butt ends to flail away at his attackers. Wilkes Henry joined Underwood, side by side, covering the retreat to the boat, putting his pistol and bowie knife to good use until both he and Underwood were felled by clubs flung from behind by the attackers.

Alden, aided by a fresh breeze, rapidly sailed for shore. Before the launch touched bottom, the lieutenant and his men leapt from the boat and made for shore, firing their muskets as they waded in the surf. By the time they reached dry land, the natives had fled into a nearby mangrove swamp.

Alden was the first to reach shore. The beach was by then nearly devoid of life. Ten paces from the waterline he discovered the naked bodies of Underwood and Henry, "their heads split open with a hatchet and lacerated to a shocking degree."[88] He dropped to his knees in the sand, lifting the bodies in a vain search for signs of life. Both Underwood and Henry breathed their last in Alden's arms. Such was the anger of the rescue party at this bloody scene that, when Alden looked up to spy a writhing native lying a few feet away and ordered him dispatched, the men ran the dying islander through repeatedly with their bayonets and then beheaded him.[89]

Miles away on another island, Wilkes had noticed that *Peacock* was hurriedly weighing anchor and heading for Malolo. He packed his gear, shoved off in his cutter, and reached the schooner just before Alden's launch arrived with the bodies of the victims. The captain, upon viewing the lifeless and mangled body of his nephew—his sister's only son—fell into a fit of insensible grief, fainting, then after being revived, "crying and moaning in the most lamentable manner."[90]

The next day, following a concealed burial of the bodies on an isolated island, Wilkes held council with his officers and plotted retribution—total destruction of the villages on the two islands and decimation of their people. This, all the members of the expedition carried out with great relish on 26 July, so much so that Wilkes had to restrain his men from exacting further revenge than he had deemed necessary.[91] Sinclair vividly described the battle for Malolo: "The scene was grand and beautiful and at the same time horrible, what with the vollies of musketry, the crackling of the flames,

Malolo Island, 26 July 1840. Sketch by Alfred Agate. "Emmons boat fight off Malolo." Source: Henry Eld Papers, Yale Collection of Western Americana, Beinecke Rare Book and Manuscript Library. Wilkes ordered a land and sea attack in retaliation for the killing of Joseph Underwood and Wilkes Henry by the inhabitants of Malolo Island.

the squealing of the pigs . . . the shouting of men and women and the crying of children. The noise was deafening, above which you could hear . . . the loud cheers of our men, with 'there they go,' 'down with them,' 'shoot that fellow,' etc., etc."[92]

Another officer recalled the tragic scene as the village was engulfed in flames. "A number of the wounded natives were burned to death in the town with some children. A child was seen to come to the gate and hold out its little hands and crying bitterly, but would not come to us, and assistance at that time was impossible, so he fell a victim to the devouring element."[93]

Wilkes had ordered that no man be spared, but as the Fiji women fought alongside the men, the officers had difficulty in preventing their party from killing them also. Slain chiefs and other natives were tossed onto great pyres, their bodies roasted "Fiji fashion" as the angry men threw yams onto the burning bodies.[94]

The attack and torching of the towns of Malolo was devastating—well over one hundred natives lost their lives, the rest were left without homes, crops, canoes, or relatives. The men of the expedition returned to their vessels that evening with just a few minor injuries and without loss of a single life. The grieving Wilkes was satisfied that he had again inflicted "a salutary lesson, as well to the actual perpetrators of the deed, as to the inhabitants of the whole group."[95] The crew was tired but exultant that they had been given the opportunity to demonstrate conclusively the "superiority" of the white race, a need that went beyond exacting revenge at Malolo. Sinclair, for one, shed no tears for the Fijians. He could philosophize that it was all for the best. "They [Fijians] brought it all on themselves and altogether it is the best thing that could have happened for us, for it has given us an opportunity of showing these cannibals the power of the white man, and the manner in which he exercises it. . . . It would have been better if this had happened when we had first came into the [island] group."[96] Only the spectacle of the remnants of the village population crawling upon their hands and knees on the following day (as ordered by Wilkes), begging for forgiveness, stayed the voyagers' hands from further revenge.

Despite later criticism of his methods, the immediate effect of Wilkes's actions was all he had hoped for.[97] His "salutary lesson" had indeed been taken to heart by the Fijians; at last he had gained the upper hand. The results could be seen in the tears shed by Tuemboooa as he weepingly implored Hudson to stay his hand and spare the towns of Muthuata, or in the way this king was reduced to groveling about his village desperately gathering the demanded quota of yams for the expedition.[98] Nor was it any coincidence that when Wilkes next visited an island (Mali), he found its villages deserted and the canoes and other possessions hidden from the Americans.[99] Where before a measure of cordiality had prevailed between the expedition and the islanders, arguments and disagreements were rife, threatening to erupt into further bloodshed.

Finally, after three months' stay in the Fiji group ("two more than we

ought to have been," in Pickering's opinion) Wilkes informed the crew that
the expedition was leaving these islands for Hawaii. Hudson paid one last
visit to the chastised king of Muthuata and informed him of the squadron's
imminent departure, asking Tuemboooa if "he was glad." He replied "that
he was."[100]

The events of the final month of their stay in the Fiji group had an
obvious negative impact upon their perceptions of the people of these
islands. Notwithstanding this, what really stands out from the recorded
observation and conclusions regarding the Fijians is not so much the tangible
animosity but a marveling at the great contrasts seemingly "inherent" in
their culture. The standards of Fijian society were totally inconsistent to
those bred on the prevailing American notions of civilization and savagery.
These islanders seemed to encompass the spectrum of traits from the most
refined courtesies to gruesome abominations. Wilkes could describe these
people as "intelligent, observing, ingenious and industrious" and in the
same breath denounce them as "revengeful, treacherous, superstitious and
cowardly . . . great thieves and liars" who are "never to be trusted." By the
time Wilkes balances the behavioral books, the only "redeeming quality"
the Fijians truly possess is their generous and thoughtful hospitality.[101]

So there you have them: revengeful, untrustworthy liars yet polite and
courteous hosts; superstitious and treacherous yet intelligent and observing;
cowardly yet industrious. Wilkes did not, at least in his narrative, deem to
probe further, nor did he conjecture where these bewildering people might
fit within humankind's family tree. For Wilkes, the practice of cannibalism
overrode any other redeeming qualities they might have exhibited, placing
them beyond the pale of civilization; "wretches in the strongest sense of
the term and degraded beyond the conception of civilized people."[102] Yet
he felt there was hope for the future. Although he judged that the "present
generation of the Feegee nation" was "irreclaimable," he envisioned a future
more promising than that which lay ahead for most of Polynesia. In Wilkes's
estimation, the solution was amalgamation, "connecting themselves" with
the white castaways on the islands (a "strategy" pursued with great relish by
sailors throughout Polynesia, albeit not with Wilkes's lofty foresight). Such
mixing would ameliorate the "savage propensities" of the Fijian "race," a
sort of genetic watering-down process. This, in conjunction with the work
of the missionaries, "could not fail to exert a most salutary [a favorite term
of Wilkes] influence over the destinies of these fine islands" and result in the
Fijians—or at least whoever is left in control of the islands—making "rapid
strides in civilization."[103]

Horatio Hale's extensive three-month study of Fijian language and eth-nology yielded valuable data concerning the origins and migrations of the Pacific islanders and their social institutions. The Fijians, he declared, could not be classified as "negro" despite their similar skin pigment and general physical traits—the typical criteria for determining race. The crew as a whole seemed to agree with this assessment; beyond the first, fleeting glances, there is no evidence that anyone confused them with "their negroes." It is interesting, however, that for Hale the real delineation between "negro" and Fijian was the polarity of temperament. According to Hale, "African Negroes" were "gay, frank, social, quick of apprehension, though deficient in steadiness and resolution, and prone to sensuality."[104] That the above "scientific definition" of a negro bears such a strong resemblance to "Jim Crow," "Zib Coon," and "Juba Coon" is a point not to be missed. Nor is the fact that the traits Hale attributes to the Fijians—"sullen, shy, treacherous, indocile, stubborn, and of a cold temperament"—were also applied to America's "archetypical savage," the American Indian.[105]

Despite such an unflattering profile of these people, Hale still had to admit there was much to admire about Fijian ways. In fact, he was at a loss to explain why their culture had always been ranked so low among the various Pacific groups, particularly when compared to the Polynesians: "They are yet spoken of by all voyagers as savages, and uniformly treated as such, while the Polynesians are regarded rather as a semi-civilized race."[106] He considered Fijian culture, from their social institutions to their "knowledge of various arts," as vastly superior to the Polynesians in nearly every respect. As for the Fijians' vaunted bad traits, Hale countered that "there are few of the Polynesian tribes to whom the same description will not apply."[107] He was particularly intrigued by the complex political system under which this group was governed. He discovered that, in essence, the islands were organized into a series of independent provinces, similar to the city-states of ancient Greece. He and his fellow scientists marveled at the sophistication— and corruption—of Fijian politics, their "intrigues and machinations," as he termed them. In Hale's eyes, the Sforzas, Medicis, and Borgias had nothing on these Pacific princes.

> Among these states constant intrigues and machinations are carried on, and that with a degree of shrewdness and craft that frequently excited our astonishment. All the arts of that baser species of state policy which we are accustomed to look upon as the growth of a corrupt civilization, are thoroughly understood and continually practiced by this extraordinary race of savages. To weaken a rival state by secretly exciting its dependencies

to revolt,—to stir up one class of society against another, in order to take advantage of their dissensions,—to make an advantageous treaty with a powerful foe, by sacrificing a weak ally,—to corrupt the fidelity of adherents, by bribing them with the anticipated spoil of their own master,—to gain a battle before it is fought, by tampering with the leaders of the opposing force,—all these, and many other tricks of the Machiavelian school, are perfectly familiar to the subtle chieftains of Viti.[108]

Despite such evidence attesting to the sophistication of the Fijians, Hale could not bring himself to consider these people as anything other than of the basest, savage sort. Indeed, while he envisioned that the Polynesians would gradually rise out of the mire of barbarism, Hale held out no such hope for the Fijians. His reasoning was thus: the vices exhibited by the Polynesians at the time of European contact were the result of their living in a state of ignorance (a variant of the eighteenth-century concept of "state of nature"), a sort of childlike bliss that simply did not recognize the sinfulness of their lascivious lifestyle. But the Polynesians, when presented with a "superior" alternative—that is, white culture—were ready to "lay aside their worst practices and adopt many of the improvements of civilization." According to Hale, it was this acquiescence in the face of white culture that in turn marked the Polynesians as "naturally" superior in character to the Fijians.

So why were the Fijians, who were considered to possess a sophistication and intelligence far in advance of any other island people, such a recalcitrant people? Hale believed that, unlike the Polynesians, whose "evil qualities . . . lie merely on the surface of the character," the Fijians "*are by nature* [italics mine] and inclination a bloodthirsty, treacherous, and rapacious people," dictated by sinister qualities that "have their roots deep in their moral organization."[109] Hence, Hale traced the "failure" of the Fijians to shed their "savage" skin to an evil and intractable nature, ignoring the possibility that the islanders saw no need to do so. "The Feejeeans," Hale concluded, "may be said to differ from the Polynesian as the wolf from the dog; both, when wild, are perhaps equally fierce, but the ferocity of the one may be easily subdued, while that of the other is deep-seated and untameable."[110] The "Feejee" as symbol becomes the ultimate savage—an irredeemable, evil, untameable beast whose very cunning and intelligence makes him all the more to be feared. To civilize in this context is to tame, to "break" the beast of its wild propensities, just as the Tahitians had been broken or as the American Negroes had been "domesticated" by their enslavement.

Like Hale, Pickering also found himself pondering the propensities of the Fijians. His observations of Fijian culture had a profound impact on his theories and conceptions of the organization of humankind. It was no coincidence that it was from this island group that he chose to write two lengthy letters to his colleague Samuel George Morton. On 7 August he drafted a description of the Fijians; the next day he followed with a lengthier compendium, summarizing the progress of his thoughts on the various races of the world. What he had to say no doubt took his Philadelphia friend by surprise. He explicitly called into question the accepted definition of the term "savage"; implicitly, he suggested that Morton reconsider his notions on race and savagery—which, of course, the craniologist was not inclined to do. "The *Feejees* are not savages, at least the Books would not call them so, for they live in towns, are adept in everything that relates to the cultivation of the soil, are excellent navigators, are a most ingenious people, and excell in various arts and manufactures—have made no mean progress in the culinary department, and are great epicures—have instruments of music. . . . If they have not written laws, they have customs which answer the same purpose. . . . The wearing of a dress adapted to the climate surely does not make them savages!"[111]

That the Fijis held no desire to imitate and adopt white culture should not disqualify them from the ranks of the civilized either, according to Pickering. Indeed, the "stamp of originality" and pride imprinted upon everything connected with these people, coupled with the sophistication of their culture, led him to the insightful conclusion that the Fijians likely saw no need to emulate others—a deduction definitely at variance with Hale's.[112] Pickering was even so bold as to suggest that, regardless of their cannibalism, the practice of parricide, and the like, "the *Feejees* are by no means without their good qualities, and I could enumerate some from which even the White man might take pattern."[113]

As a trained naturalist and an American citizen, Pickering struggled to square the existence of so anomalous a culture with the accepted images of "civilization" and "savagery." Unlike Hale, he was unwilling from his observations to write them off as an "arch-savage." Nor, like those of Morton's ilk (later to be described as the founders of the "American school" of anthropology), did he endeavor to pinpoint and quantify a supposed physical deficiency for purposes of debasement.

But a naturalist he was, driven to classification and compartmentalization in his quest for order. And so, in the quest to fit the Fijians into the prevailing paradigms as formulated by nineteenth-century Western society, Pickering found a solution—one that was in perfect harmony with his vocation. To paraphrase Foucault, Pickering set about to "build a new box" for the

Fijians that would account and allow for their variance while at the same time preserving the integrity of the accepted scheme of the classification of the races. This he explained in his letter to Morton: "If you search the dictionaries, etc., I think you will find nothing above [his description of Fijian culture] corresponding to the definition of a savage; we must therefore set down rather a *new species* of civilization [italics mine]."[114]

This solution did not come without some serious category stretching, however. "Species" was a term later reserved by Morton and others of like beliefs to separate what they considered the wheat and chaff of humankind. According to this notion, biologically superior whites were created apart from other "species" such as blacks and Indians. This was the notion of polygenesis. Pickering, however, utilized the concept to delineate differences in the *civilizations* of humankind and not their biological origins.

In any case, Pickering soon found that, in order to explain the differences that he perceived between the people of the world, Blumenbach's accepted enumeration of five races was not sufficient. More stretching and compartmentalizing was in order. In his second letter to Morton, Pickering laid out his list of the various "races of mankind." He requested confidentiality, anticipating the future need to "modify my opinions very essentially."[115] He acknowledged that his experiences on the voyage had taught him the folly of rigid preconceptions. "I have never yet," he testified, "found any place I have visited [to] correspond altogether with my preconceived notions."[116] He had begun the voyage believing that there were five races of man; now he believed that he had observed eight, "and not without expectation of my meeting with others before reaching home."[117] Whether they should be categorized as races or species—a contention crucial to Morton's theories— did not concern Pickering. His intent was not to rank the races, nor was it in his agenda to challenge the humanity of those of color. "I will not at present enter into the question of species, but as all the world seems to think, one, . . . I am content to let them have their way."[118]

He proceeded to describe his eight races, each set apart by their supposed unique combination of physical features, social characteristics, past histories, great attainments, and ignoble foibles.[119] Again, it is important to point out that he made no attempt to present them in hierarchical order. The "white race" is discussed following the Australians and before the Papuans (to which the Fijians belong)—fifth in line. His depictions of Polynesians, Australians, and Papuans—however superficial—obviously owe much to his personal observations during the expedition. What is surprising is that his discussion of the "white race" owes a similar debt to the expedition, reflecting considerable rumination over the actions and attitudes of his own tribe during the course of the voyage. He concluded that this race possessed no monopoly on "civilization." Addressing the common assertion that the white race was distinctive for having "attained a higher degree of civilization than any other, both now and formerly," he pointed out that white civilization had "never erected works so gigantic and enduring as the Mongol or Egyptian." Instead, in order to distinguish this race from the other seven, he isolated a single characteristic, one housed in only the most well-endowed of Morton's crania collection, and a trait that was observed all too often by Pickering in the course of the expedition: "One feature in its character (disposition) can hardly fail to strike those who have seen much of other races—it has always been a race of plunderers, delighting in destruction. From the Soul-inspiring works of Greece to the simple Grave of the American Indian, whatever monument has been erected, by the head or hands, has had to deal (encounter) with some other enemy than time."[120] One can only wonder how Morton—whose entire method of research was constructed upon plundering the "simple graves" of the various races— accepted Pickering's conclusions.

Finally, on the 11 August 1840, Wilkes led the squadron through the treacherous, encircling reefs of the islands and "once more welcomed the bounding waves and the free ocean atmosphere."[121] For many, it was like fleeing the gates of hell. Others, however, such as James Dana, expressed sadness at departing an island group whose beauty was matched only by the terrors of its inhabitants.[122] Pickering, in a masterpiece of understatement, called their visit "instructive." "For however well versed a person may regard himself in the knowledge of mankind, a visit to the Feejee Islands will bring new ideas."[123] It was left to Vendovi, the Fijian prisoner who was destined never to return home, to shed tears "at the last view of his native land."[124]

There were many things to remind us of home: among them was a luxuriant sward of white clover, now in full bloom, and numerous other plants that had found their way here: the trees were also familiar, and truly American. I felt that the land belonged to my country, that we were not strangers on the soil; and could not but take great interest in relation to its destiny, in the prospect of its one day becoming the abode of our relatives and friends.—Charles Wilkes

The United States Exploring Expedition at last pulled free from the world of the Fijians. Nonetheless, a pall continued to hang over the ships as they skimmed across the sea toward their next destination, the Sandwich Islands. The ships made Honolulu Bay amidst rumors that many of the crew were ready to leave the expedition and book private passage home. Wilkes expressed fears that a cabal of officers, fed up with his martinet behavior and poor seamanship, were plotting against him. Most of the scientists, too, were displeased with the progress of the voyage. They complained about Wilkes's policy of stressing surveying and hydrography at the expense of more "scientific" pursuits: exploring new terrain, interviewing natives, and collecting specimens and artifacts of all types. They attributed the tragedy at Malolo to Wilkes's fanatical desire to chart every nook and cranny of these dangerous islands. One scientist, Joseph Couthouy, parted with the expedition in Hawaii as a consequence of his continual confrontations with the captain.[1] All in all, it was an uncheerful aggregation of Americans that anchored in the bay in September of 1840.

The expedition remained moored to these islands for an extended stay of seven months. Consequently, there was ample time to visit each of the various islands in the group. Scientists moved from place to place gathering plants, shells, and the like. Exploring parties scaled the lava-spewing Mauna Loa and conducted a host of experiments that yielded valuable data on volcanic phenomena. Islanders were questioned and observed, though most

"Scene at Oahu." Hawaiians maneuvering among the commercial and military vessels. Ship in the foreground is the whaling vessel *New Bedford*. Sepia ink painting by Alfred Agate.

often under the watchful gaze of a missionary chaperon. But in the end, the Sandwich Islands represented for the expedition not only an area for intense exploratory activity but a much-needed opportunity for rest and recuperation, ship repair, and restocking of provisions. In this respect, their motives were no different than those of nearly every mariner that sailed near these strategically positioned islands. Nor did the crew behave any differently than the salty sailors that preceded them, despite Wilkes's and Hudson's best efforts to rein in the more lusty exploits of their men. The Americans took to their lengthy respite from the rigors of exploring with a gusto that drew rebukes from local authorities and disapproving looks from the ever-present clericals. For years, the missionaries had been fighting and generally losing a battle with visiting ships' captains and their crews for the "morals" of the island population. The expedition's visit represented merely another victory for lascivious "Jack before the Mast." William Reynolds was rarely hesitant about mixing with the natives of any of the Pacific Islands, particularly with the women. The Sandwich Islands were certainly no exception, as is evident in a letter sent home to a relative. "We have had both pleasant and unpleasant times—pleasant in as much as our association with the shore, particularly at Hilo Island . . . where I [lived] for 3 months in a straw hut, by the side of a sparkling stream, basking of an evening on the sand with a group of merry girls the like of which we had not seen in this cruise, and in the night resting in the arms of a delicious little Hawaiian girl, who just gave up to me her virgin charms."[2] For Reynolds the "unpleasant times" commenced when he was compelled to leave his little paradise and again face "the old song" aboard *Vincennes.*

Wilkes and others of his bent chose to ignore such indiscretions (on either side) and instead focused upon the apparent strides that the islanders, led by the missionaries, had taken toward "civilization." They found Honolulu to be an actual "city" somewhat after the fashion of Sydney. All the ingredients were there: the crowded avenues lined with shops, the great stone church rising from the rows of low buildings, the cosmopolitan makeup of the people. For the first time they witnessed an organized laboring force, which led white landowners to wax eloquent over the promise of future wealth and progress through the large-scale cultivation of sugar and cotton. Small factories as well seemed to proliferate; workers were paid in script, honored at the company store.

Other signature signs of "civilization" were evident to the men of the expedition. The Hawaiians possessed a written code of laws and a constitution. Their king and queen were resplendent in their European affectations and military uniforms; his majesty's appearance seemed to the expedition to be "more of a European Potentate than a chief of Savages."[3] After three months among the intractable Fijians, many on the expedition were ready to applaud the Hawaiians and their missionary sponsors. They were relieved that these islanders had apparently "been convinced of the perfect absurdity of many of the superstitious notions and have in consequence relinquished them."[4]

Still, it was hard to ignore the fact that despite the moralizing influence of the Protestants and the "civilizing" implementation of organized labor the Sandwich Islanders seemed eminently poorer and sadder for the experience—more so than the Fijians, or even the Tahitians and Samoans, for that matter. The injection of Protestantism and its social and cultural baggage, while enriching the white interlopers, had failed to produce material improvement for the natives or their islands. Hawaii was no longer the luxuriant paradise of Cook's narrative. Dyes, in his journal, pondered what the English explorer would now think of his discovery "if it was only possible for him to come into existence and see the change of these people. I [have] no doubt he would wish that he had never discovered them."[5] Plantations and factories, high taxes, and religious bigotry had begun to transform Cook's paradise into a land of dwindling means and declining population.[6] The weight of religious dogmatism had come crashing down upon yet another culture. The expedition had seen it all before, in Tahiti, Samoa, Tonga; the difference was only that of degree. The virulence of missionary imposition in the Sandwich Islands was stifling, with little thought to the material well-being of the inhabitants. J. Frederick Sickles, who had arrived in advance of the main squadron aboard *Relief*, took note of the islanders' plight. "It appears to me," he concluded, "that if a little more attention had been paid to things temporal, the conditions of the natives would have been infinitely better than it is."[7]

James Alden in particular was appalled at what he saw. A refined "down-easter" who hailed from Portland, Maine, he was no stranger to the Calvinistic ethics of his American brethren living in Hawaii. But he could not ignore the great damage done to the islanders, their land, and their culture.

> Many . . . if not all the Blue laws of Connecticut, if not already adopted, were about to be declared as the laws of the land . . . [by] men . . . fanatical, sectarian, and intolerant . . . ignorant of the world—zealots devoted *to no object* but the instruction of the natives in religious views and sentiments of a gloomy, forbidding and bigoted character. . . . Alas for the harvest!! . . . What a picture does the condition of things at the present time at the Sandwich Islands present to that of a period only twenty years back. . . . The habitations of the people, once celebrated for cleanliness, are now dirty and miserable. . . . A population dwindled from over 220,000 to less than 100,000, filthy, shabby and diseased in their persons, apathetic and careless of life or health, oppressed . . . to a degree only to be believed by those who have had an opportunity to know the fact from personal observations—a less quality of land that but ten years since teemed with its own fatness, which showed the skill of the cultivator and his knowledge of engineering in its irrigation, now parched, barren, or overgrown with weeds.[8]

Nor were the activities of the foreign secular element any more beneficial to the welfare of the islanders. According to Wilkes, these foreigners made no pretensions to what they had come to the islands for.

> In all cases that came within my knowledge on the islands, the object of the majority of foreign residents was solely to increase their own wealth; and on the accumulation of a sufficient amount, they withdraw from the islands, taking their capital with them. . . . So far, therefore, as their influence goes, instead of enriching the islanders, their exertions have in some degree had a contrary effect, and the result does not justify those engaged in mercantile pursuits, in attributing the advancement of the islands to themselves; on

the contrary, they leave very little but evil habits and vices behind them. Few foreigners have made any permanent improvements, and when they have, they pass into the hands of others, to the exclusions of the natives, who are looked upon and treated as slaves.[9]

Such observations reflected the growing pessimism of many on the expedition concerning the benefits and propriety of the interaction between foreigners and the native populations of the Pacific Islands. It seemed that the Sandwich Islands and their population were in fact suffering from an acute case of "civilization"; a condition far more deadly than their prior "savage" state of existence.

Nearly seven months of rest and repair restored vigor and health to the members of the expedition. The grumbling and discontent that were so evident following their stay in the Fiji Islands had also largely dissipated. Thus it was a hearty crew that set sail on 5 April 1841 for its final area of assignment—the northwest coast of the present-day United States.[10] *Vincennes* arrived off fog-bound Cape Flattery on 30 April, entering the Straits of Juan de Fuca two days later. Over the next six months the expedition would gradually work its way southward, carefully charting and surveying both the treacherous shorelines and the interior regions of the Pacific Northwest down to San Francisco Bay.

After three years' absence, the members of the expedition were able to set foot on their own continent, albeit upon its western face. For Pickering, the opportunity to explore the Pacific Northwest represented a thrilling step backward into an earlier, unspoiled, precontact era in American history. Hurrying ashore, he was overcome by the impressions of his first contact. "I shall not soon forget the rush of sensations, on my first interview in the forest, with the aboriginal proprietor. On returning to the strand, I observed that a party bringing rails and mats in their canoes, had established a temporary encampment. Indeed the whole details of aboriginal life, contributed to render this day memorable. Scarcely two centuries ago, our New England shores presented only scenes like that before me; and what was to be the result of the lapse of the third?"[11]

Others were less awed by their first contact with the original inhabitants of the Pacific Northwest. Upon entering the straits, *Vincennes* had been surrounded by a flotilla of canoes manned by Clallam Indians. This welcome reintroduced the members of the expedition to the American Indian. All during the voyage, the image of "our Indians" had served as the litmus test for "savagery." Tahitians, Samoans, Fijians, Australians, and New Zealanders had frequently been evaluated according to their supposed affinity with or dissimilarity to American Indians. As has been shown previously, the discourse concerning native culture many times led to merging of images— even to the point of identifying various peoples of the South Pacific as "Indians," consciously or unconsciously, either by design or by "slips of the pen." Such comparisons, however, seemed far from the minds of the men aboard *Vincennes* on the morning of 1 May as the first Clallams boarded the ship. Wilkes noted the shock of the crew at this encounter. "In the morning we were boarded by a large canoe, with Indians who spoke a few words of English; and we had occasion to notice the wide difference between them and the Polynesians, both in language and appearance. No contrast can be more striking than this. They seemed to have scarcely any idea of decency, and to be little less elevated in their moral qualities than the Fuegians."[12]

Short, bowlegged, and muscular, these squat, thick-set people obviously did not fit the image of the tall, stoic "noble savage" used as a reference point during the voyage. Instead, "filthy" and "disgusting" were the adjectives used most in connection with the Clallams.[13] They immediately inquired, in broken English, whether *Vincennes* was a "King George ship" or "Boston ship." When James Alden affirmed the latter, they "appeared delighted, shook hands, and commenced abusing King George (ie. Victoria)"[14] Clad in blankets and skins, they emitted such an odor that the officer was "compelled to retreat some twenty paces" before resuming the conversation.[15] Even more repulsive to some of the men were the flattened heads of the Clallams, a custom that William Briscoe felt made them "look more like monsters than human beings." Here, he concluded, was truly "a meager, dirty race of being, entirely incapable of civilization."[16] This opinion seemed well-nigh unanimous throughout the ship. Even Vendovi, that incarcerated "arch-savage" whose people had been equated with the image of the Indian by experts such as Hale, joined in, voicing his displeasure. According to Pickering, the Fijian "imbibed a profound contempt" at the sight of these people, a juxtaposition the expedition found "amusing to us, who had no very exalted opinion of the Feejeans."[17] Wilkes marveled at "the contempt our prisoner Vendovi entertained for these Indians, which was such that he would hardly deign to look at them."[18]

While the expedition was taken aback at its first encounter with native North Americans, the appearance of another "Boston ship" in the Oregon Territory was nothing out of the ordinary—in fact, it was business as usual— for the Clallams. Their business was trade, a skill at which the expedition found them very adept. To Wilkes's surprise, the Clallams "manifested little curiosity" about the presence of such a large ship entering their waters. Nor should they have, since vessels of varying size and different nationalities had been plying their shores continually for the fifty years since the voyages of George Vancouver and Robert Gray in the 1790s. An intricate and interlocking trade network had thrived among the diverse groups of the region long before white merchants had arrived with their avidity for furs. The Clallams and other tribes had readily assimilated this intrusion into their world with a marked skill, exhibiting a facility for commerce and an ability to incorporate new goods into their culture that incessantly frustrated white peddlers eager to exploit the resources and people of the Pacific Northwest. "The modern Hebrew," complained an early French trader, "could teach the Indians [of this region] nothing in the art of bargaining."[19] Lewis and Clark, who spent a winter among the Chinooks near the mouth of the Columbia River, were similarly impressed with the acumen of the northwestern people: "In traffic," the explorers recorded, "they are keen, acute, and intelligent, and they employ in all their bargains a dexterity and finesse."[20] Wilkes later found that their propensity for and insistence upon negotiating a favorable deal was "enough to tire the patience of Job himself."[21]

The Indians of the Pacific Northwest had survived and even economically thrived with the arrival of the British North West Company, Hudson's Bay Company, and John Astor's Pacific Fur Company by quickly learning to take advantage of Anglo-American competition for sea-otter and beaver pelts and salmon. A "Chinook" jargon, described as "a vile compound of English, French, American and the Chinook dialect" with Spanish, Russian, and even Japanese words thrown in, quickly emerged and functioned as an Esperanto of the Pacific Northwest trade.[22] Unfortunately, the introduction of the "cold sick" in 1830—a flu-like affliction causing high fevers, chills, muscle cramps, coughs, intestinal problems, and a death rate of fifty to ninety percent among the Pacific Northwest tribes—had tipped the economic and demographic scales in favor of the British and the ever-arriving Americans.[23] When Indian leaders such as the legendary Comcomly succumbed to the disease, their struggle against the introduction of rum as the primary trade item was lost. The dwindling populations subsequently lacked the numbers and leadership to resist the influx of settlers that would soon make the Indians a minority in their own land.

The expedition, therefore, had returned to a section of America that was shrouded in a period of cultural flux and decline of native inhabitants, an area where British-American political machinations would soon take precedence over white-Indian commerce. Land, instead of furs, would soon become the most prized commodity in the Pacific Northwest. The activities of the Exploring Expedition reflected this awareness. At no other location during the voyage were Wilkes's instructions so specific as to the necessity of comprehensive inland exploration in addition to the intensive survey of harbors and the entire coastal region. Accordingly, he dispatched expeditions north, east, and southward up rivers and into the fertile valleys of Oregon Territory to ascertain the topography and fruitfulness of the land. These were not specifically scientific excursions. Wilkes himself led one of the inland treks up the Columbia River. His reminiscences reveal much as to the purpose of the expedition's visit and to the feeling that prevailed among the men concerning the future of this land. Traveling amidst the bounteous growth of the river valley, he wistfully noted that "there were many things to remind us of home: among them was a luxuriant sward of white clover, now in full blossom, and numerous other plants that had found there [sic] way here: the trees were also familiar, and truly American. I felt that the land belonged to my country, that we were not strangers on the soil; and could not but take great interest in relation to its destiny, in the prospect of its one day becoming the abode of our relatives and friends."[24] In the mind of Wilkes, science, in this case botany, lent support to notions of manifest destiny. Even the trees, flowers, and shrubs can be identified as "truly American" and therefore "belonging to my country."

Although continuing to disclaim officially any political designs on the Pacific coast, Wilkes and his officers could barely contain their enthusiasm for what lay before them and speculation about to whom its future belonged. Further indications of these beliefs occurred after the expedition eventually made its way south to California, at that time still a Mexican province. They spent several weeks at San Francisco, where William Heath Davis, a Yankee entrepreneur residing in the town, made frequent contact with the officers of the expedition during its stay in the bay. The officers often invited the young businessman and other residents of the town on board ship for entertainments and other hospitalities. During these visits conversation often focused upon the expedition's presence and on the future importance of the area. Confiding to Davis, they intimated that "the more they became conversant with it in their surveys the more they were impressed with its importance, and they would sometimes exclaim, 'This is ours!' referring to the future, when the United States government should hold possession of this part of the country."[25]

As optimistic as Wilkes was about the Pacific coast and the inevitability of American settlement, he joined most others of the expedition in being equally pessimistic about the plight of the natives in this part of America.

He concluded that fifty years of interaction with "civilization" in the form of merchant vessels and trading posts seemed to have had no effect in ameliorating the "savage" propensities of these people. Thus, unlike the natives of Polynesia, for instance, he felt that no hope could be entertained for the "improvement" of these people. The Chinooks, those flat-headed traders par excellence who controlled the gateway to the interior of Oregon at the mouth of the Columbia River, received particularly severe condemnation from the pen of Wilkes. After noting a particularly frustrating bartering session in which Wilkes had found that these Indians had raised the price of their valued salmon by fifty percent, he foresaw extinction for the Chinooks.

> The viscious propensities of the Indians were seen here, as they appear around all the posts of the Hudson Bay Company. . . . [G]ambling is the vice to which they are most prone. Both sexes are equally filthy, and I am inclined to believe will continue so; for their habits are inveterate, and . . . there is reason to believe that they have not improved or been benefited by their constant intercourse with the whites, except in a very few cases. It is indeed probable that the whole race will be extinguished ere long, from the natural effects of their mode of life, even if no pestilential disease should come among them to sweep them off in a single season.[26]

While attempting to enumerate the actual number of Indians remaining in the Pacific Northwest, Wilkes also made note of the dramatic increase of American settlement since 1840. To him, the hand of nature and/or destiny seemed to be balancing the demographic books: "the decrease of the red race," he had no doubt, was "equivalent to the increase by [American] immigration."[27] Perhaps the most vivid example of the demographic and cultural turnover occurred when Wilkes's party ventured eastward to Fort Vancouver. There Wilkes met Casenove, chief of the Klackatack (or Cowlitz) Indians, thought to be one of the last of his tribe. He watched this "noble and intelligent-looking Indian . . . once lord of all this domain . . . quietly enter the apartment, wrapped in his blanket, and take his seat at the lonely board. . . . At the fort he is always welcome, and is furnished with a plate at meal-times at the side-table. . . . He scarce seemed to attract the notice of any one, but ate his meal in silence."[28] Though once Casenove was able to "muster four or five hundred warriors . . . he now stands alone, his land, tribe, and property all departed . . . left a dependant on the bounty of the Company. . . . I could not but feel for the situation of one who, in the short space of a few years, has not lost only his property and importance, but his whole tribe and kindred."[29] Here, Wilkes felt, was evidence of the fate that even the "noblest" of "savages" were destined to meet. These predictions of extinction also served as justification for American claims of racial superiority and eventual possession of the land from the "doomed" inhabitants.

Many others evinced some sympathy for these people. William Briscoe was moved to record in his journal a poem composed by a messmate.

> Though far from our home's, yet still in our land,
> And publish to all each side of the main
> We triumphed once & can do it again
> A problem, a problem, oh! hear great and small
> The true owners of the country are still on the soil
> Whilst Jonathan and John Bull are growling together
> For land which by right belongs not to either . . .[30]

George Emmons placed the blame for the Indians demise on "the white man generally." They were "*doomed* to vanish before the *white man*. . . . [W]hole tribes have been completely swept off—and but a few years longer at that rate & their [sic] will be none left—how melancholy the reflection! How little do we know of this once numerous people! & yet how much have we done to shorten their existence."[31]

Again, as they had done throughout the voyage, members of the expedition criticized the methods and motives of the missionaries in attempting to "civilize" the Indians. Wilkes was appalled at the habits exhibited by some of God's servants: "These missionaries are very far from what they ought to be. [They are] low, vulgar and unclean. . . . If they were Christian men and readers of their bible, they ought to practice cleanly habits. Mr. W[aller] was as filthy as any Indian I have met with in appearance & taking our nation into consideration more so. They are sent out to show an example but how little they earn their wages in preaching the Gospel a higher and Just God will determine."[32]

It seemed odd to Wilkes that American Protestants tended to settle upon land that not so coincidentally was the most fertile in the territories. The tribes of the north, whom Wilkes felt were particularly ripe for the gospel, were left to the Catholics.[33] They were disappointed that trade and land acquisition appeared to take precedence over missionary work. When the expedition questioned this, they were bombarded with stories and complaints of Indian acts of depravity and bellicosity. Their experience in the Pacific Northwest, however, taught the expedition that any hostility on the part of the Indians "in a great measure is to be ascribed to the conduct of the

Oregon Indians—cross and flag. This unfinished allegorical watercolor in the Agate Collection sums up the expedition's general attitude toward the Indians of Oregon. "How little do we know of this once numerous people! & yet how much have we done to shorten their existence." George Emmons, Journal.

whites themselves, who leave no opportunity . . . of molesting them. Cases have frequently occurred of white men shooting a poor defenseless Indian without any provocation whatever."[34] In his official report to the secretary of the navy, Wilkes found little veracity in the accusations by American settlers, which he suspected were tied to enticing American military power into the area. The expedition had listened to similar complaints at other junctures during their voyage; they knew now not to take them at face value. All in all, Wilkes considered the Indians of Oregon "an inoffensive race," and that any "depredations committed on the whites may be traced to injuries received or from superstitious motives."[35]

Of course, the anticipated imminent demise of these people served to render such sympathies moot. There were those on the expedition who seemed intent upon writing the epitaph of these western Indians, consigning to them a fate similar to those east of the Mississippi. Casenove was only one example. Such predictions also served to absolve the sympathetic of any responsibility or obligation to reverse the perceived trend toward extinction.

The Kalapuya of the Willamette Valley, whom Horatio Hale described as "cleanly, honest, and moral," were surely as doomed as the "debased" and "quarrelsome" Chinooks, whether by "the progress of disease" or "the influx of foreign population." With the objectivity of a scientist, Hale concluded that any efforts to alter their fate would be fruitless—their inevitable extinction "supercede[ing] the necessity of any further labors for their benefit."[36]

Overall, the expedition found Pacific Northwest culture a puzzling patchwork of beliefs that felt totally foreign to their sensibilities. In some ways, this feeling was even more pronounced than during their experiences in the Pacific Islands. For instance, they learned to be careful about administering medicine or otherwise attempting to treat medically the Indians for their ailments. In the Pacific Northwest, the life of a doctor, whether white or Indian, was held in surety for the success of his treatments.[37] Their systems of trade continually puzzled the crew. Though seemingly everything possessed by tribes such as the Chinooks was available for trade or barter—including sexual favors—the swapping of a few fish could entail the most protracted negotiations that it hardly seemed worth the effort. One can sense Wilkes's frustration after a particularly difficult trading encounter: "The Indians are beyond measure the most provoking fellows to bargain with that I have ever met with, and as our wants or necessities increase, their prices rise in proportion. They are not slow in perceiving your wants, or the dilemma you may be placed in—which they view with becoming *sang froid*."[38]

Never good at perceiving relative values of trade wherever they went, the expedition's members in this case were also ignorant of the intricacies of Pacific Northwest culture. Therefore, Wilkes and his men became perplexed when, near Puget Sound, they were rebuffed when attempting to purchase salmon from a native fishing party. He watched as the fishermen landed the first salmon, then rushed to purchase it for the "usual" price—about ten cents in trade items. The Indians countered by demanding the equivalent of $1.25, an offer Wilkes attributed to Indian "cupidity." The exploring party's guide, a trapper by the name of Simon Plumondon, explained to the vexed commander that in fact the Indians "had no desire to sell the fish, as they had a superstitious objection to dispose of the first fish to strangers: even if induced to sell it, they will always take the heart out and roast it for themselves; for they believe, that if the heart of the fish were eaten by a stranger at the first of the season, their success would be destroyed, and they would catch no more fish. To prevent this, they consider it requisite that a certain number of 'sleeps' or days should pass before any are sold."[39]

Thus turned away, the explorers eschewed any further negotiations and went on their way. Later, when Wilkes reached Fort Vancouver and related the incident to the white residents, he was told that "I ought to have taken the fish and paid the Indian what I thought proper"—no doubt an apt summation of white attitudes toward Indian customs at that time.[40]

Much to the dismay of the scientists, the expedition found Native American customs of the Pacific Northwest an added barrier to collecting specimens such as those prized by Samuel George Morton in Philadelphia. The Indians continually thwarted any attempts to procure skulls, their native vigilance no doubt owed in large measure to their prior experience with anthropological foragers and looters such as John Townsend. The Indians of this region revered the spirits of the dead and believed that these spirits could not rest if the bones of their ancestors were disturbed. Naturally, the expedition's collectors aimed at bagging at least one of the distinctive Flathead skulls. It was the custom of many (but not all) of the Pacific Northwest tribes to artificially flatten the forehead at infancy, a process that never failed to intrigue white visitors. The members of the expedition were no exception. James Alden, among many others, recorded the custom in detail while among the Clallams:

> They are called Flat heads, and I think judging from the heads of the men, they are rightly named, not that nature has any hand in *beautifying* these *miserables*; but 'tis a custom, & I believe universally so, to compress the head of the males during infancy which gives them the most unsightly appearance. I had an opportunity of observing the manner that this system of torture is carried out. A small piece of board or bark is provided with a sufficient number of holes in each side. The poor little sufferer is laid upon his back, then a thick layer of the fiber of bark is spread over his body up to the chin. Then the cord is passed through the holes in the board over the body from the feet to the shoulders when the ugly little devil is lashed firmly down with his arms pinned to his sides.[41]

Alden went on to note that this "system of torture," as he described it, apparently harbored no ill effects on the baby's disposition. "I thought the child would go into fits," he admitted. But instead, the procedure seemed to have a soothing affect on the child, the procedure accomplished "with the utmost *sang froid*."[42] The men learned that, when performed correctly, this custom caused no damage to the mental or physical capacities of these people, as the white merchants of the region wholly attested to. It was probably this fact that made Flathead skulls among the most sought-after specimens for ethnologists, craniologists, and phrenologists alike.

Thus it was deemed imperative that the United States government should procure these skulls for "the national trust." This, however, proved to be a difficult task. They found success three weeks after making their first landfall in Puget Sound, where, near Port Orchard, they spied "three canoes, propped on trees, containing the bodies of Indians," from whence the ship's doctor extracted a Clallam skull.[43] A later attempt by a party traveling inland near Walla Walla was thwarted, however. Expedition draughtsman Joseph Drayton came across "a large burying-place. . . . The corpses were placed above ground, in their clothing, and then sewed up in a skin or blanket; and the personal property of each deceased individual was placed near the body: over all were laid a few boards, of native construction, placed as a kind of shed to protect them from the weather."[44] Drayton moved to desecrate the bodies and remove a skull, "but, to the surprise of the party, several Indians made their appearance and prevented it."[45] Wilkes later learned that his men were lucky to be let off with a warning, as grave robbing invited a stiff penalty among the Pacific Northwest Indians. "To rob their burying-grounds of bodies," he discovered, "is attended with much danger, as they would not hesitate to kill any one who was discovered in the act of carrying off a skull or bones."[46] Such depredations were considered worse than robbery (which it was) by the Indians; these were inhumane and grotesque—savage—acts perpetrated upon their culture by whites. One wonders how Wilkes would have reacted had the Indians of the Pacific Northwest enforced *their* laws in this case. If American blood had been shed, would it have triggered acts of retribution such as those at Malolo in the Fiji Islands?

During their excursions along the Columbia River, members of the expedition visited the stately tomb of the famous and "hospitable" chief Comcomly but found it in ruins. In this instance, British science had beaten them to the punch. They were told that Comcomly's skull "is in Glasgow, having been long since removed by Dr. Gardiner."[47]

Most of the expedition gathered at Fort Nisqually to celebrate Independence Day, providing a chance to parade an American custom before the Indians, not to mention the British stationed at the fort. They announced the holiday with the traditional firing of guns, in this case two brass howitzers that had been hauled ashore for this purpose. Indians and "red-coats" alike, according to Erskine, were "thunderstruck" at the "racket" caused by the expedition and "wanted to know what we meant." In reply, the Americans "pointed them to our country's flag, which was so proudly waving in the breeze over our observatory. . . . We told them that it was Brother Jonathan's birthday. They then called us a crew of crazy Americans."[48] At nine o'clock on the morning of the fifth (the fourth being a Sunday), a patriotic procession of sailors and marines, clad in "span-clean white frocks and trousers," streamed from the observatory, flag flying, the fife piping, and drums beating a marching tune. There, bringing up the rear and accompanying the ship's dog, was the prisoner Vendovi, "dressed 'a-la-Fejee' and appearing to enjoy the occasion quite as much as any one present."[49] This occasion was the first time Vendovi had set foot ashore since he had left the Fiji Islands, a period of approximately one year.

The men spent the day feasting upon roast ox, playing "foot-ball," and racing horses. It was said that the Indians surrounded the proceedings, marveling at "the novel sight" of this American rite, no doubt trying to comprehend the significance of "brother Jonathan's birthday."[50] At no other time during the expedition—at least not since the burnings of the Fijian villages of Tye and Sualib—had the men been so joyously exuberant. Even an unfortunate accident during the firing of the howitzers, resulting in the amputation of an arm of one of the sailors (with Dr. Pickering assisting at the surgery), failed to douse their enthusiasm. After all, Wilkes noted, "Men-of-war's men are somewhat familiar with such scenes, and, although this accident threw a temporary gloom over the party, the impression did not last long."[51] The reveries went on in Fiji-like fashion until the setting sun signaled an end to the celebration of this very special day.

The expedition's stay in Oregon allowed Horatio Hale to compile data that resulted in what came to be considered his greatest contribution to the field of philology. He had begun the voyage three years previously, anticipating that his major contribution to his field lay in tracing, through the residue of language, the origin and migrations of the Pacific islanders. This he had faithfully accomplished. But now an unexpected bounty lay before him: the opportunity to compile linguistic data on scores of languages and dialects— a virtual philological cornucopia compressed within a relatively small geographical area. The Pacific Northwest, in Hale's estimation, presented a unique scientific environment for his studies. Whereas the number of distinct family languages found in most "barbarous populations" was quite small, "in Oregon, however, the contrary has occurred, and the variety of idioms has been found to be much greater than was anticipated. Probably . . . no other part of the world offers an example of so many tribes, with distinct languages, crowded together within a space so limited."[52]

The diversity of speech astounded the scientists and made significant direct communication with the Indians problematical at best. They discovered that whereas among the Polynesians one interpreter—John Sac—sufficed from Paumotu to Hawaii, here in the Pacific Northwest a linguistic chain of up to five interpreters was often required to converse at length.[53] Information collected and sifted through such a linguistic filter had to be regarded rather dubiously. Pickering considered this situation "a serious obstacle to missionary operations" as well. Foretelling the comments of twentieth-century critics of cultural anthropology, he asserted that the "professed interpreters seldom acquire a correct knowledge of these languages" and questioned "whether the people themselves have hitherto been fairly reached."[54] Hale, however, was undaunted. The challenge of bringing order to this diversity was so alluring to him that he requested—and received—permission to remain behind to continue his work in the Pacific Northwest when the expedition departed for home in November of 1841.

Hale's eagerness to study Pacific Northwest languages was not in any way fueled by even the slightest appreciation of the culture and customs of the native speakers. In fact, no other culture encountered during the expedition fared as poorly in his *Ethnography and Philology*—and this includes the Fijians. His distaste for nearly every tribe encountered went beyond aversion to the physical traits and personal habits to encompass the intellectual and moral characteristics of the northwestern people as well. Indeed, Hale could not separate the two. All Indians, he concluded, who rely on fish for their sustenance "are excessively indolent and filthy, and, as a natural concomitant, base and depraved in character . . . prone to sensuality, and chastity among the women is unknown. . . . They seem to be almost devoid of natural affection." "Their religious ideas," he determined, "are very gross and confused," apparently lacking "any distinct ideas of a god, or of the existence of a soul."[55] Not all tribes in the Pacific Northwest were primarily fishermen, of course. Many inland groups were hunters, an occupation Hale deemed more noble for Indians. The young philologist, however, dismissed their culture nearly as summarily as those of the coastal tribes.

Hale's distaste for Pacific Northwest Indian culture seemed to know no bounds, going beyond the generally negative opinions of his fellow voyagers. Wilkes, for example, in his narrative documented a cultural similarity among the various tribes of the Pacific Northwest—the "conspicuous" role played by the coyote (or "prairie wolf") in their oral traditions and histories. "This wolf," he explained, "was not an object of worship, but was supposed to be endowed with supernatural powers, and to exert them in many ways."[56] Wilkes proceeded to retell what he considered to be a typical story, as heard from the Salish:

The wolf was desirous of having a wife, and visited the tribe on the Spokane for that purpose, demanding a young woman in marriage. The request being granted, he promised that the salmon should be abundant, and for this purpose he raised the rapids, that they might be caught with facility. After he had been gratified in this first instance, he made the same request of the others, among them, of the Sketsui (Coeur d'Alene) tribe, who were the only ones to refuse; he thereupon formed the great falls of the Spokane, which have ever since prevented the fish from ascending to their territory.[57]

Hale essentially repeats the same story in *Ethnography and Philology*, he, obviously, being the source of Wilkes's account.[58] The tone, however, is quite different from that expressed in Wilkes's narrative:

Like the Sahaptin, the Salish have many childish traditions connected with the most remarkable natural features of the country, in which the prairie-wolf generally bears a conspicuous part. What could have induced them to confer the honors of divinity upon this animal cannot be imagined. They do not, however, regard the wolf as an object of worship, but merely suppose that in former times it was endowed with preternatural powers, which it exerted after a very whimsical and capricious fashion. Thus, on one occasion, being desirous of a wife (a common circumstance with him), the *Wolf*, or the divinity so called, visited a tribe on the Spokane River, and demanded a young woman in marriage. His request being granted, he promised that thereafter the salmon should be abundant with them, and he created the rapids, which give them facilities for taking the fish. Proceeding farther up, he made of each tribe on his way the same request, attended with a like result. At length he arrived at the territory of the Skitsuish (Coeur d'alène); they refused to comply with his demand, and he therefore called into existence the great Falls of the Spokane, which prevent the fish from ascending to their country. This is a fair sample of their traditions.[59]

This "fair sample" of Pacific Northwest Indian culture better serves as a fair indicative of how Hale seemed to take pains to disparage these people in the eyes of science.

In all the Pacific Northwest, only one tribe—the Sikanis—fit to any degree Hale's image of what an Indian should be. This inland group (of whom Hale likely knew only secondhand) lived in the northern regions of Oregon. Though they spoke a language similar to that of their "indolent" Tahkali neighbors, Hale reported that they shared none of the "base" "character and customs." For the Sikanis were primarily hunters—as noted previously, a more noble occupation for the "savage," in Hale's eyes. No doubt in consequence, Hale described the Sikanis as a "brave, hardy, and active people, cleanly in their persons and habits, and, in general, agreeing nearly with *the usual idea of the American Indian* [italics mine]."[60]

Herein lies an important clue as to why Hale was so disparaging toward the Indians of the Pacific Northwest. Throughout the course of the expedition, Hale's conception of the American Indian had served as his gauge for identifying and measuring "savagery." Polynesians, Australian aborigines, Maoris, and Fijians had all been ranked according to this model. At the same time, these cultures were working subtle changes upon his standards of "savagery," so that, returning to America and encountering its native population, Hale discovered that these Indians were no longer "Indians," according to his perspective. Later, during the process of integrating his ideas into a new synthesis, he reintroduced the Pacific Northwest natives into his image of the Indian and was forced to construct new groupings of "savagery." This process occurs, significantly, within his chapter on the Pacific Northwest.

> In comparing the various races with which we have come into contact, it is impossible not to be struck with a certain similarity of character between the American Aborigines in general, but more especially the natives of Oregon, and the Australians,—the latter appearing like an exaggerated and caricatured likeness of the former. The Indian is proud and reserved; the Australian sullen and haughty. The former is, at once, cautious and fierce; the latter is cowardly and cruel. The one is passionate and prompt to resent an injury; the other is roused to fury by the slightest imagined insult. The superstition of the Indian is absurd and irrational; that of the Australian is stupid and ridiculous. The Indian, who acknowledges a chief, yet renders him such deference only as he thinks proper; the Australian owns no superior, and has not even a name for such an office.[61]

Thus proposing the model, he then attempts to entice others to proceed down this trailblazed path of inquiry. "It might be a point of some interest to determine how far this similarity, in many respects, between the two races otherwise so distinct, has arisen from a similarity in their position and circumstances."[62] The noble savage, alas, had been rendered extinct.

Charles Pickering, as could be expected, used his time in the Pacific Northwest to good advantage. He took part in more than one lengthy excursion through the interior and along the coast. His adventures were numerous and occasionally harrowing, as his footrace with a bear in Oregon Territory would indicate. He wryly noted that certain Indians of the interior, as a consequence of constantly being called "savages," had subsequently "adopted the epithet, unsuspicious of the implied opprobrium."[63] Here, interestingly, where Hale had seen depravity, Pickering saw promise. He visited the Reverend Henry H. Spaulding's farm near the mission at Lapwai and observed that many of the Indians (Nez Percé) were growing wheat, maize, and various garden vegetables. The reverend termed them "an exceedingly industrious people." "Here," in Pickering's estimation, "was abundant evidence, were any needed, that the North American tribes are in nowise averse to the arts of civilization, or devoid in any respect of the common attributes of humanity."[64] It goes without saying that Pickering measured progress in proportion to the extent of their adoption of the so-called Protestant work ethic. Nonetheless, his conclusions and general optimism stand in stark contrast to Hale's cursory dismissal of their character.

Pickering's experience among the Indians of Oregon led him to conclude that they belonged to the Mongolian race. As such, they were relatives of the Chinese. With this classification came a good deal of optimism for the future of this "race." "I have already referred to the superior powers of endurance of the aboriginal American; while in perseverance, patient industry and frugality, the Chinese will, I think, be admitted to excel other nations. These are qualifications that promise to have an important bearing on the future prospects of the Mongolian race."[65] Pickering was not the first to group the Chinese and Pacific Northwest Indians into one ethnological niche—though this theory definitely lacked majority support among scientists during this period. Morton, for instance, considered the American Indian a separate— and inferior—creation. A few of Pickering's ancillary conclusions, however, were even more controversial. In his *Races of Man*, he wrote that available evidence points to a relationship between the Pacific Northwest Indians and the Aztecs of Mesoamerica. "Mexican annals," he noted, "derive the origin of the Aztecas (the intrusive Mexicans) from the North, in the direction of Oregon." As further evidence, he offered several "coincidences" to bolster the connection, some more trivial than others:

> The connexion may not be easily traced; but a coincidence has been spoken of, in the occurrence of the terminal *tl*, so characteristic of the Mexican language, among the Nootka people. I remarked that the same termination was common with the Chinooks; and I heard it even in the Nisqually tribe. The lateral fringe to the trousers, universal in Oregon, is known to occur among the aboriginal Mexicans. . . . The fashion, aboriginal with the Oregon females, of wearing the hair in two lateral braids, is also widely diffused in Spanish America; and we observed it even in Chili. The use of masks, which is also common to Mexico and the Northwest maritime

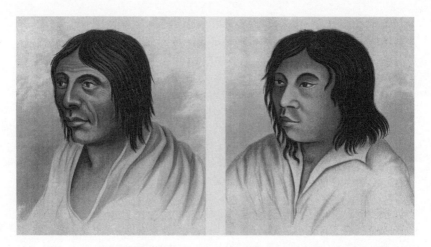

"A Kalapuya man" and "A Kalapuya lad." Drawings by Alfred Agate. Pickering classified Pacific Northwest Indians as belonging to the Mongolian race. He also felt there was a connection between the Aztecs and the Oregon Indians. Source: Pickering, *Races of Man.*

Maleka, a native of Hawaii. Both Pickering and Agate believed the Hawaiians and the Indians of California belonged to the Malayan race. Drawing by Alfred Agate. Source: Pickering, *Races of Man.*

tribes . . . and further, a distinct correspondence in style of art, is traceable, between the ancient paintings and sculptures of Mexico and Yucatan, and the carved stone pipes of Northwest America. Another fact not irrelevant to the point in question, is the observation made by the missionaries; that the tribes of Interior Oregon, are at this day "all pressing gradually towards the South."[66]

If, then, in Pickering's eyes the "connexion" were true, what of the Indians in between? Into what racial compartment did the California Indians belong? Pickering's conclusion, seconded by James Alden and expedition portraitist Alfred Agate, was that they were Malays—descendants of the Pacific islanders.[67] He formulated this idea on little more than cursory physical examinations, hardly the type of evidence to be met with credulity back home (it was not), where the savants preferred hardheaded (as in cranial) evidence. Nevertheless, his extrapolations as to the future of the California Indians, which was inexorably tied to their perceived difference in race from other tribes of America, are interesting to note. This distinction was their salvation. Perhaps, like the natives of Tahiti and unlike the "eastern tribes" of the United States, these "Malays" of North America would prove "more tractable, and not disposed to create difficulty."[68] And so, in the end, perhaps for Pickering as well, whatever scientific method the anthropologist or ethnologist chose when studying the "other," it all eventually boiled down to the binary classificatory analogy articulated by Horatio Hale in the Fiji Islands—the choice being between the "tameable" and the "untameable"— the Wolf or the Dog.

6 ETHNOGRAPHY AND THE LEGACY OF THE EXPEDITION

There is a vast deal of unintentional humbuggery in some of the accounts we have from scientific men concerning the religious institutions of Polynesia . . . obtain[ing] the greater part of their information from the retired old South-Sea rovers, who . . . know just the sort of information wanted, and furnishes it to any extent. . . . Now, when the scientific voyager arrives at home with his collection of wonders, he . . . enters into a very circumstantial and learned narrative of certain unaccountable superstitions and practices, about which he knows as little as the islanders do themselves. . . . Were the book thus produced to be translated into the tongue of the people of whom it purports to give the history, it would appear quite as wonderful to them as it does to the American public, and much more improbable.
—Herman Melville, *Typee*

At last, in November 1841, Wilkes led the expedition home, recrossing the Pacific, sailing through the Indian Ocean, around the Cape of Good Hope, and into New York harbor in June 1842. Expecting to be welcomed as heroes, the returning voyagers instead found the citizens of New York restrained in their praise. Instead of testimonial dinners and proclamations in their honor, many of the officers were swept into a series of courts-martial spanning 105 days—culminating in three weeks of trial and proceedings against Wilkes.

Upon returning to the United States, the captain had chosen to bring formal charges against those officers with whom he had had serious confrontations during the voyage. Many in turn filed accusations of their own against Wilkes. Among the twenty-seven counts included in the official proceedings against Wilkes were charges of oppression of his men; illegally flogging men in the squadron; illegally detaching enlisted men; scandalous conduct, specifically making a false entry as to the date on which he sighted land in the Antarctic; and finally, cruelty in killing natives and burning their villages in reprisal for the death of his nephew.[1] Eventually, Wilkes was exonerated of all charges save for the excessive use of the cat-o'-nine-tails, for which he received only a public reprimand from the board.[2] His actions in the Fiji Islands, in the end, were upheld.

What the general public found thrilling about the return of the voyagers was not the glory of their achievements, but the idea that a cannibal would soon be walking the streets of New York. But this "spectacle" was not to be. Vendovi had been despondent since the death of his friend and interpreter, Benjamin Vanderford.[3] Racked by consumption, the Fijian was clinging to life by the time *Vincennes* dropped anchor in New York harbor. Vendovi's deteriorating condition prompted Pickering to dash off a missive to Morton on the day of their arrival. "This is to let you know that our Feejee Cheif [*sic*] is on his last legs and will probably give up the ghost tomorrow. As you go in for *Anthropology*, it would be well worth your while to come on immediately, for such a specimen of humanity you have never seen, and the probability is, that you may never have the opportunity again."[4] There is no record that Morton availed himself of this opportunity. Perhaps he preferred to bide his time for a more detailed, scientific examination, whereby he could funnel his white pepper seed into the cranium of this soon-to-be specimen in a more "objective" clinical study than that offered by a cursory visit to the dying cannibal.

Vendovi made news even as he was carried ashore to the naval hospital. Gordon Bennett of the *New York Herald* kept his readers updated on the procession and on the condition of the Fijian. Bennett diagnosed Vendovi's illness as a prolonged abstinence from his staple diet of human flesh.[5] The *North American Review* reported that "at the sight of this massive building [the naval hospital], he [Vendovi] was said to have remarked, that it was the place where the Great Spirit waited for him." Vendovi expired soon after. Though "his body did not grace the triumph of his captors," his skull was indeed placed "among the trophies of the Expedition."[6]

Scientists in America and Europe who had been awaiting the return of the expedition were rankled that the courts-martial and the hoopla surrounding Vendovi threatened to overshadow its outstanding scientific achievements. All were eager to sample the fruits of such a wide interdisciplinary sweep of the Pacific, whether as active analysts of the collections or as reviewers of the results of such studies.[7] Unbeknownst to the scientists on the expedition, however, many of the boxes of specimens of every variety that had been shipped home during the course of the voyage had been tampered with. The boxes had been opened, in many cases, not by scientists but by politically appointed "curators" who often treated the collections as they would patronage, doling out specimens upon request to politically partisan gardener-botanists and private collectors. As a result, much of what was forwarded during the voyage was either lost or rendered useless by separating the descriptive identifying information from the specimens.[8] Nonetheless, the collections kept aboard the expedition vessels (with the exception of *Peacock*, which had run aground and broken up on a sandbar at the mouth of the Columbia River) were intact and untampered with, and much was still expected from every field of science.

No scientific discipline represented on the expedition captured the public imagination as much as ethnology. No doubt it was for this reason that the ethnological collections were among the first to be arranged and displayed for public viewing. By 1843 the *American Journal of Science and Arts* reported that one could visit the United States Patent Office in Washington (where the collections were on display) and, in a single stroll through the Great Hall of the National Gallery, learn about the "manners and customs, mode of life, superstitions and religious observances, traditions, &c. of the people met with in the course of the cruise."[9] Here Americans could see for themselves "the condition of the various tribes and races, and the degree of civilization among them. . . . By a walk through the National Gallery, we travel with more than railroad speed over the Pacific, and examine into their various productions and the relative intelligence of the savages."[10]

Surely the most impressive link in this "train of savagery" was the extensive collections brought back from the Fiji Islands, containing nearly "all the arts and manufactures of the islands." The reviewer expressed disappointment that Vendovi had not survived to act as docent for the collections—only his grinning skull remained to greet visitors. Were the Fijian still alive, "a visit to the hall with Vendovi at hand would be little less interesting than visiting the islands themselves," adding that there was "one advantage at least—no danger would be apprehended from a ferocious race of cannibals, that are ready to attack all intruders into those seas." On display were the skulls collected among these islands, including the one bartered for by the crew of *Peacock* that bore the marks of its being roasted over a fire. This skull in particular represented a most important piece of evidence "on account of the prevalent unwillingness to admit that cannibalism actually exists among savages. This was seen both by men and officers, and from the facts collected there can be no doubt of their [Fijians'] entertaining an actual relish for human flesh."[11] The collections in the Great Hall were an instant popular success, considered "the best sight in Washington" by visitor Ralph Waldo

Emerson.[12] Prominent scientists such as the Swiss-born Harvard professor Louis Agassiz traveled to the capital to inspect the collections.[13]

The federal government appointed Charles Pickering to supervise the collections. Within months, however, he resigned the superintendency in order to embark on a voyage to Egypt and its adjoining areas, seeking to fill in the ethnographical gaps of his proposed work on the races of man. Nonetheless, the task of putting the remainder of the collections into some sort of order was finally set in motion. The first fruits were produced by Wilkes. Following the courts-martial proceedings, he had collected the expedition journals of his officers and scientists and commenced writing the official narrative of the expedition. Published in 1845, the five-volume *Narrative of the United States Exploring Expedition during the Years 1838, 1839, 1840, 1841, 1842* received an initial printing of just one hundred copies, which were distributed to each state and territory in the Union and each friendly foreign power, with one extra set each for France and Great Britain.[14] Subsequent volumes were to focus on the various scientific aspects of the voyage; all told, twenty-four volumes were planned for government publication. These were to include Ethnography and Philology, Zoophytes, Mammalogy and Ornithology, the Races of Man, Geology, Meteorology, Mollusca and Shells, Crustacea, Herpetology, Ichthyology, Physics, Hydrography, and the various branches of Biology.[15] Strangely enough, no sets were reserved for American or foreign scientific institutions, an oversight roundly decried.[16]

Despite its limited publication, Wilkes's five-volume narrative quickly drew the notice of reviewers on both sides of the Atlantic. Handsomely bound and abundantly illustrated, these volumes masterfully chronicled America's entry into the mainstream of scientific exploration of a magnitude at least equal to that of the leading European powers. While the *Edinburgh Review* cautioned that the *Narrative* contained "little romantic and still less picturesque description," such as that found in the florid travel books then in vogue, the amplitude alone of such a successful undertaking elicited favorable nods from British and American publications alike.[17] All marveled at the expansive territory covered over the course of the voyage and the rich harvest of comparative scientific studies it promised to yield. The *Narrative* served, the *British Quarterly Review* declared, "to excite our wonder that so large a portion of the semi-barbarous climes of the earth should have been visited at so small a cost of human quiet and human life."[18] Such an ambitious expedition seemed to dwarf other recent scientific voyages, including that of HMS *Beagle*. Charles Darwin, the young naturalist on that expedition, had already written to Wilkes requesting an interview, hoping "to have the pleasure of conversing a short time with you, concerning your long and most interesting voyage."[19]

The *Narrative* contained little of the more detailed scientific data that scientists long anticipated. Its strength was in the wealth of ethnological information compiled on a grand sweep across the Pacific, which encouraged the comparative methodologies demanded by philologists and anthropologists alike. The *Narrative* provided a panoramic ethnological "update" on the current state of "savage" humankind and its positioning within the nations and races of the world. The results of the United States Exploring Expedition could be compared to earlier endeavors by Cook and La Pérouse so as to gauge over time the degree of "improvability" inherent in the various "barbarous tribes." Such comparisons, scientists argued, would also measure the extent to which Americans and Europeans had succeeded in "civilizing" others. According to the *British Quarterly Review*, Wilkes's account represented no less than "a sort of miniature cyclopedia of the less cultivated portions of the globe."[20] Within these volumes the "attentive reader will find help" in discovering the "solution" to the "great social questions" then being debated concerning the origins and classification of humankind.

Not surprisingly, each reviewer found the answers he sought within the sixteen-hundred-odd pages of the narrative. Some found ample evidence of the unity and improvability of humankind. Others saw proof of the permanent degradation of the "savage." There seemed to be something for everyone. The American publication *Southern Quarterly Review* considered Hale's ethnological work among the various African people held in bondage in Brazil to be particularly valuable. They praised Alfred Agate's woodcuts comparing the "distinctive physiognomies" of the captive Africans and, with possibly an eye to the future, "the marks by which they may be recognized."[21] On the other end of the spectrum, the *British Quarterly Review* concluded that the ethnological data presented in the *Narrative* once and for all confirmed the unity of humankind, striking a blow against the institution of slavery in the process. "All these nations and all these tribes are men; they are each and all members of the one great human family. . . . [T]hey have all heads to think, and hearts to feel, and souls to save. This fact can no longer be denied. Such a narrative as that of Commander Wilkes will hereafter prevent the fact from being any more blinked. Slavery has for ever lost one of its excuses."[22] This enraptured reviewer even sensed in Wilkes's account the hand of God ushering in the millennium. He found it impossible "in the survey which this book has led us to make, wholly to shut out the feeling that the wide earth is preparing for a great ordinal change, if not for the second advent of its Redeemer."[23]

Then again, there was the staid *Edinburgh Review*. Concerning the Tahitians, who generally fared well among English savants, "We cannot disguise our conviction that the Polynesians, however improvable in many respects, are, and are too likely long to continue, a very imperfect variety of the human race."

These differing interpretations of the *Narrative* reflected the debate raging in Britain between old-school philologists such as James C. Prichard, who espoused the essential unity (if not actual equality) of the human race, and those who, like Thomas Carlyle, rejected such notions as antiquated eighteenth-century nonsense.[24] For the latter, the significance of the United States Exploring Expedition was that it had confirmed the self-evident—the innate superiority of the Anglo-Saxon race—and once and for all dispelled "the dreams of Rousseau and Condorcet which represent man as weakened and depraved by the artificial training of civilization." They felt that no amount of outside influence can alter the characteristics inherent in human beings, whether "civilized" or "savage." "Neither barbarism nor civilization, powerful agents as they are, can develope propensities which do not naturally exist."[25] It was inevitable that the Fijians were cited as the most obvious cases in point.

The eyewitness accounts of Fiji cannibalism contained in the *Narrative* were seen as crucial arguments for asserting the superiority of Anglo-Saxon civilization. As mentioned earlier, the *American Journal of Science and Arts* considered such testimony, coupled with the artifacts brought back from the islands, to be not only invaluable contributions to the body of scientific knowledge but also a valuable pedantic tool with which to educate the American public. Faced with such evidence, even the *British Quarterly Review* was hard pressed to find a place for cannibals within their family of man, given the repulsion with which most Americans and Britons regarded the eating of human flesh. This particular dilemma was solved by assigning to the Fijians a satanic role within the reviewer's teleological framework. "Lest the reports we have made of the tokens of improvement visible in the world should produce an undue impression," he cautioned his readers, "[w]e advert, in conclusion, to a dark, a very black feature, which still fixes its blot on humanity. This work puts it beyond a doubt, that human sacrifices and cannibalism still survive. In the Feejee Islands, where religious opinions are found which in form resemble some that prevail around us, both human sacrifices and cannibalism are practised on a large scale, and in very revolting forms."[26] In this role, the Fijians become even more fearsome by virtue of the resemblance of their religion to Christianity. Within this perspective, what is this, if not the Antichrist?

The various reviewers found other facts in the *Narrative* equally enlightening. Analysts on both sides of the Atlantic seemed genuinely surprised and even embarrassed by the missionaries' abuse of power over the natives throughout the Pacific. Many decried the senseless interdiction of native customs such as surfing, singing, and wearing flowers in their hair.[27] John Stuart Mill's *Westminster Review* was appalled by Protestant missionary behavior as recounted in the *Narrative*. The evidence presented by Wilkes concerning the disputes between Catholics and Protestants on Tahiti led the reviewer

> to doubt whether Catholic forms, and Catholic toleration of innocent amusements, would not have been much more successful as a means of introducing the real elements of civilization than the sour asceticism and cold formalities which incompetent teachers have introduced in the name of Christianity. We read with impatience of schools founded only to teach catechisms, and lay the most severe restraints upon the sports of childhood. Children are not to play, nor are their parents to sing or dance, or smoke tobacco. These restrictions we meet with occasionally in the methodistical connexion of England, but it was new to us to find them extended even to the cultivation of *flowers*. So, however, it is. . . . Blind teachers of the blind![28]

Mill's journal was not merely highly critical of "civilization's" injunctions against "savagery." It went so far as to call to account Wilkes's and the expedition's actions in the Fiji Islands, considering the work done there "disfigured by . . . reprisals upon the savage for injuries sustained by the expedition."[29] The reviewer considered the incident at Malolo "a sad story to connect with objects of science. The expedition was not sent out to punish crimes carelessly provoked. . . . The natives of Malolo have doubtless been taught not to trifle with the armament of a man-of-war; but how will this benefit the crew of an unprotected merchant-vessel touching at the same island?"[30] The reviewer admitted, with fully bared sarcasm, that "the fearful retaliation, however, of the Vincennes had some redeeming features. The crew did not quite descend to a level with the savage. Seventy-five men were killed to revenge the loss of two, but Captain Wilkes did not eat his prisoners, as the natives would have done. This is gratifying."[31] A discussion of the practice of cannibalism was transformed by the reviewer (Mill?) into a weapon to harpoon his political opponents. While "we must confess our disapprobation of the practice . . . our own ancestors were not free from this reproach, and we can easily imagine the progenitor of the editor of the 'Times' newspaper picking the bones of an ancestor of the Poor-Law Commissioners with a degree of hearty satisfaction, which might possibly still be extended to the plump limbs of a Somerset-house functionary, roasted or boiled, but for a certain fastidiousness of stomach which has been occasioned by a change of dietary, and the fact that the dish alluded to is difficult to be had."[32]

Such criticism of Wilkes's methods was not indicative of majority sentiment, however. More typical was the *Southern Quarterly Review*, which deemed the commander's actions against the Fijians "not only justifiable, but humane and politic" by "impressing upon the Polynesians, the Malays, and the savage pirates of every sea, that a signal vengeance awaits them if they fail to respect our flag."[33]

While the *Narrative* elicited a gamut of reaction, it was Charles Pickering's *Races of Man and Their Geographical Distribution*, published in 1848, that provoked the most controversy. Pickering had not tarried long in the United States upon the expedition's return. Before leaving for Egypt, however, he had invited Samuel George Morton to Washington DC to view the expedition's collection of skulls, at the same time confessing that he had not as yet read Morton's *Crania Americana*.[34] Pickering returned to America in 1845 fully prepared to publish the most sweeping study of humankind ever based on direct observation. But it was not to be so easy. He (and Wilkes, whose responsibility it was to supervise the completion of the various scientific volumes) discovered that to speculate on the origins of mankind was to trespass on the hallowed ground of Mosaic revelation. Thus it was that Pickering was informed that his work would be reviewed by a congressional committee in charge of the expedition publications, headed by Benjamin Tappan.[35] The usually mild-mannered doctor adamantly refused at first to comply with the wishes of the committee. Therefore, for the next two years Wilkes found himself in the difficult position of trying to secure Pickering's manuscript while at the same time reassuring the committee that the work contained nothing that upset popular notions of biblical creation and the origins of races. Since Tappan and the committee had only hearsay on which to base their apprehensions, it is likely that Pickering was deemed guilty by association with his friend Morton and George Gliddon, whose notions of separate species Tappan and the others no doubt found both morally and politically unacceptable.[36]

At last, after much stalling, threats, and delays by both Pickering and the committee, *Races of Man* was published in 1848.[37] The organization of the book is part narrative and part racial grouping, held together by clear, eloquent prose and bolstered by the weight of direct observation of his subjects. The book lacks the prodding of interwoven analysis (though not as noticeable an omission to those still under the aegis of the Baconian method, as many naturalists were at that time). The author too often relied on rather superficial evidence and "intuitive" methods from which to form his conclusions.[38] His greatest handicap, however, was not of his own making; it was having to operate under the pre-Darwinian time frame of creation—a paradigmatic straitjacket from which Pickering (and most others, for that matter) did not struggle much to free himself.

Historians and scientists in the twentieth century have too often lumped *Races of Man* with other contemporaneous works emanating from the "American school" of anthropology—in particular Morton's *Crania Americana* and *Crania Aegyptiaca*, George Gliddon's and Josiah Nott's *Types of Mankind*, and works by Ephraim George Squier and Louis Agassiz.[39] To do so is to create a misleading picture of Pickering's ideas as expressed in his books, field notes, and letters dealing with the Exploring Expedition and subsequent travels to the Middle East, Africa, and India. It is significant that few of his contemporaries equated Pickering with the American school.[40] No wonder. Not only does *Races of Man* contradict many of the main tenets of Morton and the polygenesists, but its conclusions also put it at odds with those intellectuals from either side of the Atlantic who were championing the Caucasus Mountains as the birthplace of the Anglo-Saxon. And as for the congressional committee, the only supposition that could be considered objectionable to those of Tappan's ilk was that Pickering chose not to buttress his conclusions with religious material.

In a brief chapter toward the end of *Races of Man*— significantly titled "Zoological Deductions"—Pickering laid out his conclusions regarding the origins and dispersal of humankind. As a naturalist, he saw "no reason why the order of nature should be set aside for the special accommodation of physical man."[41] He therefore began with the assumption that since humans had been "placed on the globe in unison with the rest of creation, and subject to the same general laws which guide us in investigating other beings; we may proceed to search for his place of origin, in the same manner as for that of other natural productions."[42]

One of his first tasks was to rule out the assertion advanced by European and American "Anglo-Saxonists" that "man was originally planted on frosty Caucasus." Pickering declared this an impossibility because of humans' "physical discordance with the surrounding natural objects."[43] Next, he distanced himself from the American school by ruling out the possibility of a separate origin—and hence, species—for the American Indian on "zoological grounds." There was no separate Indian race or species according to Pickering.

Pickering felt that in terms of geography, it could be shown "that the races of men could all be conveniently derived from the same two centres; the one, in the East Indies; and the other, in Africa . . . if we could suppose separate species."[44] If Pickering was to stop at this point, historians would have some justification for placing him in the camp of the polygenesists. But "zoological considerations" led him to a different conclusion. "Analogy with the rest of the organic world," he stated, "implies a central point of origin."[45] According to Pickering, that "point of origin" was not the Caucasus, nor any other white-centered area of population; instead, it was in Africa.

From this cradle of humanity, Pickering envisioned an outward pulse of dispersion of the races of mankind, "sending forth streams of population; and at the same time prohibiting a return" to the original source.[46] Anthropologists today would brook no argument with pinpointing Africa as the wellspring of humanity, but few in the 1840s were willing to accept African origins, whether on religious, moral, or racial grounds. This conclusion, coupled with his omission of an implicit Mosaic framework, was bound to upset Americans such as Tappan while at the same time alienating Anglo-Saxonists. His refusal to isolate the American Indian as a separate, inferior species contradicted the findings of Morton, Gliddon, Nott, and Squier. Finally, none of the above could have been pleased that Pickering imposed no hierarchical scheme upon his enumeration of the races, which, of course, was the cornerstone of the beliefs both of the American school and Anglo-Saxonists.

Pickering's professional differences with Morton were readily apparent throughout the Exploring Expedition and are again manifested in *Races of Man*. His trips to Egypt further magnified these differences. In his letters to Morton, Pickering challenged many of the findings expressed in *Crania Aegyptiaca*. He disputed data listing Egyptian crania as undersized and therefore intellectually diminished.[47] Even more disturbing to Pickering was Morton's and Gliddon's contention that black Africans in ancient Egypt served exclusively as slaves—which was seen as proof for continuing the "natural" institution of American slavery in the South. Pickering's examination of Egyptian artifacts during his travels found that no such racial hierarchy existed in ancient Egypt.[48] While he acknowledged "the possibility of distinguishing the races by the skull," he was never willing to impose a hierarchical structure to these differences.[49]

All of the above help to explain in part the lack of recognition afforded Pickering's work with the expedition. Another factor was the very limited official distribution of the first edition of *Races of Man* (subsequent foreign editions, however, expanded its circulation). His reliance on his observation of a limited—though diverse—sample of populations also did not endear him to those preferring Morton's supposedly more data-based methods. Those interested in questions of race and species ultimately found Morton's work eminently more useful. Southerner William Brown Hodgson acknowledged this utility in a letter to Morton in 1844. A grateful Hodgson wrote that "your [Morton's] conclusions as to the unvarying physical characteristics of races, must explode Dr. Prichard's one-sided arguments [as to the unity of humankind], and in the South, we shall not be so much frightened hereafter by the voices of Europe or of Northern America."[50] Morton's "scientific" classificatory system, which relegated blacks to a position of permanent inferiority, provided many Americans a tangible, "scientific" foundation for upholding and defending the institution of slavery; *Races of Man*, in contrast, provided no such ammunition to besieged southern slaveholders.

One prominent northerner who took the time to read and compare Morton's work with Pickering's was Oliver Wendell Holmes Sr. Holmes was dean of Harvard Medical School in 1849 when he wrote to Morton, thanking him for the cranial catalogue Morton had sent him. He had found the catalogue immensely useful in "preparing a lecture or two on the Races of Mankind." He particularly found the "measurements of (intellectual) capacity . . . of great interest and importance." Not so with Pickering's book, however. "Is not Pickering's book the oddest collection of fragments that was ever seen? I have been more puzzled to find the law of association by which many of his observations are brought together than the savan[t]s ever were by the Rosetta stone. . . . It seems to me that Pickering has heaped his materials together with a pitchfork—that his book is amorphous as a fog, unstratified as a dumpling and heterogeneous as a low priced sausage."[51] In the dean's opinion, the unacceptable, "unstratified" nature of Pickering's work was all the more deficient when compared with Morton's findings. "The more I read on these subjects," Holmes confided to Morton, "the more I am delighted with the severe and cautious character of your own most extended researches, which from their very nature are permanent data for all future students of ethnology."[52] Undoubtedly, Dean Holmes found such data most relevant and helpful the following year, when he revoked the conditional admissions of three black men—the first ever to enter Harvard Medical School—after white students and faculty refused to sit in classes with Negroes.[53]

Samuel George Morton died in May 1851, just two months after the skulls collected by the Wilkes Expedition were temporarily placed in his care.[54] The *New York Tribune* eulogized Morton and his accomplishments, placing him "in the front rank of archaeologists and ethnographers throughout the world." "Few scientific works," the *Tribune* said, "ever provided a stronger or more durable impression on the philosophic mind, or have had a more powerful effect in directing the course of future investigations."[55] Charles Pickering, on the other hand, turned his attention to ethnobotany—specifically, the correlation of the movement of humankind and the dispersion of plants and animals. This sweeping field consumed his interest through the Darwinian revolution until his death in 1878. In ethnobotany Pickering had found a safe haven from the hierarchical, social, and political implications of anthropology.

If Pickering's digest on humankind was by and large rejected by his contemporaries, the work of Horatio Hale initially fared much better within the scientific community. Hale's arrival in Philadelphia in May of 1842 had preceded the expedition's return by one month; he therefore managed to sidestep the political quagmire in which their return bogged down. Hale immediately set to work on his assigned volume. The result was volume 6 of the United States Exploring Expedition: *Ethnography and Philology*, published in 1846.

Hale's work was met with unqualified praise among the scientific and literary community, which was a welcome change from the unfulfilled expectations and criticisms that seemed to be endemic to the history of the expedition. No doubt owing to these past problems, and aware of the author's youth, some had braced themselves for the worst when reviewing Hale's work, "expect[ing] but little more than a few imperfect vocabularies" to be, at best, the sum total of the expedition's ethnological contributions. Instead, the *American Journal of Science and Arts* discovered in volume 6 "evidence throughout of great labor, directed by a clear and philosophical mind."[56] A much-relieved Asa Gray, who had been critical of the processing of the expedition's scientific data since its return, spoke well in *North American Review* of his friend Hale's efforts. He assured readers that Hale's work "will do credit to himself and to the country."[57] The consensus was that the mature and comprehensive nature of volume 6 would help to redeem the tarnished reputation of the Exploring Expedition in the eyes of American science.

Ethnography and Philology is basically divided into three sections. Hale began with the ethnological descriptions of the various cultural groups encountered during the voyage. He concluded his discussion of Polynesia with a chapter entitled "Oceanic Migrations." This section is marked by his innovative use of language to trace the origins and subsequent movement of the islanders of the South Pacific. Approaching the various dialects comparatively, he traced the evolution of the meaning and pronunciation of the word *Hawaii* as the islanders had migrated east to west across the ocean. Polynesian culture, according to Hale, had originated in Samoa and Tonga. He devoted the remainder of the volume to a compilation of vocabularies and grammars of the languages heard in the course of the voyage, again making liberal use of comparative methodology.

Such a comprehensive, comparative sweep of Pacific culture and language by a trained, firsthand observer was unprecedented. Americans such as Asa Gray were confident that Hale's data and conclusions would "stand in the foremost rank" among ethnological research. Anthropologists agreed with this assessment. R. G. Latham, author of *Man and His Migrations* and other works on the varieties of humankind, considered Hale's work to be "the greatest mass of philological data ever accumulated by a single inquirer."[58] As the years passed and South Pacific culture and language became increasingly diluted by white civilization, Hale's data took on added significance for later anthropologists such as Daniel Brinton, who turned to *Ethnography and Philology* as the last "pure" source for Pacific culture.[59] A century later, Hale's information on the Fiji Islands was still considered the authoritative source by many ethnographers.[60]

Along with the philological portion of the volume, contemporaries gave equal praise to his section on ethnography. A book of assorted grammars and vocabularies, however valuable, was considered shallow if not placed within a framework or system to give the data meaning and importance. Hale's ethnography furnished such a framework. In Gray's estimation, this section provided not only "an excellent introduction of Philology" but also the "intellectual superstructure" upon which to arrange and comprehend the collected data of language.[61] Hale's discussion of ethnography created a comfortable system from which to view other cultures. "This arrangement," Gray noted, "is sound and rational"; his methods and organization "succeed in giving a certain classical completeness to his work."[62] He further commended the "remarkable acuteness and tact in discerning the characteristic peculiarities of the numerous tribes" covered in the ethnographical section, particularly the "many curious analogies between barbarous institutions and those of the most refined nations."[63]

Following the publication of *Ethnography and Philology*, Hale collaborated with the dean of American philology—the aged Albert Gallatin—to publish an ethnography of the Pacific Northwest Indians for the Transactions of the American Ethnological Society in 1848.[64] At this juncture, however, having achieved the acclaim of his peers and a solid reputation as scientist—all before his thirtieth birthday—Hale took a curious path away from the scientific mainstream. He ceased his research and turned to the study of law. After achieving the bar in 1855, he married, packed up, and moved to the Canadian frontier town of Clinton, Ontario. For the next twenty-five years he was known to neighbors as a kindly but eccentric lawyer who had erected an "enormous wigwam" in his fruit orchard to accommodate the various Indians from Canada and the United States who came to call on the aging ex-philologist.[65]

Remarkably, Hale reappeared on the scientific scene while in his sixties, emerging to debate leading American ethnologist Lewis Henry Morgan. Morgan had succeeded in amalgamating Darwinian evolution with the older notions of savagery and civilization to create a well-marked anthropological road map of race hierarchy. According to Morgan, while there was no longer any doubt as to the common ancestry of humankind, not all took the same path "upward" toward civilization. The goal of the anthropologist was to discover why some groups have "succeeded" and others have "failed to progress" over the eons now agreed upon as having passed since the beginning. "It is both a natural and proper desire to learn, if possible, how all these ages upon ages of past time have been expended by mankind; how savages, advancing by slow, almost imperceptible steps attained the higher condition of barbarians; how barbarians, by similar progressive advancement, finally attained to civilization; and why other tribes and nations have been left behind in the race of progress—some in civilization, some in barbarism, and others in savagery."[66] Among other things, Morgan pointed to the "progressive evolution" from matrilineal to patrilineal social systems as a key step in the process. Language too, he claimed, was a key indicator of progress from the simple to the complex. Hale, through his study of languages on the Exploring Expedition, knew that neither was true. And so he entered the fray, vigorously refuting Morgan's assumptions and constructs. In a commentary to the American Association for the Advancement of Science in 1881, Hale struck at the hierarchical assumptions of cultural superiority as fatal to the study of anthropology. "As there could be no sound astronomy while the notion prevailed that the earth was the center of the universe, and no science of history while each nation looked with contempt upon every other people, so we can hope for no complete and satisfying science of man and of human speech until our minds are disabused of those other delusions of self-esteem which would persuade us that superior culture implies superior capacity, and that the particular race and language which we happen to claim as our own are the best of all races and languages."[67]

This statement, arguing for a relativistic approach to anthropology, leads one to contemplate just what had transpired to transform a young philologist who, forty years earlier, had summarily dismissed assorted cultures and tribes as incapable of rising from their almost bestial state, and who had confidently ranked "savages" according to their "tameability." Was it an epiphany of old age or perhaps disaffection with the direction anthropology and "race thinking" had taken since his years on the Exploring Expedition? Possibly an interest in women's rights inherited from his mother, Sarah Josepha Hale, had mitigated his earlier conclusions. Or had the years spent in communion with the various Indian groups that came to call at his orchard wigwam taught him that aspects of culture should not and could not be compartmentalized and ranked according to a hierarchical dominant perspective? Finally, what drove Hale, in his twilight years, to reenter a branch of science that seemingly had radically changed since his time on the Exploring Expedition in the 1830s and 1840s?

One motivation, surely, was fear. By the 1880s it was evident to scientists, as well as to the population at large, that, based on the rapid downward trajectory of the Native American population coupled with the efforts of reformers to eliminate Indian culture through forced adoption of white ways, anthropologists would soon be relegated to sifting through museum pieces and exhumed bones in order to study Indians. For linguists, who, unlike anthropologists, did not possess the power of Elijah to "make the bones come to life," there would be even less to go by. This apprehension for the fate of Native Americans was not necessarily a humanitarian impulse. According to anthropologist Jacob Gruber, among the "civilized" nations there rose a "haunting fear that the impending extinction of the Indian and the destruction of his culture would destroy data of great value for the solution of significant ethnological and historical problems."[68] So, while American government institutions such as the Smithsonian, the Bureau of American Ethnology, and the Bureau of Indian Affairs hurriedly dug for, foraged, and otherwise appropriated as many artifacts of Indian culture as their museums could store,[69] the British Association for the Advancement of Science called for a sweeping study of the "physical characters, languages, industrial and social conditions of the North-western tribes of the Dominion of Canada."[70] The brunt of this great commission fell upon the seven Canadian members of the association, one of whom was Horatio Hale.

Of these members it was Hale, then nearing seventy, who provided the energy and thrust for the pursuit of this quest. The urgency of this project was such that in 1884 Hale readied to carry out the field research in the Pacific Northwest himself, as he had done nearly a half-century earlier on the Wilkes Expedition. The body would not respond to the urging of the mind, however, and by 1888 it was evident that someone else would have to venture westward for the association. Fortunately for Hale, the British association, and the future of anthropology in general, a noted young German ethnographer— Franz Boas—happened to be seeking a sponsor for an extended study in that very region of the Pacific Northwest. In a propitious alliance the Canadians acquired a proven field researcher, while Boas received the financial and institutional backing he needed at this crucial point in his career, not to mention eventual enshrinement as the father of modern anthropology.

Jacob Gruber's 1967 article "Horatio Hale and the Development of American Anthropology," based on correspondence between Hale and Franz Boas during the time of this research, recounts Hale's guidance and influence on Boas's work among the Native American groups in the Pacific Northwest— supervision that the German at times resented as meddlesome and irritating. When reading the letters that passed between the two, one cannot help being struck by the sense of urgency embodied in Hale's explicit and detailed instructions to the young ethnographer working in the field. No doubt the above-mentioned fear of the approaching demise of Native American cultures played a role in triggering such anxiety—there was no time to lose. But very possibly, Hale's actions emanated from another, more personal source—one that becomes evident only when comparing Hale's accounts of the Wilkes Expedition with his correspondence with Boas fifty years later: the realization that his ethnographical conclusions from the expedition were marred by the very flaws for which he had indicted Lewis Henry Morgan before the American Association for the Advancement of Science.

The commission of the British association was Hale's last chance to rectify for posterity the mistakes of his youth. Unable to take to the field because of his age, he instead utilized Boas as a conduit for his quest. As Gruber points out, "it is difficult to avoid the conclusion that Hale . . . saw the activities of the younger man as an extension of his own work which had begun, but was never finished, a half-century earlier."[71]

Hale, as we have seen, had relegated the Pacific Northwest Indians and their respective cultures to the lowest rungs on the ethnological ladder in *Ethnography and Philology*. From this perspective, he had amassed a seemingly objective collection of philological data on the myriad language groups and dialects of the region. Forty years later, eminent anthropologists such as Friedrich Müller considered this work "still the best authority on the Oregon tribes."[72] Now, in his seventy-first year, Hale expressed his regret to Boas:

> I do not know whether you have seen my account of the Oregon tribes, written more than forty years ago. You will find it in Vol. 7 [*sic*] of the U. S. Exploring Expedition under Wilkes—the volume of Ethnography and Philology. . . . You will find many deficiencies, as I had but about three months [Hale actually spent far more time there] for a large territory of whose ethnology hardly anything was known. I had to travel hundreds of miles through a wild country, with no companions but Indians and half-breeds, and often very few interpreters. I gave my attention chiefly to the languages, and less to customs, traditions, arts, and physical traits than I should now. My impression is that I rated the character of these Indians too low. I was then a young man of twenty-four, fresh from College, and ethnological science was far behind the present stage.[73]

Such an admission represented not a sudden revelation but rather a half-century of rumination and reflection upon his experiences as a member of the Wilkes Expedition. Over the course of years, Hale's perspectives on culture, formulated outside of the mainstream of anthropological thought in the mid- to late nineteenth century, had become more relativistic. The science of anthropology, conversely, had opted for the hierarchical classificatory systems first manifested in a scientifically "objective" manner by the American school. Darwin's revelations in 1859 and their subsequent adaptation by "social Darwinists" added further scientific substantiation of the belief in the successful struggle of "superior, civilized" cultures over the "inferior, savage" way of life. While Hale no doubt worried that his earlier, flawed work concerning the Indians of the Pacific Northwest would be the only extant record for the ages, there remained an even more dreaded fear: the possibility that a Lewis Henry Morgan, for example, would choose to write the final chapter on the culture of the Pacific Northwest Indians. Thus it was that Hale browbeat and pushed Boas, not only to complete the work but to do it right.

The German was fully equal to this task, succeeding beyond Hale's expectations. It was Boas's method, now famous, to access native folklore, not only for recapturing linguistic data (as Hale had so skillfully done fifty years earlier in Polynesia) but also as a key to unlock the history, social organization, and belief systems of the various Pacific Northwest tribes. This was the step Hale was unable to take in his time. And so it was, in a sense, that the concluding volume of the United States Exploring Expedition came to be written by Franz Boas, the man who ushered in a new era in the study of humankind—and who in turn served as the instrument for an old man who died in 1894, knowing that the work of the long voyage had been satisfactorily completed at last.

NOTES

Introduction

1. Sahlins, *Islands of History*; Obeyesekere, *Apotheosis of Captain Cook*; Said, *Orientalism*; Geertz, *Interpretation of Cultures*; Rosaldo, *Culture and Truth*; and Clifford, *Predicament of Culture.*
2. Winkler, "Anthropologists Urged."
3. Geertz, *Interpretation of Cultures.*
4. Many scholars preferred limiting the stages to four, omitting "enlightened"; nineteenth-century American texts, however, included this category, perhaps to further separate the new nation from their ancestors.
5. Carter, ed., *Surveying the Record.*
6. I pulled the following seven textbooks from the stacks at San Diego State University Library with publishing dates ranging from 1964 to 1998: Barnouw, *Ethnology: An Introduction to Anthropology* (1982); Haviland, *Anthropology* (1974); Kottak, *Anthropology: The Exploration of Human Diversity* (1974); Bidney, *Theoretical Anthropology* (1964); Beals and Hoijer, *Introduction to Anthropology* (1971); Harris, *Culture, People, Nature: An Introduction to General Anthropology* (1975); and Bennett, *Classic Anthropology* (1998).
7. See H. N. Smith, *Virgin Land*; Bieder, *Science Encounters the Indian*; and Drinnon, *Facing West.*
8. Takaki, *A Different Mirror*, 83. See also Fredrickson, *Inner Civil War*, and Ward, *Andrew Jackson.*
9. For a discussion of the tensions of the Jacksonian period, see Sellers, *Market Revolution*; Saxton, *Rise and Fall of the White Republic*; Wilentz, *Chants Democratic*; Johnson, *Shopkeeper's Millennium*; and T. L. Smith, *Revivalism and Social Reform.*
10. For the impact of science upon religion in early-nineteenth-century America, see Hovencamp, *Science and Religion*; Boller, *American Thought*; and Greene, *Death of Adam.* James Ussher was a seventeenth-century Anglican archbishop and biblical scholar who, by tracing the genealogy of the Pentateuch, determined the date of creation at 4004 B.C.
11. Freehling, *Prelude to Civil War*, 359–60. See also Cooper, *The South*, and Steward, *Holy Warriors.*
12. Morgan, *American Slavery*, 327–28, 386–87.
13. For a fuller discussion of Morton and the American school, see Stanton, *Leopard's Spots*, and Gould, *Mismeasure of Man.*

14. Smedley, *Race in North America*, and Daniels, *American Science*.
15. See Porter, *The Eagle's Nest*. By the nineteenth century the study of plants had been uprooted from the exclusive domain of the gentleman gardener-botanist and transplanted in the drawing rooms and laboratories of scientific societies and colleges.
16. Stanton, *Leopard's Spots*, 10.
17. Keeping with American naval tradition, black sailors were allowed to join the U.S. navy during this period. A small, undetermined number were on board during the expedition.

1. *Motivations and Preparation*

1. Takaki, *Iron Cages*, 284.
2. Kazar, "United States Navy," and Stanton, *Great United States*.
3. Smith, *Virgin Land*; Ward, *Andrew Jackson*.
4. Viola and Margolis, eds., *Magnificent Voyagers*, 9; Stanton, *Great United States*, 8.
5. John Cleves Symmes (Jr.) to Elisha Kent Kane (1851?), Kane Papers.
6. Henderson, *Hidden Coasts*, 30.
7. Henderson, *Hidden Coasts*, 31.
8. Goetzmann, *New Lands, New Men*, 261–64.
9. Reynolds, *Address*, 15, 72.
10. *Public Statutes at Large of the United States of America*, 5:29.
11. Thomas ap Catesby Jones to Mahlon Dickerson, 9 September 1836, Exploring Expedition Records, roll 1.
12. Navy Department General Order, 22 June 1838, Cruises and Voyages.
13. Jones to Dickerson, 30 June 1836, Exploring Expedition Records, roll 1.
14. Dickerson to Jones, n.d., Exploring Expedition Records, roll 2.
15. Davis, *Seventy-Five Years*, 97–98.
16. Pierre Du Ponceau (1760–1844) was a French-born lawyer and philologist who specialized in the study of North American Indian languages. He was elected president of the American Philosophical Society in 1828.
17. Committee of the American Philosophical Society to Mahlon Dickerson, 17 October 1836, Papers, American Philosophical Society (APS), Philadelphia.
18. The Swiss-born Albert Gallatin (1761–1849), in addition to his distinguished service as secretary of the treasury under Thomas Jefferson, is considered "the father of American ethnology" for his pioneering study of American Indian languages. He founded the American Ethnological Society in 1842. Committee to Dickerson, 17 October 1836.
19. Committee to Dickerson.
20. Raynell Coates to Mahlon Dickerson, 26 September 1836, Exploring Expedition Records, roll 1.
21. Sherlock Gregory to the Department of the Navy, 18 November 1838, Exploring Expedition Records, roll 5. Unfortunately, I have not been able to uncover any additional biographical information on Gregory.
22. Gregory to Navy Department.
23. "Hear the word of the Lord, O ye nations, and declare it in the isles afar off, and say, He that scattered Israel will gather him, and keep him, as a shepherd doth his flock."
24. Gregory to Navy Department.

25.   The expedition library contained many books relating to the ethnology and philology of the Pacific Islands. The majority were narratives of prior expeditions, such as those of Cook, Bligh, Kotzebue, Flinders, and Vancouver. Humboldt's works were also brought along. Two interesting inclusions were Fraser's *Tour to the Himalaya Mountains* and Franklin's two expeditions in search of the northwest passage. Missionary accounts, such as William Ellis's *Polynesian Researches*, provided valuable grammars and lexicons.

26.   Stanton, *Great United States*, 53.

27.   For an excellent description of the battle between philologist Albert Gallatin and the American school, see Horsman, *Race and Manifest Destiny*.

28.   Dutch Anatomist Pieter Camper (1722–1789) attempted to classify man by his "facial an-gle," the interior angle that the face makes with a horizontal plane. Belgian astronomer Quételet (1796–1874) searched for the "average man," insisting upon quantitative anal-ysis and statistical method. Swedish anatomist Anders Retzius (1796–1860) introduced the "cephalic index"—the ratio of the length to the width of the head—to the portfolio of the nineteenth-century anthropologist.

29.   Blumenbach (1752–1840) was a German physiologist, comparative anatomist, and collector of skulls whose measurements of crania led him to separate humankind into five races—Caucasian, Mongolian, Malayan, Ethiopian, and American.

30.   While European physicians in the eighteenth and nineteenth centuries were interested in detecting skeletal differences between the accepted races of humankind, they focused their comparative studies on the differences between male and female skeletons and skulls. According to historian Londa Schiebinger, this preoccupation reflected a desire by scientists to maintain male hegemony and power by "objectifying" and "proving" female inferiority that existed in European society. As we shall see, American scientists and physicians sought similar fixed "objective" determinants to buttress American racial hegemony. In both societies it was a "closed system." Since white males had "proven" that women and nonwhites were physically incapable of scientific reasoning, it was deemed unnecessary to allow the latter groups access to any means of "scientific" rebuttal. Schiebinger, "Skeletons in the Closet," 42, 71–72.

31.   "Prospectus of a Course of Sixteen Lectures on Phrenology to be Delivered by Mr. George Combe of Edinburgh," 1838, Morton Papers, APS.

32.   William Ruschenberger (1807–1895) was a naval surgeon, naturalist, and president of the Academy of Natural Sciences (1870–1882) who published accounts of two of his naval voyages in the 1830s. Ruschenberger to Samuel Morton, 3 March 1833, Morton Papers, APS.

33.   Ruschenberger to Morton, 15 February 1836.

34.   Samuel George Morton, Lecture No. 4, "North American Indians," Morton Papers, The Library Company (TLC).

35.   Zina Pitcher to Samuel Morton, 4 March 1834, Morton Papers, APS. Zina Pitcher (1797–1872) was yet another physician-naturalist who supplied information about the flora, fauna, and American Indians of the Great Lakes to Morton, Asa Gray, John Torrey, and Henry Schoolcraft, among others.

36.   William Wood to Daniel Drake, 28 September 1833, Morton Papers, APS.

37.   William Burrough to Samuel Morton, 13 March 1835, Morton Papers, APS.

38.   William Bird Powell to Samuel Morton, 12 August 1839, Morton Papers, APS. Powell

(1799–1866), a southern "eclectic" physician and scientist, also collected and studied human skulls.

39. Samuel Morton to John Townsend, 3 March 1836, Scientific Letters, APS.
40. Townsend to Morton, 20 September 1835, Morton Papers, APS. Townsend had to endure other trials in his pursuit of science in the American wilderness. Besides encountering Indians unwilling to contribute their "data" to the American school, Townsend found his own employees no more enlightened. He described the loss of several reptile specimens:

> I had them in a large gallon bottle of whiskey, and almost immediately after we arrived here some of the men of the party, in a drunken frolick, got possession of my bottle and pledged their companion, in the decanted liquor. . . . I would have given the beasts 20 galls. of liquor if they would have spared my reptiles, but it is useless to lament it. The sneaking dogs did not tell me of it for some weeks afterwards, so that when I looked at the bottles, the lizards, salamanders, and serpents had united into a filthy mass that I never could make anything of and I was compelled to toss the whole into the river.

41. Charles Pickering to Samuel Morton, 16 July 1836, Morton Papers, APS.
42. Joseph Couthouy to Samuel Morton, 27 May 1837, Morton Papers, APS.
43. Asa Gray, "Memorial." Reprinted in a collection of eulogies preceding Pickering's monumental posthumous work, *The Chronological History of Plants*.
44. Pickering's father, Timothy Jr., was a Harvard graduate who died in 1807. Timothy Sr., a Revolutionary War officer who had served in Washington's cabinet, brought the two-year-old Charles and his mother Lurena Cole Pickering to his farm in Wenham, Massachusetts. There Charles spent his boyhood.
45. From a collection of eulogies preceding Pickering's *Chronological History of Plants*.
46. John Pickering to Mahlon Dickerson, 1 June 1838, Cruises and Voyages.
47. Henry Patterson to Mahlon Dickerson, 2 September 1837, Exploring Expedition Records, roll 3.
48. List of Supplies, n.d., Exploring Expedition Records, roll 3.
49. Henderson, *Hidden Coasts*, 34–38; Viola and Margolis, *Magnificent Voyagers*, 189–95.
50. Jaffe, *Stormy Petrel*, 8–9.
51. J. R. Poinsett to J. K. Paulding, 29 July 1838, Cruises and Voyages.
52. John Pickering to J. R. Poinsett, 1 June 1838, Cruises and Voyages.
53. Pickering to Poinsett, 1 June 1838.
54. Josiah Gibbs to J. R. Poinsett, 25 May 1838, Cruises and Voyages.
55. Gibbs to Poinsett, 25 May 1838.
56. Fred C. Sawyer, introduction to Hale's *Ethnography and Philology*.
57. Horatio Hale to Mahlon Dickerson, 16 July 1837, Exploring Expedition Records, roll 2.
58. Wilkes, *Narrative*, 1:xxii–xxiii; Wilkes, Journal, 31 August 1838, Exploring Expedition Records, roll 5.
59. Wilkes, *Narrative*, 1:367–68.
60. List of Trades Items Compiled by Commander Jones, 11 July 1835, Exploring Expedition Records, roll 4.
61. Wilkes, *Narrative*, 1:xxviii.

2. Around the Horn

1. Stuart, Journal, November 1838.
2. Wilkes, *Narrative*, 1:54.
3. Wilkes, *Narrative*, 1:55.
4. Wilkes, *Narrative*, 1:57.
5. Wilkes, *Narrative*, 1:64.
6. Stuart, Journal, December 1838.
7. Anonymous, Journal, 25 December 1838.
8. Erskine, *Twenty Years*, 38.
9. Colvocoresses, *Four Years*, 31.
10. Pickering, *Races of Man*, 183.
11. Wilkes, *Narrative*, 1:45.
12. *Peoples of the Earth*, 7:110.
13. *Peoples*, 7:121–22.
14. The guanaco is the largest animal in Patagonia and a close relative to the Peruvian llama. It is described as possessing "the neigh of a horse, the wool of a sheep, the neck of a camel, the feet of a deer, and the swiftness of the devil." *Peoples*, 7:111.
15. Wilkes, *Narrative*, 1:114.
16. Anonymous, Journal, 22 January 1839.
17. Wilkes, *Narrative*, 1:115.
18. Gilchrist, Journal, 21 January 1839.
19. Wilkes, *Narrative*, 1:114–15.
20. Anonymous, Journal, 22 January 1839.
21. Erskine, *Twenty Years*, 50–51.
22. Sanford, Journal, n.d.
23. Wilkes, *Narrative*, 1:121.
24. Anonymous, Journal, n.d.
25. Erskine, *Twenty Years*, 44.
26. Wilkes, *Narrative*, 1:122; Clark, *Lights and Shadows*, 47.
27. Emmons, Journal, 25 February 1839.
28. James Dana to Asa Gray, 6 May 1839, Gray Papers.
29. Long, Journal, 31 January 1839.
30. Dana to Gray, 6 May 1839.
31. Dana to Gray, 6 May 1839.
32. Dana to Gray, 6 May 1839.
33. Clark, *Lights and Shadows*, 44.
34. Wilkes, *Narrative*, 1:125.
35. Dana to Gray, 6 May 1839.
36. Wilkes, *Narrative*, 1:125.
37. Wilkes, *Narrative*, 1:125.
38. Clark, *Lights and Shadows*, 49.
39. Stanton, *Great United States*, 105.
40. Wilkes, *Narrative*, 1:128.
41. Wilkes, *Narrative*, 1:126–27.

42. Wilkes, *Narrative*, 1:125; Anonymous, Journal, February 1839; Clark, *Lights and Shadows*, 45.
43. Wilkes, *Narrative*, 1:122.
44. William Reynolds, Journal, quoted in Stanton, *Great United States*, 107.
45. Exploring Expedition Collection, Smithsonian Institution.
46. Wilkes, *Narrative*, 1:122.
47. Pickering, Journal, 15 April 1839.
48. Pickering, *Races of Man*, 20.
49. George Combe to Samuel George Morton, 28 February 1840, Morton Papers, APS.
50. Pickering, Journal, 25 May 1839.
51. Pickering, Journal, 14 May 1839.
52. Stanton, *Great United States*, 112.
53. Pickering, Journal, 14 May 1839.
54. Wilkes, *Narrative*, 1:245.
55. Pickering, Journal, 27 May 1839.
56. Pickering, Journal, 29 June 1839; Wilkes, *Narrative*, 1:280–81; Underwood, Journal, 28 June 1839.
57. Underwood, Journal, 28 June 1839.
58. Poesch, ed., *Peale and His Journals*, 148.
59. Poesch, *Peale and His Journals*, 148.

3. Across the Pacific

1. Erskine, *Twenty Years*, 67; Wilkes, *Narrative*, 1:311.
2. The name of these groups of islands was changed from Paumotu to Tuamotu in 1852, following protests by delegates from the Dangerous and Disappointment Islands that Paumotu is Tahitian for "conquered islands."
3. Wilkes, *Narrative*, 1:309.
4. Wilkes, *Narrative*, 1:308–9.
5. Report Number 47, 15 September 1839, Cruises and Voyages.
6. Pickering, *Races of Man*, 54.
7. Pickering, Journal, 14 August 1839.
8. Pickering, Journal, 14 August 1839.
9. Erskine, *Twenty Years*, 67.
10. For a further discussion of the sociological basis of such attitudes, see Omi and Winant, *Racial Formation*.
11. Wilkes, *Narrative*, 1:313.
12. Emmons, Journal, 14 April 1839.
13. Wilkes, *Narrative*, 1:314.
14. Wilkes, *Narrative*, 1:314.
15. Alden, Journal, 18 August 1839.
16. Wilkes, *Narrative*, 1:315.
17. Poesch, *Peale and His Journals*, 151.
18. Poesch, *Peale and His Journals*, 151.
19. Stuart, Journal, 26 August 1839.
20. Wilkes, *Narrative*, 1:319; Pickering, Journal, 25 August 1839.

21. Wilkes, *Narrative*, 1:319.
22. Tapa is a form of cloth formed by laboriously pounding strips of bark from the paper mulberry tree (*Broussonetia papyrifeira*) for hours on end.
23. Poesch, *Peale and His Journals*, 152.
24. Stuart, Journal, 26 August 1839.
25. Poesch, *Peale and His Journals*, 152.
26. Pickering, Journal, 26 August 1839; Pickering, *Races of Man*, 57.
27. Pickering, Journal, 26 August 1839.
28. Wilkes, *Narrative*, 1:322.
29. Wilkes, *Narrative*, 1:324.
30. Wilkes, *Narrative*, 1:324.
31. Wilkes, *Narrative*, 1:324.
32. Sinclair, Journal, 25 August 1839.
33. Pickering, *Races of Man*, 58.
34. Pickering, *Races of Man*, 61.
35. Wilkes, *Narrative*, 1:328.
36. Pickering, *Races of Man*, 61.
37. Wilkes, *Narrative*, 1:330.
38. Wilkes, *Narrative*, 1:330.
39. Pickering, Journal, 10 September 1839.
40. Hale, *Ethnography*, 9. It is interesting that at the same time the expedition was visiting the Tahitians and Samoans, Morton was publishing his *Crania Americana*, which among other things "proved" the superior cranial capacity of whites. Of the over one thousand skulls in his collection, however, only three were listed as "Polynesian." In fact, they were from New Zealand—one supposedly being that of a elderly woman. Morton, *Crania Americana*; Morton, *Catalogue of Skulls*.
41. Pickering, Journal, 10 September 1839.
42. Wilkes, *Narrative*, 2:10.
43. Wilkes, *Narrative*, 2:8.
44. Wilkes, *Narrative*, 2:210.
45. Erskine, *Twenty Years*, 76.
46. Wilkes, *Narrative*, 2:13; Clark, *Light and Shadows*, 70.
47. Emmons, Journal, 29 September 1839.
48. Gilchrist, Journal, 28 September 1839. Continuing, he pinpointed what he felt the real problem was: "There is no Physician in the Islands and the treatment of the sick is in the hands of the missionaries—It had much better be in the hands of the natives."
49. Wilkes, *Narrative*, 2:12–13.
50. Pickering, Journal, 21 September 1839.
51. Henry Eld, Journal, quoted in Stanton, *Great United States*, 125.
52. Erskine, *Twenty Years*, 71.
53. Erskine, *Twenty Years*, 74.
54. Pickering, Journal, 21 September 1839; Wilkes, *Narrative*, 2:23.
55. Stuart, Journal, 12 September 1839.
56. Pickering, Journal, 11 September 1839.
57. Anonymous, Journal, 14 September 1839.

58. Pickering, Journal, 11 September 1839.

59. Pickering, *Races of Man*, 69.

60. Pickering, Journal, 17 September 1839.

61. Pickering, Journal, 17 September 1839.

62. Pickering, Journal, 17 September 1839.

63. Pickering, Journal, 17 September 1839.

64. Pickering, Journal, 17 September 1839.

65. Wilkes, *Narrative*, 2:56.

66. Wilkes, *Narrative*, 2:57.

67. Wilkes, *Narrative*, 2:57.

68. Pickering, Journal, 26 September 1839.

69. Wilkes, *Narrative*, 2:55.

70. It is difficult to determine the precise number of black sailors assigned to the voyage. The roll of sailors, officers, and scientists who served on the expedition is given in volume 1 of the *Narrative*. Information on race, however, must be gleaned from journal accounts. The few references most often regarded comparisons of their skin color to that of the natives. An exception was when Assistant Surgeon Charles Guillou referred to an ordinary seaman named John Dean. According to Guillou, Dean "belonged in the sloop-of-war *Vincennes*, but Capt. Wilkes left him behind in Astoria [Oregon]." Dean's name, however, does not appear on any ship's roster. Hence blacks, though part of the expedition, were nearly invisible. Indians, on the other hand, while not physically present in the South Pacific, were never far from the thoughts of the expedition members.

71. Admiral Matthew Perry treated Japanese dignitaries to a similar performance, with similar results, during his expedition to open Japan to American influence in the early 1850s.

72. Pickering, Journal, 7 October 1839.

73. Erskine, *Twenty Years*, 85.

74. Stuart, Journal, October 1839.

75. Wilkes, *Narrative*, 2:93, 124.

76. Wilkes, *Narrative*, 2:81.

77. Wilkes, *Narrative*, 2:81.

78. Sinclair, Journal, 31 October 1839.

79. Stanton, *Great United States*, 134, 136.

80. Pickering, Journal, 8 October 1839.

81. Wilkes, *Narrative*, 2:135–37; Erskine, *Twenty Years*, 84.

82. Poesch, *Peale and His Journals*, 161.

83. Wilkes, *Narrative*, 2:80.

84. Pickering, Journal, 10 November 1839.

85. Pickering, Journal, 23 October 1839.

86. Pickering, Journal, 1 November 1839; Pickering, *Races of Man*, 77.

87. Poesch, *Peale and His Journals*, 162.

88. Poesch, *Peale and His Journals*, 162.

89. Pickering, Journal, 22 October 1839.

90. Wilkes, *Narrative*, 2:103.

91. Wilkes, *Narrative*, 2:89.

92. The French explorer Jules Dumont D'Urville, in command of *Astrolabe* and *Zelee*, had been trying for two years to force his way through the thick southern polar ice to locate the magnetic South Pole. The Englishman James Ross, a veteran of polar exploration, hoped to edge out Wilkes as well.

93. Pickering, Journal, 30 November 1839.

94. Wilkes, *Narrative*, 2:163.

95. Pickering, Journal, 3 December 1839.

96. Erskine, *Twenty Years*, 96–97.

97. Clark, *Lights and Shadows*, 98; Erskine, *Twenty Years*, 97.

98. Clark, *Lights and Shadows*, 98.

99. Wilkes, *Narrative*, 2:186.

100. Pickering, Journal, 10 December 1839. This point is very significant. In an era before the advent of photography, artists played a crucial role in creating a popular image of a people, particularly those of an "exotic" or unknown nature. Fortunately, the American expedition included three excellent artists: Titian Peale, Joseph Drayton, and especially Alfred Agate. Dana, in a letter to Asa Gray, assured his fellow scientist that Agate was compiling "an admirable series of portraits—Unlike those of the French voyages, they may be trusted not only as characteristic, but as accurate likenesses of the *individuals*." Dana to Gray, 15 June 1840, Gray Papers.

101. Pickering, Journal, 10 December 1839.

102. Pickering, *Races of Man*, 147; Pickering, Journal, 10 December 1839.

103. Pickering to Morton, 8 August 1840, Morton Papers, APS.

104. Pickering, Journal, 10 December 1839; Wilkes, *Narrative*, 2:262.

105. Pickering, Journal, 10 December 1839.

106. Pickering, *Races of Man*, 140.

107. Pickering, Journal, 10 December 1839; Pickering, *Races of Man*, 140.

108. Conjectures such as these were common among scientists. A scientific puzzle of similar ilk contemporaneous with the Wilkes Expedition concerned the origins of the massive mounds of Cahokia near St. Louis, Missouri. Samuel Morton and others felt it imperative to discover the architects of these mounds; up to that time few believed that Indians could have completed such works, preferring to attribute them to Welshmen or the Ten Lost Tribes of Israel. See Bieder, *Science Encounters the Indian*, 104–20.

109. Hale, *Ethnography*, 116.

110. Anonymous, Journal, 16 December 1839.

111. Hale, *Ethnography*, 108. A common misconception of nineteenth-century science was to equate minimalist technology with a simple social structure. For example, marriage is a complex and complicated institution for Aborigines, who consider European modes of matrimony little more than indiscriminate and animal-like mating. Hale certainly could not have comprehended the Aboriginal concept of time. In addition to the "here and now," the Aborigines acknowledged an open-ended parallel dimension that translated to "dreamtime," a timeless original world that was revisited while asleep.

112. Wilkes, *Narrative*, 2:186.

113. Hale, *Ethnography*, 109.

114. Hale, *Ethnography*, 109; Wilkes, *Narrative*, 2:187.

115. Hale, *Ethnography*, 109.

116. Wilkes, *Narrative*, 2:184.

117. Pickering, Journal, 10 December 1839.

118. Pickering to Morton, 8 August 1840, Morton Papers, APS.

119. Pickering, Journal, 3 December 1839.

120. Wilkes, *Narrative*, 2:276.

121. Pickering, Journal, March 1840.

122. Pickering, Journal, March 1840; Clark, *Lights and Shadows*, 128.

123. Clark, *Lights and Shadows*, 127–29.

124. Hale, *Ethnography*, 34.

125. Wilkes, *Narrative*, 2:397.

126. Wilkes, *Narrative*, 2:402.

127. Anonymous, Journal, 30 March 1840.

128. Titian Ramsay Peale to John Kane, 5 April 1840, Papers, APS.

129. Wilkes, *Narrative*, 2:375–76.

130. Pickering, *Races of Man*, 80.

131. Wilkes, *Narrative*, 2:380. Wilkes may have had other reasons in mind for opposing annexation besides bemoaning the plight of the Maori. American merchants stood to suffer from British regulation and, according to the captain, were now prohibited from owning land. Wilkes's attitudes toward the British had also deteriorated as a result of his competition with James Ross for the honor of discovering the Antarctic land mass. Stanton, *Great United States*.

132. At least the Maori were spared the indignity of a "Trail of Tears." The British were denied this option, New Zealand being an island.

133. Wilkes, *Narrative*, 2:380–81.

134. Wilkes, *Narrative*, 2:380–81.

135. The results of Wilkes's attempt to be the first discoverer of land in Antarctica were and are controversial. See Stanton's work and Joyce, "James Alden."

136. Erskine, *Twenty Years*, 126–27.

137. Erskine, *Twenty Years*, 127.

138. Clark, *Lights and Shadows*, 124.

139. Erskine, *Twenty Years*, 137.

140. Wilkes, *Narrative*, 2:399–400.

141. Titian Peale to Franklin Peale, April 1840, Peale-Sellers Papers, APS.

142. It was among these waters that Captain Bligh was cast adrift in a dinghy following the mutiny on the HMS *Bounty*.

143. Wilkes, *Narrative*, 3:10. Tongans, like all other people, were no strangers to warfare. What set this confrontation apart was the open assault on traditional Tongan culture encouraged by the missionaries.

144. Among them was Taufa'ahau, also known as King George, a dignified and athletic-looking ruler of two neighboring islands who was destined to unite all of Tonga within five years of the expedition's visit.

145. Sinclair, Journal, April 1840.

146. Quoted in Stanton, *Great United States*, 187.

147. Anonymous, Journal, 2 May 1840.

148. Charles Wilkes to James Paulding, 4 May 1840, Exploring Expedition Records, roll 6.
149. Pickering, Journal, 24 April 1840.
150. Wilkes to Paulding, 4 May 1840.
151. Quoted in Stanton, *Great United States*, 187.
152. Pickering, Journal, 24 April 1840.
153. Wilkes, *Narrative*, 3:12; Pickering, Journal, 24 April 1840.
154. The construction of which they had learned from the Fijians.
155. Pickering, Journal, 24 April 1840.
156. Pickering, *Races of Man*, 86.
157. Wilkes, *Narrative*, 3:20.
158. Wilkes, *Narrative*, 3:20; Dyes, Journal, 28 April 1840.
159. Alden, Journal, 26 April 1840.
160. Pickering, Journal, 26 April 1840.
161. Pickering, Journal, 25 April 1840.
162. Pickering, Journal, 25 April 1840.

4. The World of the Feejee

1. Charles Wilkes to Navy Department, n.d., Area Files, A-10.
2. According to Pickering, merchants were unable to secure insurance for a voyage to these "cannibal islands." Pickering, Journal, 7 May 1840.
3. Pickering, *Races of Man*, 168.
4. Pickering, Journal, 8 May 1840.
5. Pickering, *Races of Man*, 146.
6. Emmons, Journal, 23 June 1840. Such observations were quite consistent with observations and attitudes expressed by British and French settlers and government officials when the Fiji Islands were brought under the late-nineteenth-century European colonial umbrella. Sir Arthur Hamilton Gordon, first British governor of the islands, noted that the Fijians, referred to as "damn niggers . . . are not niggers at all, but of a warm light bronze colour." A German visitor in the 1870s noted the common perception of the Fijians as "a set of lazy niggers." Author Nicholas Thomas has stated that "nigger" was the "standard term among settlers and some traders." Thomas, *Entangled Objects*, 164.
7. Hale, *Ethnography*, 49.
8. Sinclair, Journal, 15 June 1840.
9. Pickering to Morton, 7 August 1840, Morton Papers, APS.
10. Anonymous, Journal, June 1840.
11. Anonymous, Journal, June 1840.
12. Wilkes, *Narrative*, 3:352–53.
13. Dyes, Journal, May 1840.
14. Pickering, *Races of Man*, 150.
15. Pickering, *Races of Man*, 150.
16. Wilkes, *Narrative*, 3:247.
17. Poesch, *Peale and His Journals*, 170.
18. Erskine, *Twenty Years*, 156–57.
19. Sinclair, Journal, August 1840.

20. Wilkes, *Narrative*, 3:350.
21. Pickering, Journal, 13 May 1840.
22. Dana to Gray, 15 June 1840, Gray Papers.
23. Pickering, Journal, 17 June 1840.
24. Dana to Gray, 15 June 1840.
25. Wilkes, *Narrative*, 3:48–49.
26. Anonymous letter, n.d., Area Files, A-10; Sinclair, Journal, 15 June 1840.
27. Anonymous letter, n.d.
28. According to George Colvocoresses, Tanoa remained silent "for a considerable time" after the proceedings had begun. Eventually the king communicated through an interpreter that he was puzzled at Wilkes's breach of diplomatic etiquette, pointing out that the commander had not fired an appropriate salute upon his boarding *Vincennes*. Colvocoresses, *Four Years*, 140.
29. Wilkes, *Narrative*, 3:56–57.
30. Wilkes, *Narrative*, 3:57.
31. Thomas, *Entangled Objects*, 54–63, 190.
32. *Peoples*, 8:84–93.
33. *Peoples*, 8:84–93.
34. Pickering, Journal, 13 May 1840.
35. Pickering, Journal, 20 May 1840.
36. Wilkes, *Narrative*, 3:118.
37. Wilkes, *Narrative*, 3:128.
38. Erskine, *Twenty Years*, 161; Wilkes, *Narrative*, 3:130.
39. Stuart, Journal, 18 May 1840.
40. Pickering, *Races of Man*, 157.
41. Stanton, *Great United States*, 200.
42. Pickering, Journal, 22 May 1840.
43. Pickering, Journal, 22 May 1840.
44. Quoted in Stanton, *Great United States*, 200.
45. Dana to Gray, 15 June 1840, Gray Papers.
46. The Fijian proved particularly helpful in piloting his captors through the treacherous reefs and shoals of his islands.
47. Stuart, Journal, 23 June 1840.
48. Pickering, Journal, 3 July 1840.
49. Pickering, Journal, 3 July 1840.
50. Pickering, Journal, 3 July 1840; Wilkes, *Narrative*, 3:234.
51. Wilkes, *Narrative*, 3:234; Stuart, Journal, 3 July 1840.
52. Dyes, Journal, 3 July 1840.
53. Stuart, Journal, 3 July 1840.
54. Wilkes to Navy Department, n.d., Area Files; Pickering, Journal, 3 July 1840.
55. Stuart, Journal, n.d.
56. Pickering, Journal, 3 July 1840; Wilkes, *Narrative*, 3:234.
57. Pickering, Journal, 3 July 1840.
58. Sinclair, Journal, August 1840. For a recent analysis of Fijian cannibalism, see Sahlins, "Raw Women, Cooked Men."
59. Pickering, Journal, 12 July 1840.

60. Wilkes, *Narrative*, 3:241.

61. Wilkes, *Narrative*, 3:242.

62. Clark, *Lights and Shadows*, 144.

63. Anonymous, Journal, 13 July 1840; Clark, *Lights and Shadows*, 145.

64. Anonymous, Journal, 13 July 1840.

65. Stuart, Journal, 13 July 1840.

66. Anonymous letter, n.d., Area Files.

67. Wilkes, *Narrative*, 3:244.

68. Anonymous letter, n.d.

69. Dana to Gray, 15 June 1840, Gray Papers.

70. Wilkes, *Narrative*, 3:126.

71. Emmons, Journal, 15 May 1840.

72. Wilkes, *Narrative*, 3:136.

73. Wilkes, *Narrative*, 3:216.

74. While surveying a harbor or shoreline could ostensibly be considered a "neutral" or "scientific" activity on the part of the expedition, in fact such work was often used by ships' captains as a way of establishing their presence in foreign waters. See Joyce, "James Alden." In 1853 Admiral Perry sent out boats to survey Tokyo Bay to send just such a message to Japanese authorities who had forbidden him to remain in the harbor. Wiley, *Yankees in the Land of the Gods*. For an interesting analysis of the differing cultural connotations of placing foreign staffs on native soil, see Sahlins's description of the Maori-English wars of the 1840s in *Islands of History*.

75. Pickering, Journal, 2 August 1840.

76. Clark, *Lights and Shadows*, 149; Anonymous, Journal, 30 July 1840.

77. Wilkes, *Narrative*, 3:426.

78. Wilkes, *Narrative*, 3:426.

79. Colvocoresses, *Four Years*, 156.

80. Wilkes, *Narrative*, 3:427.

81. Wilkes, *Narrative*, 3:427.

82. Wilkes, *Narrative*, 3:428.

83. Wilkes, *Narrative*, 3:428.

84. Wilkes, *Narrative*, 3:428.

85. Wilkes, *Narrative*, 3:269.

86. Clark, *Lights and Shadows*, 156.

87. Colvocoresses, *Four Years*, 158.

88. Briscoe, Journal, 27 July 1840.

89. Briscoe, Journal, 27 July 1840; Anonymous, Journal, 31 July 1840. Pickering later questioned persons living among the Fijians about the incident, who told him that had the men on shore given up their weapons and trade goods, they would have been allowed to depart safely. Apparently the difficulties Underwood had incurred in trading arose from the fact that the Fijians saw no need to barter for things that, as a result of the grounded boat, already belonged to them. Pickering, Journal, 2 August 1840.

90. Anonymous, Journal, 31 July 1840.

91. Wilkes, *Narrative*, 3:266.

92. Sinclair, Journal, 27 July 1840. All during the defense of their town, the Fijians impressed the expedition with their bravery in resisting the attack. Wilkes, Sinclair, and others

were amazed at the seeming ability of the natives to actually dodge musket balls fired at them from close range, "falling flat on the ground at the flash of the gun powder."

93. Anonymous, Journal, 31 July 1840.

94. Dyes, Journal, 27 July 1840; Anonymous, Journal, 31 July 1840.

95. Wilkes, *Narrative*, 3:295–96.

96. Sinclair, Journal, 27 July 1840.

97. Wilkes, upon his return to the United States, was brought before a naval court martial board on various charges, among them the use of excessive force during the revenge upon Malolo. He was acquitted of these charges.

98. Stuart, Journal, 30 July, 1 August 1840; Wilkes, *Narrative*, 3:299.

99. Clark, *Lights and Shadows*, 166.

100. Pickering, Journal, 8 August 1840.

101. Charles Wilkes to Navy Department, 11 August 1840, Exploring Expedition Records, roll 6.

102. Wilkes, *Narrative*, 3:363.

103. Wilkes, *Narrative*, 3:363; Wilkes to Navy Department, 11 August 1840.

104. Hale, *Ethnography*, 45.

105. Hale, *Ethnography*, 45.

106. Hale, *Ethnography*, 50.

107. Hale, *Ethnography*, 50.

108. Hale, *Ethnography*, 51.

109. Hale, *Ethnography*, 50.

110. Hale, *Ethnography*, 50.

111. Pickering to Morton, 7 August 1840, Morton Papers, APS.

112. Pickering to Morton, 8 August 1840.

113. Pickering to Morton, 8 August 1840.

114. Pickering to Morton, 8 August 1840.

115. Pickering to Morton, 8 August 1840.

116. Pickering to Morton, 8 August 1840.

117. Pickering to Morton, 8 August 1840.

118. Pickering to Morton, 8 August 1840.

119. Pickering's eight races were (1) Mongol or the Malay, (2) Egyptian, (3) African Negro, (4) "Australian or ———," (5) White, (6) Papuan, Oriental, or Asiatic Negro, (7) Andaman or Tamany, and (8) Ethiopian.

120. Pickering to Morton, 8 August 1840.

121. Pickering, *Races of Man*, 165.

122. Dana to Gray, 15 June 1840, Gray Papers.

123. Pickering, *Races of Man*, 165.

124. Wilkes, *Narrative*, 3:316.

5. Return to America

1. Not, however, before he managed to extract several skulls from ancient cemeteries on the islands of Maui and Kauai; Wilkes to Navy Department, n.d., Exploring Expedition Records, roll 6.

2. William Reynolds to Dr. Reynolds, 9 May 1841, Area Files, A-9.

3. Long, Journal, 19 September 1839.
4. Sanford, Journal, 23 September 1840.
5. Dyes, Journal, 14 February 1841.
6. Briscoe, Journal, 14 December 1840.
7. J. Frederick Sickles, Journal, 19 September 1839.
8. Alden, Journal, April 1841.
9. Wilkes, *Narrative*, 5:264.
10. Wilkes sent *Peacock* and *Flying Fish* to explore the Kingsmill and Marshall Islands in December 1840. For an account of this mission, see Stanton, *Great United States*, 232–46.
11. Pickering, *Races of Man*, 23.
12. Wilkes, *Narrative*, 4:297.
13. Although bathing frequently, many Indians of the Pacific Northwest rarely, if ever, washed their garments. They frequently anointed their bodies with fish oils, which provided an added distraction for whites. Ruby and Brown, *Chinook Indians*, 47.
14. Testimony from English vessels indicated that the Indians could be just as delighted with the "King George" vessels, and just as abusive of the "Bostons," depending on the circumstances. Ruby and Brown, *Chinook Indians*, 79.
15. Alden, Journal, 1 May 1841.
16. Briscoe, Journal, 3 May 1841.
17. Pickering, *Races of Man*, 24.
18. Wilkes, *Narrative*, 4:297.
19. Ruby and Brown, *Chinook Indians*, 67; Trafzer, *Chinook*.
20. Quoted in Ruby and Brown, *Chinook Indians*, 91.
21. Wilkes, *Narrative*, 4:419.
22. Ruby and Brown, *Indians of the Pacific Northwest*, 66; Ruby and Brown, *Chinook Indians*, 112. Hale gave particular attention to this trade jargon during his philological research in the Pacific Northwest.
23. An affliction whose introduction the Indians correctly blamed on the whites; the Americans and British blamed it on the wet weather and God's providence. Ruby and Brown, *Chinook Indians*, 185–200.
24. Wilkes, *Narrative*, 4:321.
25. Davis, *Seventy-Five Years*, 98.
26. Wilkes, *Narrative*, 5:116.
27. Wilkes, *Narrative*, 5:141.
28. Wilkes, *Narrative*, 4:369–70.
29. Wilkes, *Narrative* 4:369–70. In fact, the Cowlitz have not "disappeared"; members of this group still reside today in the Pacific Northwest. It is also interesting to note that in Wilkes's diary no mention is made of Casenove being the "last of his tribe." Such romantic embellishment of Indians as "last of the race" has a long literary history in the United States, a topic that I am currently researching.
30. Briscoe, Journal, 12 June 1841.
31. Emmons, Journal, 8 August 1841.
32. Wilkes, Diary in the Pacific Northwest, 10 June 1841. The *Narrative*, while critical of the missionaries, was not as blunt in its observations as Wilkes's original diary.
33. Charles Wilkes, Report on Oregon, Exploring Expedition Records, roll 6.

34. Wilkes, Report on Oregon. At one point, Wilkes confronted a French trader, Michel La Framboise, about the shooting of Indians on the trail from Oregon to California. He was told that no battles had actually occurred, but that it was "necessary to keep them always at a distance." When Wilkes persisted in his accusations, Framboise, "Frenchman like, shrugged his shoulders and answered: 'Ah, monsieur, ils sont des mauvaises gens: il faut en prendre garde et tirer sur eux quelquefois.' " Wilkes, Narrative, 5:143.
35. Wilkes, Narrative, 5:143.
36. Hale, Ethnography, 217.
37. Wilkes, Narrative, 4:325, 370.
38. Wilkes, Diary, 19 May 1841. Another fascinating instance where these Indians failed to live up to Wilkes's image of them took place on the Columbia River. Wilkes spent the day and evening in a canoe with nine Cowlitz Indians, "all quite young and full of merriment & fun laughing the live long day." At first he was amused and surprised at finding such non-"sullen" Indians. When the gaity continued, however, Wilkes "felt at last wearied by this incessant gaity." Wilkes, Diary, 21 May 1841.
39. Wilkes, Narrative, 4:324.
40. Wilkes, Narrative, 4:324.
41. Alden, Journal, 23 May 1841.
42. Alden, Journal, 23 May 1841.
43. Wilkes, Narrative, 4:479; Sanford, Journal, n.d.
44. Wilkes, Narrative, 4:389–90.
45. Wilkes, Narrative, 4:389.
46. Wilkes, Narrative, 4:368.
47. Wilkes, Narrative, 4:321. This skull was eventually returned over a century later.
48. Erskine, Twenty Years, 236.
49. Colvocoresses, Four Years, 235.
50. Wilkes, Narrative, 4:412.
51. Wilkes, Narrative, 4:413.
52. Hale, Ethnography, 223.
53. Pickering, Races of Man, 31.
54. Pickering, Races of Man, 37.
55. Hale, Ethnography, 203. One wonders if Hale intended to include other "fishing tribes" such as the Portuguese or, for that matter, American Cape Cod fishermen, under this umbrella of indolence!
56. Wilkes, Narrative, 4:449.
57. Wilkes, Narrative, 4:449. For a compilation of the many versions of these stories, see Trafzer, ed., Grandmother, Grandfather, and Old Wolf.
58. Hale later accused Wilkes of plagiarizing large sections of Hale's journal in the Narrative. If true, this fact ironically opens another window into Hale's firsthand observations during the voyage, as Hale's original journal was reportedly destroyed in a fire shortly after his death.
59. Hale, Ethnography, 209.
60. Hale, Ethnography, 204
61. Hale, Ethnography, 200.
62. Hale, Ethnography, 200.
63. Pickering, Races of Man, 29.

64. Pickering, *Races of Man*, 36.
65. Pickering, *Races of Man*, 49. Pickering's view received a confirmation of sorts from an unexpected source. During the return leg of the voyage, while visiting Singapore, "our Feejeean, Vendovi, was now, for the first time, brought in contact with a body of Chinese; and he at once identified them with his old acquaintances, the tribes of Northwest America." Pickering, *Races of Man*, 46.
66. Pickering, *Races of Man*, 41.
67. Pickering, *Races of Man*, 101.
68. Pickering, *Races of Man*, 101. Hale, not surprisingly, did not share Pickering's evaluation of the California Indians. "They are the lowest in intellect of all the North American tribes, approaching to the stupidity of the Australians. . . . The experiment, which was successfully tried, of collecting them, like a herd of cattle, into large enclosures called missions, and there setting them to work, would probably never have been undertaken with the Indians of Oregon,—and, if undertaken, would assuredly have failed." Hale, *Ethnography*, 199.

6. Ethnography and the Legacy of the Expedition

1. Wilkes Court Martial, n.d., Exploring Expedition Records, roll 27.
2. Navy Department to Charles Wilkes, 22 September 1842, quoted in Henderson, *Hidden Coasts*, 212.
3. Erskine, *Twenty Years*, 265. Vanderford was an experienced captain from Salem whose merchant vessel had run aground in the Fiji Islands over ten years prior to the expedition's visit. He served as Wilkes's chief Fiji interpreter and was well liked both by Vendovi and Wilkes. He died on the return voyage off the east coast of Africa.
4. Pickering to Morton, 10 June 1842, Morton Papers, APS.
5. Stanton, *Great United States*, 280.
6. Review in *North American Review*, 80.
7. "U.S. Exploring Expedition," *North American Review*, 257.
8. For a more detailed discussion of this distressing scenario, see Viola and Margolis, *Magnificent Voyagers*.
9. "U. S. Exploring Expedition," *American Journal*, 398.
10. "U.S. Exploring Expedition," *American Journal*, 399.
11. "U.S. Exploring Expedition," *American Journal*, 399–400.
12. Stanton, *Great United States*, 301.
13. Marcou, ed., *Louis Agassiz*, 1:286.
14. Commanders Wilkes, Hudson, and Ringgold of the expedition, the Naval Lyceum of Brooklyn, and the Library of Congress also received sets. Subsequent abridged editions, personal narratives, and other unofficial editions combined to greatly expand the narratives in print within a few years.
15. Not all were completed. For a summation of the expedition's contribution to each of these fields, see Viola and Margolis, *Magnificent Voyagers*.
16. Gray, review of *Ethnography and Philology*, 211–12.
17. Review in *Edinburgh Review*, 431.
18. Review in *British Quarterly Review*, 629.
19. Charles Darwin to Charles Wilkes, n.d., Charles Darwin Letters, APS.

20. Review in *British Quarterly Review*, 629.
21. Review in *Southern Quarterly Review*, 11.
22. Review in *British Quarterly Review*, 629–30.
23. Review in *British Quarterly Review*, 630.
24. For more on this debate, see Horsman, *Race and Manifest Destiny*, 52–53, 62–77.
25. Review in *Edinburgh Review*, 430, 434–35.
26. Review in *British Quarterly Review*, 631.
27. Review in *Southern Quarterly Review*, 32–33.
28. Review in *Westminster Review*, 489.
29. Review in *Westminster Review*, 478.
30. Review in *Westminster Review*, 481.
31. Review in *Westminster Review*, 481.
32. Review in *Westminster Review*, 484.
33. Review in *Southern Quarterly Review*, 64.
34. Pickering to Morton, 9 December 1842, Morton Papers, APS.
35. Benjamin Tappan was an Ohio senator who found few friends besides Wilkes among former members of the expedition or the scientific community. Asa Gray, for one, blasted the decision to place Pickering's work before a committee chaired by Tappan, whom he called "the most obstinate, wrong-headed, narrow-minded, impracticable ignoramus that could well be found." Asa Gray to J. D. Hooker, 31 December 1845, in Gray, ed., *Letters of Asa Gray*, 1:335–36.
36. Stanton, *Leopard's Spots*, 94–96.
37. Stanton, in *Great United States*, suggested that, under pressure from the committee and from Wilkes, Pickering was forced to give up many of his "strange notions" concerning ethnology. While such pressure was indeed exerted to some degree, a comparison of his field notes, journal of the expedition, and letters written during the voyage with *Races of Man* clearly exhibit a consistency of thought from voyage to publication.
38. Bartlett, "Reports of the Wilkes Expedition," 650.
39. See Stanton, *Great United States* and *Leopard's Spots*; Viola and Margolis, *Magnificent Voyagers*; Kazar, "United States Navy"; Bartlett, "Reports," 646–50.
40. Stanton, *Great United States*, 344–48.
41. Pickering, *Races of Man*, 302.
42. Pickering, *Races of Man*, 302.
43. Pickering, *Races of Man*, 303.
44. Pickering, *Races of Man*, 305.
45. Pickering, *Races of Man*, 306.
46. Pickering, *Races of Man*, 306.
47. Pickering to Morton, 31 December 1849, Morton Papers, TLC.
48. Stanton, *Great United States*, 347.
49. Pickering to Morton, 17 December 1849, Morton Papers, TLC.
50. W. B. Hodgson to Samuel Morton, 29 March 1844, Morton Papers, TLC.
51. Oliver Wendell Holmes Sr. to Samuel Morton, 27 November 1849, Morton Papers, TLC.
52. Holmes to Morton, 27 November 1849.
53. Takaki, *Iron Cages*, 137–39. One of the three students, Martin Delany, was destined to

become, among other things, a notable explorer in his own right, leading an expedition up Africa's Niger River in the 1850s.

54. Unidentified to Samuel Morton, March 1851, Morton Papers, APS.
55. *New York Tribune*, 16 May 1851. Obituary found in the Morton Papers, APS.
56. "Migrations in the Pacific Ocean," 318.
57. Gray, review of *Ethnography*, 225.
58. Horatio Hale to John Wesley Powell, 14 May 1881, quoted in Gruber, "Horatio Hale," 37.
59. Bartlett, "Reports," 637; Sawyer, introduction to *Ethnography*. Today, compilations such as Hale's prove to be valuable sources for native peoples attempting to resurrect and reinvigorate the use of their languages.
60. Bartlett, "Reports," 637.
61. Gray, review of *Ethnography*, 227.
62. Gray, review of *Ethnography*, 226–27.
63. Gray, review of *Ethnography*, 228.
64. Horatio Hale, "Hale's Indians." Gallatin furnished the introduction, Hale the text.
65. Sawyer, preface to *Ethnography*.
66. Morgan, *Ancient Society*, 5.
67. Quoted in Gruber, "Horatio Hale," 18.
68. Gruber, "Horatio Hale," 23.
69. See Rydell, *All the World's a Fair*.
70. Quoted in Gruber, "Horatio Hale," 23.
71. Gruber, "Horatio Hale," 26.
72. Horatio Hale to Franz Boas, 1 March 1888, Boas Letters.
73. Hale to Boas, 1 March 1888.

Bibliography

Primary Sources

UNPUBLISHED DOCUMENTS

Alden, James. Journal. Mariners Museum, Newport News VA.

American Philosophical Society. Papers. Philadelphia.

Anonymous. Journal. Records Relating to the United States Exploring Expedition under the Command of Charles Wilkes, 1836–1842 [hereafter Exploring Expedition Records]. Record Group [RG] 45. National Archives, Washington DC [hereafter NA]. Roll 10.

Area Files, A-9, A-10. RG 45. NA.

Boas, Franz. Letters. American Philosophical Society, Philadelphia.

Briscoe, William. Journal. Exploring Expedition Records. RG 45. NA. Roll 13.

Cruises and Voyages, Subject File O-1842 (OC), E-464, RG 45. NA.

Darwin, Charles. Letters. American Philosophical Society, Philadelphia.

Dyes, John W. W. Journal. Exploring Expedition Records. RG 45. NA. Roll 11.

Emmons, George. Journal. George Emmons Papers, Yale Collection of Western Americana, Beinecke Rare Book and Manuscript Library, Yale University.

Gilchrist, Edward. Journal. Exploring Expedition Records. RG 45. NA. Roll 14.

Gray, Asa. Papers. American Philosophical Society, Philadelphia.

Kane, Elisha Kent. Papers. American Philosophical Society, Philadelphia.

Long, Andrew K. Journal. Exploring Expedition Records. RG 45. NA. Roll 18.

Morton, Samuel George. Papers. American Philosophical Society, Philadelphia.

Morton, Samuel George. Papers. The Library Company, Philadelphia.

Peale, Titian Ramsay, and Sellers. Papers. American Philosophical Society, Philadelphia.

Pickering, Charles. Journal. Academy of Natural Sciences, Philadelphia.

Records Relating to the United States Exploring Expedition under the Command of Charles Wilkes, 1836–1842. RG 45. 27 rolls. NA.

Sanford, Joseph Perry. Journal. Exploring Expedition Records. RG 45. NA. Roll 19.

Sickles, J. Frederick. Journal. Exploring Expedition Records. RG 45. NA. Roll 16.

Sinclair, George T. Journal. Exploring Expedition Records. RG 45. NA. Roll 21.

Stuart, Frederick. Journal. Exploring Expedition Records. RG 45. NA. Roll 20.

Underwood, Joseph. Journal. Yale Collection of Western Americana, Beinecke Rare Book and Manuscript Library, Yale University.

United States Exploring Expedition Collection, 1838–1885. Record Unit 7186. Smithsonian Institution Archives, Washington DC.

Wilkes, Charles. Diary in the Pacific Northwest. Yale Collection of Western Americana, Beinecke Rare Book and Manuscript Library, Yale University.

PUBLISHED WORKS

Clark, Joseph. *Lights and Shadows of Sailor Life*. Boston: Benjamin B. Massey & Co., 1848.

Colvocoresses, George M. *Four Years in the Government Exploring Expedition*. New York: J. M. Fairchild & Co., 1853.

Davis, William Heath. *Seventy-Five Years in California: 1831-1906*. San Francisco: John Howell, 1929.

Erskine, Charles. *Twenty Years Before the Mast*. Boston: Morning Star Press, 1890.

Gray, Asa. "Memorial." *Proceedings of the Academy of Arts and Sciences*, 13 (1878).

————. Review of *Ethnography and Philology*, by Horatio Hale. *North American Review* 63 (July 1846): 211–36.

Gray, Jane Loring, ed. *Letters of Asa Gray*, 2 vols. Boston: Houghton Mifflin & Co., 1893.

Hale, Horatio. *Ethnography and Philology*. Philadelphia: C. Sherman, 1846.

————. *Hale's Indians of the North-West America, and Vocabularies of North America, with an Introduction*. Transactions of the American Ethnological Society. Vol. 2 (Washington DC, 1848), xxiii–clxxx, 1–130.

Marcou, Jules, ed. *The Life, Letters, and Works of Louis Agassiz*. 2 vols. New York: MacMillan, 1896.

"Migrations in the Pacific Ocean." *American Journal of Science and Arts*, 2d ser., 1 (May 1846): 317–332.

Morgan, Lewis Henry. *Ancient Society*. New York: H. Holt, 1877.

Morton, Samuel George. *Catalogue of Skulls of Man and the Inferior Animals in the Collection of Samuel George Morton*. Philadelphia: Merrihew & Thompson, 1849.

————. *Crania Americana*. Philadelphia: J. Dobson, London, Simpkin, Marshall, 1839.

Pickering, Charles. *The Chronological History of Plants: Man's Record of His Own Existence Illustrated through Their Names, Uses, and Companionship*. Boston: Little, Brown & Co., 1879.

————. *The Races of Man and Their Geographical Distribution*. Philadelphia: C. Sherman, 1848.

Poesch, Jessie, ed. *Titian Ramsay Peale, 1799–1885, and His Journals of the Wilkes Expedition*. American Philosophical Society Memoirs. Vol. 52. (Philadelphia, 1961).

Public Statutes at Large of the United States of America. Vol. 5. Boston: Charles C. Little & James Brown, 1846.

Review of *Narrative of the United States Exploring Expedition*, by Charles Wilkes. *British Quarterly Review* 17 (1853): 627–632.

Review of *Narrative of the United States Exploring Expedition*, by Charles Wilkes. *Edinburgh Review* (April 1846): 431–52.

Review of *Narrative of the United States Exploring Expedition*, by Charles Wilkes. *North American Review* 61 (July 1845): 54–107.

Review of *Narrative of the United States Exploring Expedition*, by Charles Wilkes. *Southern Quarterly Review* 15 (July 1845): 1–69.

Review of *Narrative of the United States Exploring Expedition* by Charles Wilkes. *Westminster Review* 44 (September–December 1845): 469–96.

Reynolds, Jeremiah N. *Address, On the Subject of a Surveying and Exploring Expedition to the Pacific Ocean and South Seas.* New York: Harper & Brothers, 1836.

"United States Exploring Expedition." *American Journal of Science and Arts* 44 (April 1843): 393–408.

"United States Exploring Expedition." *North American Review* 61 (April 1843): 257–70.

Wilkes, Charles. *Narrative of the United States Exploring Expedition during the Years 1838, 1839, 1840, 1841, 1842.* 5 vols. Philadelphia: Lea & Blanchard, 1845.

Secondary Sources

Bancroft, Hubert Howe. *The New Pacific.* New York: Bancroft Co., 1899.

Barnouw, Victor. *Ethnology: An Introduction to Anthropology.* 4th ed. Vol. 2. Homewood IL: Dorsey Press, 1982.

Bartlett, Harley Harris. "The Reports of the Wilkes Exploring Expedition and the Work of the Specialists in Science," in *Centenary Celebration of the Wilkes Exploring Expedition of the United States Navy, 1838–1842.* Ed. Edwin G. Conklin. Proceedings of the American Philosophical Society, vol. 82. Philadelphia, 1940.

Beals, Ralph L., and Harry Hoijer. *An Introduction to Anthropology.* 4th ed. New York: Macmillan, 1971.

Bennett, John W. *Classic Anthropology.* New Brunswick NJ: Transaction Publishers, 1998.

Bidney, David. *Theoretical Anthropology.* New York: Columbia University Press, 1964.

Bieder, Robert. *Science Encounters the Indian, 1820–1880.* Norman: University of Oklahoma Press, 1986.

Boller, Paul. *American Thought in Transition: The Impact of Evolutionary Naturalism, 1865–1900.* Chicago: Rand McNally, 1969.

Carter, Edward C., II, ed. *Surveying the Record: North American Scientific Exploration to 1930.* American Philosophical Society Memoirs, vol. 231. Philadelphia, 1999.

Clifford, James. *The Predicament of Culture: Twentieth-Century Ethnography, Literature, and Art.* Cambridge MA: Harvard University Press, 1988.

Cooper, William J. Jr. *The South and the Politics of Slavery, 1828–1856.* Baton Rouge: Louisiana State University Press, 1978.

Daniels, George H. *American Science in the Age of Jackson.* New York: Columbia University Press, 1968.

Drinnon, Richard. *Facing West: The Metaphysics of Indian Hating and Empire Building.* Minneapolis: University of Minnesota Press, 1980.

Fredrickson, George M. *The Inner Civil War: Northern Intellectuals and the Crisis of the Union.* New York: Harper & Row, 1965.

Freehling, William. *Prelude to Civil War: The Nullification Controversy in South Carolina, 1816–1836.* New York: Harper & Row, 1966.

Geertz, Clifford. *The Interpretation of Cultures.* New York: Basic Books, 1973.

Goetzmann, William A. *New Lands, New Men: America and the Second Great Age of Discovery.* New York: Penguin Books, 1986.

Gould, Stephen Jay. *The Mismeasure of Man.* New York: W. W. Norton & Co., 1981.

Greene, John. *The Death of Adam: Evolution and Its Impact on Western Thought.* Ames: Iowa State University Press, 1969.

Gruber, Jacob. "Horatio Hale and the Development of American Anthropology." *Proceedings of the American Philosophical Society* 111 (1967): 5–37.

Harris, Marvin. *Culture, People, Nature: An Introduction to General Anthropology.* 2d ed. New York: Thomas Y. Crowell, 1975.

Haviland, William A. *Anthropology.* New York: Holt, Rinehart & Winston, 1974.

Henderson, Daniel. *The Hidden Coasts.* New York: H. Wolff, 1953.

Horsman, Reginald. *Race and Manifest Destiny: The Origins of American Racial Anglo-Saxonism.* Cambridge MA: Harvard University Press, 1981.

Hovencamp, Herbert. *Science and Religion in America, 1800–1860.* Philadelphia: University of Pennsylvania Press, 1978.

Jaffe, David. *The Stormy Petrel and the Whale.* Baltimore: Port City Press, 1976.

Johnson, Paul E. *A Shopkeeper's Millennium: Society and Revivals in Rochester, New York, 1815–1837.* New York: Hill & Wang, 1978.

Joyce, Barry Alan. "James Alden: Naval Officer, Scientist, and Explorer." M.A. thesis, San Diego State University, 1990.

Kazar, John D. "The United States Navy and Scientific Exploration, 1837–1860." Ph.D. diss., University of Massachusetts, 1973.

Kottak, Conrad Phillip. *Anthropology: The Exploration of Human Diversity.* New York: Random House, 1974.

Melville, Herman. *Typee: A Peep at Polynesian Life during a Four Month's Residence in a Valley of the Marquesas.* New York: Wiley & Putnam, 1846.

Morgan, Edmund. *American Slavery, American Freedom: The Ordeal of Colonial Virginia.* New York: W. W. Norton & Co., 1975.

Obeyesekere, Gananath. *The Apotheosis of Captain Cook: European Mythmaking in the Process.* Princeton: Princeton University Press, 1992.

Omi, Michael, and Howard Winant. *Racial Formation in the United States.* New York: Routledge & Kegan, 1986.

Peoples of the Earth. 20 vols. London: Danbury Press, 1973.

Porter, Charlotte. *The Eagle's Nest: Natural History and American Ideas, 1812–1849.* Tuscaloosa: University of Alabama Press, 1986.

Rosaldo, Renato. *Culture and Truth: The Remaking of Social Analysis.* Boston: Beacon Press, 1989.

Ruby, Robert H., and John A. Brown, *Indians of the Pacific Northwest: A History.* Norman: University of Oklahoma Press, 1981.

———. *The Chinook Indians: Traders of the Lower Columbia River.* Norman: University of Oklahoma Press, 1976.

Rydell, Robert W. *All the World's a Fair: Visions of Empire at American International Expositions, 1876–1916.* Chicago: University of Chicago Press, 1984.

Sahlins, Marshall. *Islands of History.* Chicago: University of Chicago Press, 1985.

———. "Raw Women, Cooked Men, and Other 'Great Things' of the Fiji Islands." In *Ethnography and the Historical Imagination.* Ed. John and Jean Comaroff. Boulder CO: Westview Press, 1992.

Said, Edward W. *Orientalism.* New York: Vintage Books, 1979.

Saxton, Alexander. *The Rise and Fall of the White Republic: Class Politics and Mass Culture in Nineteenth-Century America.* London: Verso, 1990.

Schiebinger, Londa. "Skeletons in the Closet: The First Illustrations of the Female Skeleton in Eighteenth-Century Anatomy." In *The Making of the Modern Body: Sexuality and Society in the Nineteenth Century.* Ed. Catherine Gallagher and Thomas Laqueur. Berkeley: University of California Press, 1987.

Sellers, Charles Grier. *The Market Revolution: Jacksonian America, 1815–1846.* New York: Oxford University Press, 1991.

Smedley, Audrey. *Race in North America: Origin and Evolution of a Worldview.* San Francisco: Westview Press, 1992.

Smith, Henry Nash. *Virgin Land: The American West as Symbol and Myth.* Cambridge MA: Harvard University Press, 1970.

Smith, Timothy Lawrence. *Revivalism and Social Reform in Mid- Nineteenth-Century America.* New York: Abingdon Press, 1957.

Stanton, William. *The Great United States Exploring Expedition of 1838–1842.* Berkeley: University of California Press, 1975.

——. *The Leopard's Spots: Scientific Attitudes towards Race in America, 1815–1859.* Chicago: University of Chicago Press, 1960.

Steward, James Brewer. *Holy Warriors: The Abolitionists and American Slavery.* New York: Hill & Wang, 1976.

Stocking, George W. Jr. *Victorian Anthropology.* New York: Free Press, 1987.

Takaki, Ronald. *A Different Mirror: A History of Multicultural America.* Boston: Little, Brown & Co., 1993.

——. *Iron Cages: Race and Culture in Nineteenth-Century America.* New York: Oxford University Press, 1990.

Thomas, Nicholas. *Entangled Objects: Exchange, Material Culture, and Colonialism in the Pacific.* Cambridge MA: Harvard University Press, 1991.

Trafzer, Clifford E. *The Chinook.* New York: Chelsea House, 1990.

——, ed. *Grandmother, Grandfather, and Old Wolf.* East Lansing: Michigan State University Press, 1998.

Viola, Herman, and Carolyn Margolis, eds. *Magnificent Voyagers: The United States Exploring Expedition, 1838–1842.* Washington DC: Smithsonian Press, 1985.

Ward, John W. *Andrew Jackson: Symbol for an Age.* New York: Oxford University Press, 1955.

Wilentz, Sean. *Chants Democratic: New York City and the Rise of the American Working Class, 1788–1850.* New York: Oxford University Press, 1984.

Wiley, Peter Booth. *Yankees in the Land of the Gods: Commodore Perry and the Opening of Japan,* with Korogi Ichiro. New York: Viking Penguin, 1990.

Winkler, Karen J. "Anthropologists Urged to Rethink Their Definitions of Culture." *Chronicle of Higher Education,* 14 December 1994, A18.

INDEX

Page references in italics indicate an illustration.